Cultural Values of
American Ethnic Groups

Harper's Social Science Series
Under the Editorship of
F. Stuart Chapin

Cultural Values
of American
Ethnic Groups

SISTER FRANCES JEROME WOODS, C.D.P.

Associate Professor of Sociology and Social Work

Our Lady of the Lake College

HARPER & BROTHERS, PUBLISHERS
NEW YORK

TO
WILLARD,
HOPE, AND PETE

CONTENTS

PART IV: CONCLUSION

EDITOR'S INTRODUCTION

The members of the helping professions of social work, counselors in education and family groups, physicians and psychiatrists, not to mention lawyers, clergymen, and personnel officers in economic institutions, are often faced with the dilemma of conflict and tensions between the personality structures of their clients, on the one hand, and, on the other hand, the all-pervading influences of differences in culture patterns of ethnic groups. Sister Frances Jerome Woods has applied a sympathetic and informed analysis to this area of problems; an analysis which should be of practical aid in these helping professions. It is easy to confuse personality disorders with cultural and ethnic differences among clients. This book presents a penetrating and scholarly analysis of examples drawn from case records, interviews, personal history documents, and also from secondary sources.

Theoretical implications and orientation are not neglected in this analysis. It offers systematic discussion of cross-cultural influences, modal personality structures, and cultural complexities. Such institutional factors as language, religion, magic, authority of government, economic values, recreation, education, and the family, are carefully examined. Specific personal roles such as the paternal, the maternal, children, and sex roles are systematically discussed for several ethnic groups—American, Oriental, Mexican, European,

Jewish, Negro, etc.—in the social setting of the United States. Sister Frances Jerome Woods has shown unusual discrimination, tolerance, and imagination in her task of interpreting the subtle influences of interaction of culture and personality.

F. STUART CHAPIN

PREFACE

The study of ethnic peoples has always intrigued me, and when I was asked to give an institute on "Cultural Factors in the Case-worker-Client Relationship" at the Texas Social Welfare Conference in 1953, I sought for an approach which would be of help to such a professional group. I decided to focus the analysis around the sociological concepts of values and roles, an approach which was little emphasized in the literature of the profession and which later was well received by the institute participants. Since this information appeared to be especially meaningful to social workers who deal with clients of differing ethnic backgrounds, it seemed logical that it would also be valuable to persons in other allied professional fields or who were preparing for them. With this impetus, and the encouragement of friends and students who volunteered case illustrations, the study developed.

Although many criticisms and suggestions of readers were found helpful, others could not be incorporated into the study without broadening the scope considerably. The analysis of the dominant American cultural group was, perhaps, subjected to the most criticism. A few critics expressed surprise that the dominant group was classified as Protestant, and that little emphasis was placed upon Catholicism. Generalizations about the non-official values of the dominant group were not always well received, and more stress upon official values was recommended. Representatives of the professional groups, moreover, wished to have a more detailed analysis of the official, traditional values relative to their respective professions. Such a comprehensive development was judged to be beyond the scope of the present study. Similarly, Negro readers often resented the generalizations made about lower-class Negroes in the rural South, and suggested the inclusion of additional information on middle-class urban Negroes. Other readers believed that undue emphasis was placed upon the ethnic groups found in the West, South, and Southwest. Decisions in these instances were ultimately based upon the numerical importance of the ethnic groups, or of the sub-groups (religion, class level, etc.), and upon the availability of material.

It would be impossible to mention the names of all the persons who have contributed to this study. My students have shared with me their personal as well as their subsequent professional experiences. The college chapter of Pi Gamma Mu has generously provided me with many of the necessary secondary source materials. Colleagues and friends have given graciously of their time to discuss problems and ideas, locate materials, and read manuscript. I am especially indebted to Daniel A. O'Connor, C.S.V., Margaret Bedard, Dorothy Roeser, Mary Louise Ross, Elizabeth Nuelle, Jennie Gares, and Dorothy F. O'Neill. Special mention must also be given to Sister M. Francisca and Sister Margaret Rose for their critical reading of the entire manuscript, to Sister M. Dorcas, who typed the final draft, and to Mother M. Mercedes, my sister, who was a constant source of encouragement.

Finally, I wish to express my gratitude to Dr. F. Stuart Chapin, the editor of Harper's Social Science Series, and to the cartoonists and publishers who permitted me the use of their copyrighted materials.

S. F. J. W.

San Antonio, Texas
January, 1956

Part I

THE FRAMEWORK

1

Theoretical Background

INTRODUCTION

AMERICA is generally acknowledged to be a land of varied ethnic composition. The aborigines were gradually displaced by waves of immigrants from many parts of the world. Although immigration lost momentum after the enactment of the quota system[1] in the post-World War I era, the late nineteenth- and early twentieth-century immigrants tended to retain much of their original culture. Even third-generation ethnics often identify, at least in some respects, with the original cultural group.

World War II gave new impetus to the movement of peoples. Many servicemen and women stationed overseas chose their spouses from other cultural groups. In addition, many displaced persons, as a result of special legislation, sought refuge and a permanent home in America. These immigrants undoubtedly have contributed to American cultural diversity, and the impact of their culture will continue to be felt in the future. With the exception of the Puerto Ricans and other nonquota groups, these recent immigrants have come primarily from Europe or the Orient. There are, however,

[1] American immigration policy is based on a restrictive quota system. The quota for any nationality is determined by finding out what proportion that nationality contributed, by birth or descent, to the total population of 1920, and applying this percentage to the total quota, which is at present 154,000. For a critical analysis of this policy see Hubert H. Humphrey, Jr., *The Stranger at Our Gate,* New York, Public Affairs Committee, 1954.

3

other large cultural groups, many of whom have long resided in America. Approximately every tenth American is Negro, every fortieth person is Jewish, and every fiftieth person is Mexican[2]—not to mention the number of surviving American Indians who have retained their cultural identity.

The analysis of cultural values which this study proposes is a socioanthropological approach to some of the problems encountered by persons in such helping professions as social work, counseling, teaching, and medical care. A theoretical framework within which to view cultural values and an ability to recognize and appreciate the significance of the cultural elements in specific case situations is believed to be helpful and, at times, essential to effective practice.

As a preliminary test in recognition of cultural factors, consider the following cases taken from actual experience:

A tubercular Mexican woman made the announcement that she was feeling much better than she did at the time of her last appointment.

"Then you have been following your diet and the doctor's recommendations, haven't you?" she was asked.

"No," replied the woman, "it was not what the doctor told me to do that helped me, but what one of my friends told me. She said a cat stew would be the best thing for me, so I caught a live cat and ate all of it. Since then I have been feeling stronger."[3]

Would the average professional worker attribute this phenomena to personality disorders or would he be able to analyze the underlying cultural motives?

This case exemplifies a very prevalent form of magic. It is commonly believed that by eating animal or even human flesh, one

[2] Numbers derived from table on estimated number of minorities in the United States in 1950 in Charles F. Marden, *Minorities in American Societies,* New York, American Book Company, 1952, p. 15.

[3] This is an instance of imitative magic. For a more detailed account of this particular kind of magic see Chapter 3 of this study and also James George Frazer, *The Golden Bough,* abr. ed., New York, The Macmillan Co., 1922, Chapter 51, "Homoeopathic Magic of a Flesh Diet."

will acquire not only the physical, but even the moral and intellectual qualities which characterize that animal or man. The cat is an energetic little animal and there is an old saying—not unknown to Americans—to the effect that a cat has nine lives. By eating the cat, the woman probably believed that she would assimilate some of the cat's energy and prolong her own life.

A second case which illustrates the dominance of cultural factors is narrated by a social worker in these words:

> The public housing authority evicted an immigrant family[4] from a housing unit and reported to the social agency that all the bathroom fixtures had been torn out of the floor and smashed or bent beyond repair. It appeared to be a case of wanton destruction, although the family had had no previous trouble with the housing authority nor had the authority any reason to suspect dissatisfaction.
>
> When interviewed by the social worker, the father of the offending family admitted that he was guilty, but was unable or unwilling to verbalize specific reasons for his action. The worker suspected that the bathroom fixtures symbolized American culture to the family and that the action was an expression of cultural revolt. Subsequent developments verified this assumption inasmuch as the action could not be attributed to other factors such as employment difficulties, ill health, or family troubles.

The bathtub is generally regarded as a symbol of American culture. "Nothing is more warmly rejoiced in than our superiority to the grimy Europeans in the matter of bathtubs," says one commentator. "Cleanliness," he adds, "is far ahead of godliness."[5] A Chinese ethnic remarks that the acquisition of a bathtub symbolized his family's "progress upward in the scale of the American standard of living, with its emphasis upon material creature com-

---

[4] The particular group to which this immigrant belonged was not noted because almost any immigrant might visualize bathroom fixtures as symbolic of the dominant culture.

[5] Bergen Evans, *The Natural History of Nonsense,* New York, Alfred A. Knopf, Inc., 1946, p. 261.

forts." "This receptacle," he says, "was certainly our symbol of progress," for it "embodied all our American hopes and fears."[6]

As these cases illustrate, a knowledge of cultural values may be essential to an analysis of a case situation. An appreciation of cultural values, it will be noted later, is also important in establishing rapport or a working relationship with an ethnic client and in determining a plan of treatment.

DEFINITIONS OF KEY TERMS

Culture

Culture is a "composite of specific ways of thinking, feeling, and acting which differentiates one group from another."[7] It is the manner which the group devises to meet those problems of adjustment that all human beings have in common. All men, for example, establish basic societies to regulate the family, authority in the larger community or state, and religion. One's attitudes and behavior in all these areas are learned from one's forebears, stored up in the memories of men or in books, and transmitted to succeeding generations. Like an accurate and readable map, culture shows one his "way around in the life of a society."[8] Although an analyst may not be intimately acquainted with the majority of the people belonging to a cultural group, if he has information about their culture, he may be said to possess "some a priori information about their system of values."[9]

Since culture is learned and not biologically transmitted as in-

[6] Pardee Lowe, Father and Glorious Descendant, Boston, Little, Brown & Co., 1943, pp. 178-179.
[7] Otto Pollak's condensation of Clyde Kluckhohn's analysis of culture. "Cultural Dynamics in Casework," Social Casework (July, 1953), 34:280.
[8] Clyde Kluckhohn, Mirror for Man, New York, McGraw-Hill Book Co., 1949, pp. 28-29.
[9] Jurgen Ruesch and Gregory Bateson, Communication, New York, W. W. Norton & Company, Inc., 1951, p. 48.

stincts are in animal life, there is a wide range of cultural potentialities. Ruth Benedict maintains that this plasticity should be "man's proudest boast," because it gives evidence of his superiority over the animal.[10] In actuality, however, man's proudest boast seems to be rather the supposed superiority of his own brand of culture—called ethnocentrism. The way in which he does things becomes "second nature" to him and tends to be equated with "human nature." The traditional manner of doing things becomes the only reasonable or logical way and people who are different are beyond the pale—lesser beings, so to speak. The names by which some American Indian tribes designated their own groups illustrate this attitude. Navaho means "the people," and the tribal names of Kiowa, Zuñi, and Déné were native terms for "the human beings," that is, themselves.[11]

At the present time ethnocentrism still prevails. Even professionally trained workers need to be reminded of the relativity of cultural norms. "There has never been a time," says Ruth Benedict, "when civilization stood more in need of individuals who are genuinely culture-conscious, who can see objectively the socially conditioned behaviour of other peoples without fear and recrimination."[12]

Values

Culture has been envisioned as the means devised by a group to meet its needs. Some needs, such as the regulation of the family, the establishment of law and order, and relations toward superhuman powers are more basic than other derived needs, such as economic organization, education, and recreation. In all these instances, however, values are involved. Values concern not only

[10] Ruth Benedict, *Race: Science and Politics*, Rev. ed., New York, The Viking Press, 1943, p. 138.
[11] Ruth Benedict, *Patterns of Culture*, New York, Penguin Books, Inc., 1934, p. 6.
[12] *Ibid.*, pp. 9-10.

the needs themselves, or the ends of action, but also the selection of adequate means to achieve these ends.[13] Among all cultural groups attitudes prevail toward the systems or institutions developed to regulate and standardize behavior in matters upon which group welfare and survival depend. Once tested and accepted, these important needs and the means of meeting them become values and tend to be regarded as the natural and even the *right* way of doing things. Values are so meaningful to those who hold them that they come to be accepted without question.[14]

It is only natural, then, that these culturally approved, institutionalized means of meeting basic needs are, as a rule, changed only slowly and reluctantly.[15] Any attack on them, especially in the nature of ridicule, is deeply resented. Others are expected to respect them, if not to accept them. In fact, one's values are usually regarded as desirable for other persons, and differences in values "form the base for the most violent personal and group attractions and repulsions."[16]

The term "value" is commonly used as a device which renders incomparable things commensurable, such as rating the cost of an evening's entertainment against that of a wedding dress. Value also has reference to "preference," where there are alternate or even multiple choices. Bilingual or multilingual persons, for instance, may prefer to use one language rather than another as a medium of communication. Other definitions of value stress "attention or emphasis." Among one cultural group the emphasis in daily living and in conversation may be placed upon the fine arts and literature;

[13] Robin M. Williams, Jr., *American Society*, New York, Alfred A. Knopf, Inc., 1951, p. 376.

[14] Milton L. Barron, *The Juvenile in Delinquent Society*, New York, Alfred A. Knopf, Inc., 1954, p. 203.

[15] Cf. Joseph K. Folsom, "Changing Values in Sex and Family Relations," *American Sociological Review* (October, 1937), 2:719.

[16] Abram Kardiner and Lionel Ovesey, *The Mark of Oppression*, New York, W. W. Norton & Company, Inc., 1951, p. 35.

another cultural group may emphasize the supernatural. A value, moreover, may be identified by the use of social sanctions. Behavior that is valued is rewarded and praised, while that which deviates from the valued patterns is censured, disapproved, and punished. The extent of praise or punishment is often an index to the importance of the value.[17]

The following criteria give some indication of the subordinate and dominant values for a group: extensiveness of the value in total activity of the group; duration, or length of time over which the value has persisted; intensity with which the value is sought as shown by choices, verbal affirmation, and by reactions to threats to the value; and prestige of the value carriers, whether they be persons, objects, or organizations.[18]

Not everyone in a culture group gives the same appraisal to all values. At different ages or under different circumstances, the same individual may rate some values higher than others. According to a recent survey on religion, it was found that young and elderly people are more inclined to be concerned with the next world than are those in the prime of life.[19] Students who returned to college after their experience in the armed forces during World War II tended to do a better job scholastically than they did prior to their entrance into the service.[20]

In analyzing values, allowances must be made for both the official and the unofficial. The former are found in the sacred documents of a society, while the latter are informally and unsystematically conveyed. Unofficial values are predominantly "anti-" or

[17] Williams, *op. cit.*, pp. 378-380.

[18] *Ibid.*, pp. 382-383.

[19] "What the U.S. Thinks of Life: Here and Hereafter," *Catholic Digest* (May, 1953), 17:76.

[20] At Brooklyn College a study of 900 returned veterans in the summer of 1946 revealed that 73 percent had achieved a better total record as veterans than the total record prior to their induction. Joseph Justman, "Educational Services for Veterans at Brooklyn College," *School and Society* (September 20, 1947), 66:212.

laden with negativism, suspicion, and skepticism, and they are logically incompatible with official values.[21] In American culture, for example, democracy is an official value in terms of which it is considered desirable that an individual "stand on his own feet" and "work out his own destiny in his own way." He should be self-reliant and independent and the equal of every other individual. The voice of the majority shall rule, and in the long run it will speak the truth "because men are rational creatures who can and must bear the responsibility for jointly charting their own course."[22]

In practice, however, unofficial values tend to operate. Americans wink at official democratic values where ethnic minorities are involved. The latter are often made to endure exploitation and discrimination simply because they are minorities. Similarly, the values which Judeo-Christian society officially places on the inviolability of private property and respect for authority are not always adhered to in practice. Unofficially, dupery and dishonesty are viewed as "shrewdness" and "enterprise," and resistance to authority becomes "rugged individualism."[23]

Social Class

Any discussion of cultural values must, of necessity, also make allowances for class differences. Individuals and the groups to which they belong are ranked on a "scale of superiority-inferiority-equality, according to some commonly accepted basis of valuation."[24] Criteria of evaluation often include such factors as membership in a kinship unit, possessions, education, authority, and personal qualities. On the basis of such criteria, individuals and groups are said to belong to social classes ordinarily designated as "upper," "middle," and

[21] Mary Ellen Goodman, "The Anthropological Dimension," *Adult Leadership* (April, 1954), 2:15; Barron, *op. cit.*, 212. Goodman uses the terms "core" and "fringe" values while Barron prefers "official" and "unofficial."

[22] Goodman, *loc cit.*

[23] Barron, *op. cit.*, pp. 203-210.

[24] Williams, *op. cit.*, p. 80. In italics.

"lower," with subdivisions in each category. Only after cultural groups are refined in this fashion can values be scientifically considered.

In analyzing economic values, for example, social class may be a factor in the following fashion. The American lower classes tend to focus upon the means of subsistence through work; the middle classes wish, in addition, for status or prestige either through capital investment or through membership in a business hierarchy; the upper classes aim primarily at prestige and power. In one instance, the value may be one's last meal and in the other, one's last yacht.[25]

Ethnic

The term "ethnic" denotes a feeling of belonging to a group because of racial or cultural similarities, or both. American Negroes, for instance, constitute a racial group as do Chinese and Japanese Americans. European immigrants, however, are not racially distinct from native Americans. The term "ethnic" is broad enough to include all these groups, whether the differences be racial, cultural, or both.

Race has reference to physical appearance. It is possible for a person to be culturally identified with a group and have the same racial background, but in appearance to be an "ugly duckling." The Negro who is an albino could fall into this category if he had all the other Negroid physical characteristics except color. An Italian war bride's troubles appear to have had their roots in this same factor.

Mrs. C., a twenty-six-year-old Italian war bride of World War II, married a Mexican who is presently stationed in Mississippi. She has been in the United States for seven years and has learned to speak English well and to use United States currency. She says she went through some school in Naples, Italy, but is not as well educated as the rest of her family. Her father is a doctor, and her brothers and sisters are

[25] Cf. Kardiner and Ovesey. *op. cit.,* p. 378.

educated musicians. She was the only light-haired, light-complexioned girl in the community and she was so different in appearance that her parents were ashamed of her and kept her fairly well hidden until she was almost grown. She felt that everyone made fun of her and knew no one would marry her, despite the fact that she is an unusually attractive person judged by American standards. Mr. C. was stationed in her home town and she married him to get away. The marriage has been unhappy, and she feels that she is rejected by her husband. She finds life lonely and difficult. She is fearful of friendships, and feels that people are always talking about her. Her paranoid tendency to feel persecuted evidently originated in early childhood when her color deviation was unaccepted.

One may have a feeling of belonging to an ethnic group without having any apparent racial or cultural affinity with it. Some Negroes, for example, could easily "pass" into the dominant white group, but they have a feeling of belonging to the Negro group and choose to be identified as such. Belongingness is the assurance of being inwardly at home as well as outwardly accepted by a group. Sometimes a member of a minority group wishes to be identified with the dominant group, and consequently lacks a feeling of belonging to either his own cultural group or to the dominant group. The following case illustrates this situation.

Joseph H., a sixteen-year-old boy, was referred to an agency because of his refusal to attend school. His father was of Scotch-Irish extraction, while his mother was Latin-American. The family had formerly lived in the state of Washington, but moved to Texas the preceding summer in order to be near the maternal grandmother.

When attending high school in Washington, Joseph was very prominent in athletics, popular on the campus, and had many friends of both sexes. It was reported by his mother that since their arrival in Texas the boy was finding it difficult to make new friends, and generally remained withdrawn.

In the initial interview Joe brought out the feeling that he never would be a big man on the campus here, but indicated no reasons for so feeling. At a subsequent interview the boy was able to verbalize his inability to establish relationships since he moved from Washington.

He spontaneously brought up the fact that one area which seemed to give him trouble was the racial problem in Texas, mentioning that he was particularly concerned about the discrimination against Negroes. The worker then briefly raised the possibility that Joseph might be somewhat concerned about his Latin-American ancestry, but Joseph quickly denied this. The worker concluded that the boy was not yet ready to handle his own conflict in this area and was merely displacing the race question to Negroes where it was safely handled. It is interesting to note that Joseph did not possess Latin features.

Apparently it made little difference to Joseph whether or not he "belonged" to the Mexican ethnic group as long as he lived in an area where there were very few Mexicans. When his family moved to an area where Mexicans were numerous, however, "belongingness" took on a new significance and Joseph preferred not to belong.

American

"American" is a rather loose term that is applicable to all peoples of the two American continents. When it is used in reference to the people of the United States, other Americans tend to resent the ethnocentricity implied by such usage. It is as if the citizens of the United States ignored the fact that there are twenty other American republics and considered themselves *the* Americans.

As used here, "American" does refer only to the people of the United States although it is recognized that there are many other cultural groups that have as legitimate a claim to that term. Such usage does not imply any superiority over other peoples of the Americas. It is simply used as a matter of convenience, since both in speaking and writing about the people of the United States the term "American" is commonly employed.

In reference to ethnic groups, the term "American" is here used in a restricted sense. The American ethnic group is the dominant cultural group. Hence, the term "American" as used in this work is not applicable even to the Negro who, strictly speaking, is American by virtue of citizenship, generations of residence, and cultural heritage. The Negro constitutes a minority and is set apart from the dominant group especially by racial characteristics.

Social Institutions

Values, it has been seen, are the group-approved attitudes toward basic needs and the means devised for meeting them. Both ends and means are rooted in social institutions. A social institution may be defined as the "organized system of practices and social roles developed about a value or series of values, and the machinery evolved to regulate the practices and administer the rules,"[26] or as a "set of institutional norms that cohere around a relatively distinct and socially important complex of values."[27] Cultural norms that are institutionalized are generally distinguished by the degree of consensus with which they are supported and by the intensity of the sanctions. Thus, the major social institutions—family, church, and government—are thought to embody the ultimate values that a people have in common. Hence, people have a sense of loyalty to these systems which meet persistent needs.

Some ethnic groups prefer to meet welfare needs through primary social institutions, especially that of the family. Where the family extends beyond the conjugal unit to consanguinal and spiritual relationships as it does among the Chinese, Mexicans, and Italians, most welfare needs will seek to be satisfied within the family institution. The church may also afford such assistance.[28] Organized social work or counseling services as known in America, however, may be completely alien to the culture of many ethnic groups. Counsel may be traditionally the function of the family or of the clergy.

[26] Edward Byron Reuter, *Handbook of Sociology*, New York, The Dryden Press, Inc., 1941, p. 129.

[27] Williams, *op. cit.*, p. 29; see also F. Stuart Chapin, *Contemporary American Institutions*, New York, Harper & Brothers, 1935, pp. 319-320.

[28] See William Gioseffi, "The Relationship of Culture to the Principles of Casework," *Social Casework* (May, 1951), 32:195.

Analyzing the Dominant Culture

Throughout this study the cultural values of the majority American group will be analyzed and placed in juxtaposition to those of ethnic minorities. Although it may be popularly believed that the American man in the street is familiar with his own culture, there are, nonetheless, strong motives for making an analysis of the dominant culture.

Difficulties in Self-Knowledge

Apart from methodological considerations which will be seen later, there are real obstacles to a clear vision of the culture with which one identifies. It is usually difficult to view with detachment a culture whose values color one's own attitudes and emotions. Values, by their very nature, tend to be accepted uncritically. Outsiders who do not share these values are in a position to evaluate them with less bias. Hence, the generalizations concerning American culture are, in large part, drawn from such sources. Where generalizations by Americans are utilized, they are predominantly those of critical and well-informed commentators.

Furthermore, in analyzing one's own culture there is a tendency to become a victim of myopia, for closeness to a culture ordinarily precludes clarity of vision. It is generally more difficult to perceive and analyze contemporary affairs than it is to deal with those of the past.

The complexity of American culture leads to still further complications. Even when the middle classes are viewed as typical, one must take account of gradations—religious, economic, occupational, educational, recreational, and age and sex variations—to say nothing of regional differences within these classes. To draw conclusions about American culture with any degree of reliability, then, intensive as well as extensive knowledge is necessary.[29]

American culture is also highly mobile, a fact which precludes a leisurely analysis which will endure for any length of time. Mobility brings one into contact with new patterns of behavior which tend to modify the traditional patterns. Americans move physically from one neighborhood to another, from one community to another, and from one region of the country to another, as is attested by the census reports. French travelers in this country commented on American nomadism in these words: "It can almost be said that an American is a man who possesses a head, two arms, two legs, a car, and a road with a bridge at the end of it."[30] Americans also appear to move up and down the ladder of status with much more ease than do people of other cultures. All these factors contribute to the difficulties which beset the American who attempts to analyze his own culture.

Cultural Conditioning of Professional Persons

Professional persons are as culturally conditioned as are their clients.[31] The caseworker, counselor, teacher, doctor, or nurse must "first be able to understand himself, his own emotional drives and impulses, before he can truly accept the . . . feelings [of] . . . others."[32] It is only by understanding his own motivation and by

[29] See "A Note of Caution," pp. 21-24.

[30] Pierre and Renée Gosset, "The U.S.A. Through a French Looking Glass," *The Reader's Digest* (December, 1953), 63:39.

[31] The term "client" will be used to refer to all recipients of professional services, including pupils and patients. On the cultural conditioning of professional workers cf. Isabel Burns Lindsay, "Race as a Factor in the Caseworker's Role," *Journal of Social Casework* (March, 1947), 28:102; Maurine Bois La Barre, "Cultural and Racial Problems in Social Case Work with Special Reference to Work with Negroes," *Cultural Problems in Social Case Work*, New York, Family Welfare Association, 1940, p. 16.

[32] Gordon Hamilton, *Theory and Practice of Social Case Work*, New York, Columbia University Press, 1940, pp. 31-32.

accepting himself that he is able to understand and accept others.

The professional person's attitudes, like those of his client, reflect his own life experiences and values. Among other things, his family, social class status, and religious and economic background are factors influencing his attitudes toward himself, his job, and his client. His personality has been formed in a cultural environment that has left its impact. For instance, the professional worker who has lived in the South may feel that a Negro client with small children should find employment because "Negro women with small children always work." Again, the worker who has lived a long time in a region that has large numbers of impoverished ethnics may conclude that these ethnic clients do not need the same amount of assistance as nonethnics in identical situations, since "they have low standards of living anyhow." An awareness of the impact of one's own cultural conditioning should be conducive to more effective and meaningful practice.[33]

Self-Knowledge an Aid in Therapy

The professional person's culturally instilled attitudes will tend to influence his conception of acceptable solutions to a client's problems. This is especially the case where the problem involves a cultural conflict. American values are prone to be viewed as superior, and pressure may be used to influence the client to accept "the American way" rather than to leave him free to make the most comfortable cultural adaptation.[34] Introspection may reveal that, although the professional worker intends to allow the principle of self-determination to operate, unconsciously he may have indicated his personal cultural preferences, thereby exerting pressures on the client to conform to American culture.

[33] Cf. Sol W. Ginsburg, "The Impact of the Social Worker's Cultural Structure on Social Therapy," *Social Casework* (October, 1951), 32:320.

[34] Gioseffi, *op. cit.*, p. 195.

Insecurities Common to Americans

One of the functions of culture, it has been noted, is to provide guideposts for action, thus insuring a sense of security. No culture, however, fulfills this function completely and perfectly. There are areas of insecurity which vary from culture to culture and from time to time. In assisting the client to make a cultural adjustment, the professional person should be aware of certain insecurities which the client will probably face in accepting the dominant culture.

Two prominent aspects of American culture which facilitate the development of psychic insecurity are its competitiveness and its complexity.[35] If the client belongs to a cultural group which is simple and noncompetitive he may incur severe psychic injury in attempting to adopt the American competitive pattern. A thoughtful spokesman for the American Indian believes that the federal government should not yet relinquish its wardship of certain Indians, leaving them completely free to manage their own property. "Individually and by tribes," he says, "Indians have demonstrated that when properly motivated they can compete in a white man's world." However, there "has been a failure to understand the role of culture, a failure to see that culture shapes many of our ends, however much we try to hew them out by the forces of reason." Instead of starting with an understanding of the Indians' values and building in the desired direction to prepare them for competition in the white man's culture, administrators of Indian affairs have exhibited "impatience, bewilderment, and frustration."[36]

The complexity of American culture adds to the problem of analysis. People from simpler rural environments are in a better position to comprehend the factors responsible for certain conditions. Economic difficulties, for example, may be attributed to

[35] Robert F. Winch, *The Modern Family*, New York, Henry Holt & Co., Inc., 1952, p. 165.
[36] D'Arcy McNickle, "A U.S. Indian Speaks," *Americas* (March, 1954), 6:27.

climate, soil, or lack of effort. In a complex urban environment, however, it is more difficult to understand the forces underlying depressions and technological change.[37]

The impersonal relationships common to complex societies are not conducive to security. In simple societies everyone knows his neighbors, but in a more complex environment a friendly overture or hesitant inquiry may be ignored or even met with a rebuff. Such a response engenders a feeling of isolation rather than of belonging.

Other aspects of American culture which frequently constitute a threat to security include the relative lack of function for the aged, the utilization of institutions for sick, aged, and dependent members, and the emphasis on individual achievement for status and success.

METHODOLOGICAL CONSIDERATIONS

Purpose

This study aims to provide a conceptual framework within which to view and appraise cultural factors as they relate to the helping professions. An awareness of values, it is assumed, will acquaint the professional person with the most significant cultural factors. Values are emotionally bound and resistant to change, and where they are rooted in social institutions, change may damage psychic security. By placing the values of specific ethnic groups side by side with those of the dominant American group, the professional person should be better able to appreciate the nature of the choice which confronts the client who is experiencing a cultural conflict.

Method

Values will be approached through the major social institutions—family, church, state, economics, education, and recreation. Since

[37] Cf. Winch, *op. cit.*, p. 165.

the family is the primary and most basic social institution, inasmuch as it is the first one with which a person comes into contact, and it is, moreover, the one upon which all others rest, the values pertaining to it will receive special emphasis in Part III. Values deriving from the other social institutions will be treated in Part II. Language, the chief medium of culture transmission and treatment, will be included under the framework in Part I.

Much of the source material is primary, such as case records, personal documents, personal experiences, and other information derived from interviews. All undocumented illustrations are taken from these primary sources, and, with few exceptions, refer to situations prevailing since 1950. Secondary sources are also freely utilized. Although many of the data under consideration in this study are of an anthropological nature—inasmuch as culture is the domain of that science—the approach to cultural factors will be a sociological one. The concepts of "values" and "roles" are primarily sociological. The framework within which these concepts are used, that of social institutions, is likewise sociological. It is within this socio-anthropological framework that cultural problems common to groups of people will be viewed.

An anthropological or cross-cultural approach highlights and gives perspective to the values of the various subgroups which constitute a society. One anthropologist likens this approach to standing "on a mountain top overlooking the island-dotted ocean." Each island represents a different culture, and from this vantage point one can get an unusual perspective on the scene. This approach makes it possible to obtain an impartial and dispassionate view of the differing value systems, including one's own.[38]

Studies of national character attempt to generalize about whole "ethnic islands" on the assumption that all people in a culture are exposed to so many uniform institutions that they develop similar

[38] Goodman, *op. cit.*, p. 13.

characteristics of personality and behavior.[39] Actually there is a great variety of individual personality characteristics and patternings in any society, but the modal personality structure appears with considerable frequency. American advertisers, radio commentators, film producers, and even cartoonists, for example, assume a "recommended, applauded, underlined pattern,"[40] which has some measure of reliability. This institutionalized behavior of individuals acting in their social roles is also revealed in the literature and documents relative to a given population.[41]

A Note of Caution

In generalizing about entire ethnic groups, however, certain qualifications must be made. The more complex and heterogeneous the culture, the greater the number of exceptions to any generalization. American culture, then, is apt to be highly susceptible to variation. The child reared in this culture does not see harmonious, repetitive behavior upon which he can model his own behavior. As Margaret Mead says: "The hand held out in greeting, to still a tear, or to help up a strange child that has stumbled, is not sure that it will be taken, or if taken, taken in the sense in which it is offered."[42] When a young girl smiles, or laughs, or casts down her eyes, the cue has a definite significance if patterns of courtship are clear. In America, however, "the same smile may evoke a casual answering grin, embarrassed averted eyes, an unwelcome advance, or may even mean being followed home along a deserted street, not because each boy who answers feels differently about the girl, but

[39] Mischa Titiev, *The Science of Man,* New York, Henry Holt & Co., Inc., 1954, p. 438.
[40] Margaret Mead, *Male and Female,* New York, William Morrow & Co., Inc., 1949, p. 263.
[41] Cf. Alex Inkeles and Daniel J. Levinson, "National Character: The Study of Modal Personality and Sociocultural Systems," *Handbook of Social Psychology,* Cambridge, Mass., Addison-Wesley Publishing Company, Inc., 1954, II, p. 1013.
[42] Mead, *op. cit.,* p. 252.

because each understands differently the cue that she gives."[43]

Many American ethnic groups also come from societies that are highly complex. China, for example, is a vast country with multiple cultural variations. The dialects spoken in one part of China cannot be understood in another, and the lack of communication and speedy transportation has resulted in great cultural diversity.[44] The Chinese who came to America to reside permanently, however, tend to have much in common when compared with other groups. At any rate, they are more like each other than they are like native Americans. To a certain degree the same can be said for the homogeneity of other ethnic groups.

Extent of acculturation is a factor which has a bearing on ethnic patterns. Cultural forms as they prevail in the mother country[45] will still predominate among recent immigrants, but will be modified considerably by American culture patterns among the second, third, and later generations. The post-World War II immigration, for example, has altered the prevailing ethnic values. Newly arrived immigrants tend to reinforce cultural patterns that may have begun to show adaptations to American culture. To appreciate fully the complexity of culture analysis, it must also be borne in mind that changes have taken place in the culture of the homeland in the past three or more decades, and the culture of the new immigrants varies from that which older immigrants from the same place may have attempted to preserve. As yet, there are no adequate means of determining the impact of post-World War II immigration upon ethnic patterns.

There are variations not only in the rates of assimilation but also

[43] Ibid.

[44] Ernest G. Osborne, "Problems of the Chinese Family," Marriage and Family Living (Winter, 1948), 10:8.

[45] In several instances in Part II reference is made to the mother country since it is the source from which ethnic cultures were derived. With these few exceptions, generalizations apply to the cultural group in America. In Part III the approach to family values makes provision for consideration of the original source.

in the retention of certain values in preference to others. The Jews, for instance, have tended to accept most American values, but their religion and historical tradition set them apart. Another ethnic group may compromise economic values, but retain others associated with family roles.

Variations will also occur within a single ethnic group. One generation will differ from another, and there will also be age and sex variations. Allowances are made for the factors of age and sex in considering family roles, but less provision is made for such differences in the analyses of other values because of the dearth of information.

Cultural patterns and the values attached thereto will fluctuate from one social class to another within an ethnic group. The values of the urbanized middle classes are viewed as representative of American culture inasmuch as most Americans consider themselves middle class,[46] and it is believed that the middle classes lead in diffusing their values.[47] In considering other ethnic groups, class variations cannot be as clearly differentiated. For the most part, these groups are lower on the social ladder than the American middle classes and their values, then, will reflect the attitudes of a lower class level. To a certain extent, however, even lower classes have the values of the upper classes as ultimate goals.[48] The values of the upper classes, moreover, tend to be emphasized in source materials.

Allowances must also be made for inconsistencies in differentiating between official and unofficial values. American culture is purposely presented from an unidealistic point of view in order to help the American professional person view his own culture critically. Seeing ourselves as others see us may, at times, be salutary,

[46] In a public opinion poll 79.2 percent of the Americans polled classified themselves as middle class. "The People of the U.S.A.—A Self-Portrait," *Fortune* (February, 1940), 21:14.

[47] Barron, *op. cit.*, p. 212.

[48] Cf. Williams, *op. cit.*, p. 90.

and, as one American commentator wrote of European critics, "no mirror can distort a non-existent object."[49] In dealing with the values of other cultural groups, however, the official values are more often emphasized, because they are the ones stressed in many of the available sources.

The diverse ethnic groups are not weighted proportionately, although an attempt has been made to give more space to the numerically larger and less assimilated groups. Perhaps the Mexican group is used by way of illustration most frequently. Again, the availability of material on this group accounts for the stress given it.

With all these limitations and qualifications, an attempt is made to give a cross-cultural view of the values of American ethnic groups —the dominant group as well as the minority groups. The source materials or instruments through which these cultures are seen may not be perfectly focused for the purpose of making valid scientific comparisons. Nonetheless, they do afford some insight into cultural values.

---

[49] Joseph M. Duffy, Jr., "Europe's Image of America," *The Commonweal* (July 9, 1954), 60:336.

2

Language as a Value

INTRODUCTION

LANGUAGE is the medium through which culture is transmitted. It is one of the first things the child learns and, once acquired, it becomes a key which opens to him the rest of his culture. From the anthropological point of view there are as many different worlds as there are languages, for each language guides its users "in observing, in reacting, [and] in expressing" themselves in a special way.[1] It is through language that symbolic values are imparted and "group consciousness, rapport, solidarity, and integration" are maintained.[2] Language makes man "heir to the thought, the wisdom, the imagination" of his ancestors. It is "the poor man's literature and folklore, it is his history and tradition, . . . it is his fund of music and song, it is the repertory of his prayers, it is the source of his wise maxims; in it he gives vent to his feelings, to his hopes and fears. . . ."[3]

Language is, moreover, the primary instrument of expression for many professional persons. Caseworkers depend largely upon oral communication in interviewing, and group workers use it as the

[1] Kluckhohn, *Mirror for Man, op. cit.,* p. 160.
[2] J. O. Hertzler, "Toward a Sociology of Language," *Social Forces* (December, 1953), 32:112.
[3] P. S. Dineen, as quoted by Robert E. Park, *The Immigrant Press and Its Control,* New York, Harper & Brothers, 1922, p. 12.

chief technique to produce action. Teachers, counselors, and others in the helping professions use it to incite behavior by exhortation, provocation, or command.[4] The client, too, depends primarily upon language to reveal his experiences and his attitudes. He makes known his needs through verbalization, and this verbalization may be the first step in organizing a chaos of experience.[5] His ability to impart the nature of his problems will depend, to a large extent, upon the facility with which he can express himself. In the permissive attitude of the social agency or counselor's office the client is encouraged to release his feelings of anxiety and hostility. Whether or not he has a satisfying release of tension, however, will be determined largely by his ability to express himself and also by the extent of cultural restraints.

CULTURALLY PRESCRIBED RETICENCE

American culture permits its bearers to be relatively articulate in the presence of strangers.[6] There was a time when certain things were not openly talked about in American society. The "gamier facts of life" were deemed unsuited to public knowledge, and the "gaudier private histories" were largely curtained off. When it was considered bad form to refer to people's respectable diseases, it must have been quite unthinkable to discuss their unseemly ones.[7]

As people became more "emancipated," however, they demanded less privacy for themselves and had less respect for the privacy of others. In an age of "interviewers, of gossip columnists, of TV con-

---

[4] Hertzler, loc. cit.

[5] May Irvine, "Communication and Relationship in Social Casework," *Social Casework* (January, 1955), 36:14.

[6] Cf. Mary Bosworth Truedley, "American Cultural Themes and Social Work," *Social Forces* (March, 1950), 28:294.

[7] Louis Kronenberger, *Company Manners*, Indianapolis, The Bobbs-Merrill Company, Inc., 1954, p. 128.

fessions and camera exposés," Americans have become more curious about the private lives of strangers. Oddly enough, there is keen widespread interest displayed toward individuals who are neither celebrities nor personal acquaintances. Americans listen to gossip about "who's-dating-whom, the rumors of divorce, the shifts in affection, the speculations as to marriage" and other intimate titbits.[8] Nothing is sacred and nothing private to the advertisers, whether it be filial devotion, religion, health, or cleanliness. Radio and television depict highly emotional real-life happenings, and it is believed that "few people seem to mind such invasion of privacy."[9] One radio program uses tape recordings of actual situations. On one such program a husband and wife had the following words with each other after the police questioned them about their runaway son.

Husband: "Officers, that's what I have to put up with. I say one word to the boys and she jumps on my throat. . . . I'm just a dog around here, but by ———, I'm a dog no longer."
Wife: "Please, I can't go on like this. . . . He called me a parasite and a paranoiac parasite and everything. Just because he's working hard . . . How can I go on?"[10]

The radio actor, Donn Reed, who originated the show, maintains that it has been easy to get legal releases to use the voices of prisoners and witnesses. Apparently, then, American culture offers relatively few obstacles to expressing one's feelings, a fact which facilitates counseling or the casework process.

It is more difficult, however, for the professional helping person to form a relationship with members of cultural groups who are trained not to share certain experiences with outsiders. Indians, for

[8] *Ibid.*, p. 129.
[9] "How Real Can It Get?" *Time* (April 26, 1954), 63:106. According to Jacques Freymond, Europeans remark that Americans "lay bare their own private lives as freely as they pry into the lives of others." "America in European Eyes," *Annals of the American Academy of Political and Social Science* (September, 1954), 295:38.
[10] *Ibid.*, p. 104.

instance, do not find silences awkward or embarrassing, and they may "size up" strangers during a prolonged silence. The professional person who is unfamiliar with this cultural pattern may react in the manner of the social worker who remarked that "interviews [with Indians] must be slow-paced and can be maddening when other cases need attention," or the worker who wrote, "I find it almost impossible to wait for answers to my questions and must make a conscious effort to adapt my pace to the leisurely tempo of my patients."[11] Domestic friction, especially where womenfolk are involved, is discussed with great reluctance by the Italian immigrant.[12] The Greek, too, is culturally bound never to expose "the inner core of his being, and particularly his shortcomings" outside his immediate circle.[13] Family discord is something to be borne in silence. The Oriental is, however, the classic example of self-control and reserve. This is particularly true of the Chinese. Even small children skillfully conceal suffering and resentment, and sometimes joy. An Oriental father may tell of the death of his wife with no outward show of feeling, or with a smile.[14]

The Oriental, Italian, or Mexican mother may be reticent in expressing an opinion if she believes the matter under discussion to be in her husband's sphere. That sphere is often quite inclusive when the family is patriarchal. Caseworkers in one juvenile office noticed that many a Mexican mother who gave every indication of having attitudes different from those of the father never voiced any difference in joint interviews or before the court. The father

[11] Sol W. Ginsburg, *On Cultural Factors in Casework*, New York, National Travelers Aid Association, 1954, p. 6.
[12] Gioseffi, "The Relationship of Culture to the Principles of Casework," *Social Casework, op. cit.*, 32:194.
[13] Dorothy Lee, "Some Implications of Culture for Interpersonal Relations," *Social Casework* (November, 1950), 31:358.
[14] Eileen Blackey, "Some Cultural Aspects of Social Casework in Hawaii," *Cultural Problems in Social Case Work*, New York, Family Welfare Association of America, 1940, pp. 51-52.

represented the family to outsiders and when he expressed himself, he had the support of the family.

There are also "taboo words" which culture prohibits or permits only under certain circumstances. Some relate to mystical and sacred things, such as the use of the name of God. Others are in the nature of obscenities, referring to such functions as sex and excretion. Culture also offers euphemisms or polite substitutes such as "the Almighty" for God and "to pass away" or "to kick the bucket" for "to die."[15] Apart from psychological factors, a person relatively unfamiliar with culturally approved expressions may be at a loss to express himself in these areas.

Many ethnics have no intention of sharing intimate experiences with the professional person who is trying to help, even though they have an adequate vocabulary. Culturally instilled attitudes restrain them from seeking counsel or assistance in certain areas. To many ethnics, reserve bespeaks manliness and strength of character while a free expression of all difficulties is indicative of weakness and inability to handle their intimate affairs.

Use of Courtesy Titles and Epithets

Apart from these instances where cultural groups value reticence, the professional person may experience other difficulties in communicating with the client and in establishing rapport with him. For example, the use of a courtesy title has deep significance to the Negro. Before emancipation it was customary to address a Negro by his given name only. Slaves seldom had surnames, for a surname symbolizes status. If it were necessary to distinguish between "Toms" or "Johns," the accepted form was "John belonging to Mr. Brown." In case the given name was not known, "boy" or "girl" was used, regardless of the age of the slave. Thus one "good

[15] Hertzler, op. cit., p. 116.

boy" had been a blacksmith thirty years, and was the father of at least ten children.[16]

Carl Rowan relates an incident that occurred when he was traveling with some friends in Tennessee. They were stopped by some highway patrolmen, one of whom said:

". . . Boy, we got a tip that y'all are hauling liquor."

"No, sir. Where did you get any tip like that?"

"That ain't for you to know. All you boys get out."

I pushed my suitcase out before me and stepped onto the highway. As the last man got out, one patrolman pulled the rear seat into the street. No liquor.

"You, boy, what you got in that grip?"

It had been a long time since I had been called "boy." Evidently this patrolman did not know that, in getting my Navy commission, I had become a gentleman, by act of Congress. . . . I didn't think it was the time or place to apprise him of such happenings, however. "Clothing," I replied in a voice that was high-pitched in anger.

"Zoot-suit clothes?" he continued.

"Just plain old everyday clothing."

"Aw, surely some of you black boys can dance," the patrolman said.

The eyes of five Negro veterans met silently. I knew that we all thought the same thing. One smart word and they might shoot us, and then swear that we "acted biggity." . . .

"You boys git," said one with finality. "Guess you boys ain't the bootleggers."[17]

To use the given name or to omit the courtesy title "Mr.," "Miss," or "Mrs." when addressing a Negro may lead the client to infer that the professional worker is unwilling to accord him status as a person or free agent. One of the functions of etiquette is to preserve the rank and order of individuals and classes in organized societies, and the Negro is especially sensitive to any

[16] Bertram Wilbur Doyle, *The Etiquette of Race Relations in the South*, Chicago, University of Chicago Press, 1937, pp. 17, 54.

[17] Carl T. Rowan, *South of Freedom*, New York, Alfred A. Knopf., Inc., 1952, pp. 17-18.

deviation. The implication is that the Negro is inferior, and that he belongs to the category of children or of slaves.

A Negro usually prefers to be called "Negro" or "Colored," but dislikes "negress" or "negra." "Nigger" is nearly always resented, and even derivatives may be disturbing, such as "niggertoe" for Brazil nut, "niggerhead" for a type of tobacco, or the use of the word "niggardly."[18]

Literature abounds with reactions of Negroes to such names. Elizabeth Adams says, "I think every Colored person in the world can recall the first time he or she was called by this uncomplimentary title," and she relates her own experience thus:

> One day a stranger arrived at school. We called her the "new girl" because we had never seen her before. When Mary asked her to join our game she shook her head and refused. Pointing in my direction she declared:
> "I won't play with her because—*she's a nigger.*"
> That was the first time I had ever heard—the word.[19]

Even when the term "nigger" is used by well-meaning persons who are unaware of the implications, it usually gives offense. A distinguished sociologist relates a personal experience of this kind. He was hitchhiking in a region where Negroes are seldom seen and was befriended by a kindly white couple who gave him a meal and offered him a place to sleep in their home. Whenever they addressed him, though, they said "little nigger," a fact which distressed him even though he was grateful for their kindness. Finally, he asked them not to call him by that "insulting term."

> "Who's insultin' you, son?" said the man.
> "You are, sir—that name you're always calling me."
> "What name?"

[18] S. I. Hayakawa, *Language in Thought and Action,* New York, Harcourt, Brace & Co., 1949, p. 91.
[19] Elizabeth Laura Adams, *Dark Symphony,* New York, Sheed & Ward, 1942, pp. 16-17.

"Uh . . . you know."

"I ain't callin' you no names, son."

"I mean your calling me 'nigger.' "

"Well, what's insultin' about that? You are a nigger, ain't you?"[20]

The professional worker who has heard such expressions as "wop," "dago," "bohunk," "mescin," "nigger," "greaser," "kike," "chink," or "heinie" freely used during childhood may use them inadvertently, and unwittingly create hostility. Even though the client makes reference to members of his own group in this manner, it is not advisable for the worker to infer that he, too, can use the term without giving offense. The probabilities are that the client is testing the professional worker in order to discover his attitudes toward the group in question.

Incongruities Arising from Differing Mediums of Communication

Some cultural groups make much greater use of gestures in communicating than do Americans, and a vigorous, animated sign language may appear incongruous. Many Italians, for example, use gestures freely as an accessory to ordinary conversation. They tend to talk rapidly, use their hands sweepingly by way of illustrating points, and greet each other effusively. When they become excited or emphatic, gestures appear to be used with still greater abandon. Gestures may have fairly definite patterns, however, and convey specific meanings.[21]

Jews who have retained much of their original culture also gesticulate more than Americans. In the ghetto "it was taken for granted that hands had their place in speech, that conversation was

[20] Hayakawa, *op. cit.*, p. 90.

[21] Irvin L. Child, *Italian or American?* New Haven, Yale University Press, 1943, p. 22; see also Joost A. M. Meerloo, *Conversation and Communication,* New York, International Universities Press, Inc., 1952, pp. 14-15.

to be intense."[22] Speech was animated and laughter was whole-hearted. To Americans it would seem that the Jews were highly demonstrative, but what "one society considers gauche . . . another society regards as in perfectly good taste."[23]

The Mexicans, too, tend to become very animated when speaking publicly, and often resort to what appears to be aimless, exaggerated gesturing. A political leader who was conducting a rally became so excited that he literally danced along the platform and used his arms and hands with equal freedom. Present in the audience was a newly arrived social worker who became greatly amused over the performance. He leaned toward the stranger at his side and made a remark about the speaker's actions. Unfortunately, the stranger had ethnic ties with the politician and took offense at the remark. As a consequence, a rumor was circulated to the effect that the new social worker was unsympathetic toward Mexicans.

An American woman who married a Mexican and went to live in Mexico wrote that "Mexicans all talk at the same time and at the top of their lungs," replacing half of the words by gestures. She had to learn "the whole lexicon of what is meant by each movement of shoulders, hands, wrists, eyebrows, forehead, and head." Children are taught elocution, and a good performance evokes "laughter, wags of the head, tears, applause."[24]

The professional person with a good sense of humor will have to be on guard and refrain from laughter when English is misused by the client. Such circumstances as the following are apt to occur. In attempting to describe his house to the worker, the client said it was a "bluff" house, referring to its "buff" color. On being introduced to a member of a client's family, the worker said, "I'm pleased

[22] Milton Steinberg, *The Making of the Modern Jew,* Indianapolis, The Bobbs-Merrill Company, 1934, p. 235.

[23] *Ibid.*

[24] Elizabeth Borton De Treviño, *My Heart Lies South,* New York, Thomas Y. Crowell Co., 1954, pp. 15, 217.

to meet you," and the response was a gracious "Thank you, just the same." Another client explained his delay in keeping an appointment by saying that he had forgotten the floor number and was "riding up and down in the radiator."

The difficulty of mastering the English language is best realized by those ethnics who have another native tongue. A Chinese man relates some of the expressions which he found puzzling as follows:

> When you say you are going to dress a chicken, you mean that you are going to undress it. . . . A cow may be said to have a pretty skin, but a woman may never be said to have a pretty hide. . . . The plural of foot is feet, but the plural of boot is not beet. The plural of this is these, but the plural of kiss is not keese.

One of his friends, a Korean, who had learned that "pickle" and "preserve" have the same meaning, stood up at a prayer meeting and said, "O God, please pickle my soul."[25]

MEANS OF CULTURAL IDENTIFICATION AND COMMUNICATION

The careful selection of terminology and awareness of cultural taboos are negative measures—in the nature of precautions. On the positive side, just how meaningful is communication in one's native tongue?

Language is one of the strongest bonds uniting a cultural group. It is their "sign of recognition" and their "badge of brotherhood."[26] Immigrant groups generally name themselves by their language rather than by place of origin. Even in the twentieth century, "Syrian" societies included not simply those born in Syria, but all Arabic-speaking peoples.[27] One's own language falls pleasantly on

[25] No-Yong Park, *Chinaman's Chance*, Boston, Meador Publishing Co., 1940, p. 33.

[26] J. Vendryes, *Language: A Linguistic Introduction to History*, trans. Paul Radin, New York, Alfred A. Knopf, Inc., 1925, p. 241.

[27] Oscar Handlin, *The Uprooted*, Boston, Little, Brown and Co., 1951, p. 187.

the ear, but foreign tongues sound "nasal," "singsong," "guttural," or "squeaky"—at least until one becomes habituated to them.[28]

Language gives clues to the understanding of behavior. While the English clock "runs," it "walks" in Spanish; hence, the English-speaking person must hurry to make use of time before it runs away, but the Spanish-speaking person may take a more leisurely attitude. The English-speaking person who arrives late for work tends to say, "I missed the bus," making himself the active agent and accepting the responsibility for his tardiness. The Spanish-speaking person, however, is more apt to say that the bus left him, that the dishes fell out of his hands and broke, or that diseases are the manifestations of God's will. Language, then, is a good guide to the way a person perceives events and objects in the world about him.[29]

Each linguistic group tends to have its own rules about what to say and how to say it. There is an enjoyable process of social interaction in which outsiders cannot fully participate. When something especially significant is said, even though the group would like to share the experience with an outsider, the comment loses its savor when translated. "It is terrific in Spanish," one student commented apologetically to the nonethnics in the group, "but it doesn't sound like anything in English."

A bilingual student relates some of her own experiences in a large Southwestern community as follows:

I do not remember which language I learned to speak first—English or Spanish. At home we have always spoken both. I have the advantage that my parents know English and so I had no difficulty when I entered school. Many Spanish-speaking children do not learn English in the home and are retarded when they start school. I went to a grade school where very few of the children knew Spanish, so I spoke English at

[28] Henry Pratt Fairchild, *Race and Nationality as Factors in American Life,* New York, The Ronald Press Company, 1947, p. 42.

[29] Lyle Saunders, *Cultural Differences and Medical Care,* New York, Russell Sage Foundation, 1954, pp. 116-117.

school. After school I spoke Spanish to my playmates and to my grand-parents. I spoke both languages to my parents. I really didn't pay too much attention to the matter in grade school.

I received my high school education at a private academy for girls. Here I became a little more aware of being able to speak Spanish. In my gang were girls who spoke only English, but there were others who could speak Spanish. We were fined for speaking Spanish on the play-ground because of the number of girls from Mexico who came to learn English. In my last two years of high school the Spanish-speaking girls became more clannish and told jokes, songs, and so forth that only we could enjoy. We never lost contact with the English-speaking girls, though, and were considered a part of them.

When I entered college, however, the situation became a problem. In college those that speak Spanish definitely group together and exclude all those that do not. There have been one or two exceptions, but this is due to the fact that the person could tolerate our speaking Spanish all the time. It is said that language sometimes serves as a rallying point for a suppressed group. We were never a suppressed group, but we did go through the experience of being excluded from a social group because of our ethnicity. Therefore we banded together and spoke Spanish all the time. That was three years ago. Since then the social group has been dissolved and the scars are slowly healing. I still think we would clan together, but I don't believe it would be to the same degree that I found when I entered college. We get together because we have the same interest in dancing, music, movies, jokes, and so forth.

While language serves as a "magic key" that opens a "treasure chest of associations" for those that speak the same tongue,[30] it also sets apart from the dominant group the ethnic who seeks to conceal or lose his identification. A child who was made to feel inferior to her peers because she spoke Spanish in a region where there were many lower-class Mexicans reveals her anxiety over cultural identi-fication in the following excerpt from a case record:

Yolanda, a six-year-old girl of Latin American parents, was referred to a Child Guidance Clinic by the pediatrician because of the child's

[30] Bruno Lasker, *Democracy Through Discussion*, New York, H. W. Wilson Co., 1949, p. 267.

severe nightmares, fear of the dark, and complaints that a man was following her.

Yolanda spoke contemptuously about one of her girl friends who apparently is unable to speak English. Yolanda called this child a "Mexican" and contended that she was unable to understand a word her friend said. This seems very doubtful since Yolanda is unable to express herself very effectively in English. She appears to have some conflict in the area of racial or cultural identification.

During play sessions, Yolanda consistently draws characters with blue eyes and blond hair. She named her doll "Blondie." In the course of the session when Yolanda was painting, she tried to tell me something but could not think of the English words to express what she wanted to say. She told me that she could say it in Spanish and volunteered the information that she spoke Spanish at home. This statement was in contrast to the impression she tried to convey the first time she came to the clinic. Yolanda asked me what I was when I was a little girl, whether I was a Spanish little girl or an English little girl. I told her that when I was a little girl I spoke Chinese, and she said, "That makes you like me because I speak Spanish."

As the case of this child indicates, one may be reasonably fluent in the English language and still feel that greater fluency in speaking the foreign mother tongue sets one apart. Dialect, choice of words, and accent may, indeed, be revealing. This is often the case even with persons who speak only one language. The Southern drawl, for example, is clearly distinguishable from the clipped speech of certain Easterners, and many Negroes have a dialect which is readily discernible.

It sometimes happens that even within a family there is a language barrier. The child educated in American schools tends to discuss experiences alien to his parents, and in a language that the parents cannot understand. Futile efforts to communicate frequently grow into silences. Parents often make great sacrifices to send their children to foreign-language schools, wherever possible. The language which the child learns in these schools, however, is the standard language which may be hardly intelligible to the parents.

There are, for example, many Chinese dialects and it is impossible for a person from North China to understand one from South China. A child may learn basic grammar and vocabulary, but not how to converse with any ease, much less to write the language. When the child leaves home, then, it may become impossible for him to correspond with his family.[31]

The large families, especially among the Chinese and Japanese, are a help in overcoming this language handicap.[32] Older children smooth the way for the younger siblings since they generally speak the native language with more fluency and can serve in a liaison capacity. They explain to the parents the reasons for the alien behavior of younger siblings. Parents can rely on the older children when they feel the need of depending upon someone who knows American ways as well as the native folkways. Among the Japanese, at least, this dependence of parents upon children is culturally acceptable, for the use of an intermediary is an honored institution.[33] When the older children who have acted in the capacity of intermediaries have married and left home, however, the barriers between parents and younger children—especially that of language —may prove to be a source of misunderstanding and frustration.

A Chinese girl, whose older siblings had married and moved away from home, wrote to her older sister as follows:

Remember, Sis, before you left, what I told you? Well, it was just as I had predicted. What I was referring to was my relationship with Pop. I told you then that Pop and I could never be as close as you and he were. I just can't seem to maintain the same position that you did! I know why, too! It's the language barrier that keeps us from being closer. You just don't realize how restricting it can be and how many problems it creates.

[31] See case in Katherine Newkirk Handley, "Social Casework and Intercultural Problems," *Journal of Social Casework* (February, 1947), 28:45.

[32] Bradford Smith, *Americans from Japan*, Philadelphia, J. B. Lippincott Co., 1948, p. 53.

[33] *Ibid.*

I never deliberately set out to provoke Pop by disagreeing, but I always seem to do just that. I respect Pop for letting me express my views, but it's the manner in which I speak that "irks" him so much. Here, again, is the language difficulty. Since my Chinese is so limited, I have to use whatever words I know to try to get over the point. In doing so I sound disrespectful and "sassy" but, it's only because a person can't be tactful if he or she has command of only a few key words.

When you were home you used to take care of seeing the lawyers whenever things came up and then you explained things to Pop so he could solve problems logically. I've failed here, too. It's not because I'm disinterested; I simply have such a hard time explaining matters to Pop. Just last week Pop wanted me to look over the blue prints that the contractor had brought from remodeling the property on the East Side. Well, I looked it over and understood the plans fairly well. But when I tried to explain, I couldn't even tell him the kind of bricks they were planning to use or anything! My stuttering Chinese confused Pop and frustrated me.

Pop is a terribly lonely man in the midst of his large family. He is surrounded with his children and yet is unable to communicate even in little discussions like those concerning our daily activities. All we can do is to show our appreciation and acknowledgement of all his sacrifices for us through doing little things for him—since we can't say it. Yet, how much more meaningful our actions would be if we could speak to him.

When necessity leads the client who speaks English falteringly to an agency, he becomes painfully aware of the value of his mother tongue. If it is difficult at times to voice anxiety-laden feelings in one's own language, how much more difficult it is to attempt such an expression in another language. Translations prove awkward and are sometimes unintelligible. Frustration and increased tension may result from repeated attempts at expression in another language.

The professional person, on the other hand, who has difficulty in understanding the client must sacrifice the primary social value of speech—which "lies in getting individuals to work more effectively together and in easing social tensions."[34] The relief of tension

[34] Kluckhohn, *op. cit.*, p. 147.

may depend upon helping the client to become aware of factors of which he is unconscious. Under such circumstances, where the client cannot be explicit, the language barrier may be crucial. Nuances, the fine shades of meaning that may be highly significant, cannot be appreciated by the professional person. If the client resorts to pidgin English he has a poor tool for conveying subtle and complex feelings.

USING THE CLIENT'S NATIVE TONGUE

The professional person who can understand or, better still, respond in the native tongue of the client has hurdled an important obstacle in the formation of a working relationship. Although the professional person may not speak the language fluently, he may, in some instances, increase rapport by occasionally using meaningful words or expressions in the client's language. Spanish-speaking people tend to be favorably impressed by an outsider's effort to use Spanish in conversation, even though the outsider may speak incorrectly. The Oriental, however, may be irritated or even offended by such an attempt. Japanese, in particular, are sensitive to errors in pronunciation of their mother tongue; to them mispronunciation and laughter over mistakes are tantamount to sacrilege.[35]

A bilingual client who has an appreciation of his cultural values may prefer to speak his native language, even though he can express himself adequately in English. If the professional person happens to be in any way identified with the culture of the client—by physical characteristics or surname, for example—and is unable to converse in the native tongue, this very fact may cause him to be rejected by the client.

[35] Forrest E. LaViolette, *Americans of Japanese Ancestry*, Toronto, Canadian Institute of International Affairs, 1945, p. 55.

The following examples related by a Spanish-speaking[36] person illustrate these attitudes on the part of this particular group:

No matter where you are, if you are with a person or group of people who speak Spanish you speak Spanish to them or they might not answer you. This is true even in department stores. If you ask for something in English, the salesgirl will reply in Spanish.

I was helping my pastor take the church census some time ago. I went to a house and began to interview a lady. I spoke in English, but she would not reply. A neighbor who was on the porch asked, "What's the matter? You know English, don't you?" The woman replied, "Yes, I do, but when I speak with someone who knows Spanish, I prefer to speak Spanish."

Feelings are very strong against Mexicans who do not know Spanish. My sister is in training to be a nurse and in her class is a Mexican girl who cannot speak Spanish. To make matters worse, she looks like a Mexican. When she was caring for a Mexican woman and could not understand what the woman wanted, the woman refused to let her come back into the room. Other Mexican patients also resent having her take care of them because she does not know how to speak her own mother tongue.

Language is of such importance, then, that the professional person who is able to converse in the native tongue and chooses to use another may run the risk of being rejected. How could a person to whom the native language is not a value, the client asks himself, be sympathetic toward other cultural values?

[36] Some languages, of course, seem to have greater persistence than others, even among the third generation. One study found that Spanish ranked highest, while French ranked second and German third. Cf. Lowry Nelson, "Speaking of Tongues," *American Journal of Sociology* (November, 1948), 54:207.

Part II

VALUES DERIVING FROM SOCIAL INSTITUTIONS

3

Religion and Magic

AMERICAN RELIGION

AMONG cultural groups language is, at times, an untrustworthy standard of identification. Those speaking the same tongue may find attitudes toward religion and magic a fundamental barrier, for in these areas, more than any other, one tends to have assurance that one's own values are right and those of other groups are erroneous and injurious.[1]

An appreciation of such cultural values may be very important to the professional person who is dealing with clients who have differing values; a person cannot ordinarily be really understood apart from the religious and moral code to which he prescribes.

The complexity of American culture is exemplified in the variety of religious creeds in this country, a circumstance which was made possible by the strong tradition of religious freedom. Protestantism claims more adherents than Catholicism or Judaism, but in a multiplicity of forms. The colonies were, after all, "peopled by Protestants, and chiefly by the more radical sectarians who represented the very 'dissidence of dissent.' "[2] With such a tradition, new sects arose continuously. America's two most original religions—Mormonism and Christian Science—are noted for their practical aspects rather

[1] Cf. Fairchild, *Race and Nationality as Factors in American Life, op. cit.,* p. 44.
[2] George R. Stewart, *American Ways of Life,* New York, Doubleday & Company, Inc., 1954, p. 66.

45

than for their theological contributions. In fact, most Americans are believed to be unfamiliar with the dogmatic distinctions between Protestant denominations.[3]

Dwight D. Eisenhower typifies the prevailing American attitude toward religion. To him religion is said to be "a matter of a very simple approach to his Creator."[4] Like many Americans, he is "a very fervent believer in a very vague religion."[5] Although he could "quote Scripture by the yard," he refused to become affiliated with any denomination prior to becoming chief executive. As a military officer moving from one post to another, Dwight Eisenhower attended Army chapels "from time to time and developed a non-denominational attitude."[6] In campaigning he extolled "honesty, decency, fairness, service—all that sort of thing." He was unspecific with his "that sort of thing" generalities, but "it was Abilene speaking to 10,000 other Abilenes."[7] In one speech Eisenhower seemed to identify religion and democracy. He called himself "the most intensely religious man I know," and said: "A democracy cannot exist without a religious base," adding immediately: "I believe in democracy." One churchman criticized this statement and expressed the fear that it would encourage making a "religion of our democracy."[8]

Although religion is usually inherited as a part of culture, many Protestant Americans change denominations, or simply do not affiliate with any denomination. Some Americans state that merely because of family tradition, "they have a certain affiliation, al-

[3] Henry Steele Commager, *The American Mind,* New Haven, Yale University Press, 1952, p. 9.
[4] Paul Hutchinson quoting a Washington church leader in "The President's Religious Faith," *Life* (March 22, 1954), 36:168.
[5] *Ibid.,* p. 162.
[6] William H. Stringer, "The President and the Still Small Voice," *The Congressional Record* (April 26, 1954), 100:A2992-2993.
[7] Hutchinson, *op. cit.,* p. 162.
[8] *Ibid.,* p. 160.

though they rarely or never attend services or show any other evidence of religion."[9] They may believe that their children should be free to choose a religion when the need for it is manifest. There is no established church in America and social status is affected slightly, if at all, by changing denominations. The church in America, says Henry S. Commager, is regarded as an aged relative whose claim is vague but inescapable—something to be supported.[10] A panel of outstanding American historians, educators, and journalists who were asked to rate the most significant events in history, ranked the crucifixion of Jesus Christ fourth, a tie with four other events.[11] Much of the "uneasiness, the malaise of our time" can undoubtedly be attributed to the fact that in our politics and economy, in family life and religion the certainties of earlier centuries have disintegrated and there is "no plan of life."[12]

A century ago American churchmen were respected for their leadership in education. In 1840 the president of every important educational institution in the United States was a clergyman or had training in theology; today few clergymen occupy the presidential chair in the leading universities.[13] The outstanding quality which contemporary Americans seem to admire in their churchmen, quips a French critic, is efficiency. To support his statement he cites the case of a clergyman who is "the rector of two parishes,

[9] Stewart, *op. cit.*, p. 52.

[10] *Op. cit.*, p. 166. See also Williams, *American Society, op. cit.*, pp. 326-328, and Freymond, "America in European Eyes," *Annals of the American Academy of Political and Social Science, op. cit.*, 295:35-36. The latter is of the opinion that Americans are "unable to give an answer of positive value to those who are seeking a solution to the spiritual crisis of our time."

[11] Columbus' discovery of America ranked first; Gutenberg's development of movable type second; eleven events tied for third place; and X-ray discovered, the United States Constitution takes effect, ether makes surgery painless, and Wright brothers' plane flies tied with Jesus Christ is crucified for fourth place. "Fourth in Importance," *Time* (May 24, 1954), 63:87.

[12] C. Wright Mills, *White Collar*, New York, Oxford University Press, 1951, p. xvi.

[13] Commager, *op. cit.*, p. 167.

chaplain of a Coast Guard unit, auxiliary policeman," and to take up his "leisure time," he "works at night in the tomato canning factory of Heinz and Co."[14]

The clergyman, of course, belongs to a zealous minority which deviates from the ordinary pattern. Like the aforementioned illustration, even the clergyman's zeal may extend beyond the boundaries of clerical duties. On the whole, the urbanized, middle-class Protestant American, however, falls into the pattern delineated.

RELIGION AS AN INTEGRATING FORCE AMONG IMMIGRANTS

Religion often becomes paramount in adjusting to a new way of life; it is a refuge in a sea of bewilderment. Though other institutions are forced to adjust to the new environment, this one is transplanted intact, if possible. Among many groups there is an established church, which means that religion held a "fixed, well-defined place in their society, that it was identified with the village, that it took in all those who belonged, all those who were not outcasts."[15] To most European and Latin American immigrants, the claim of a church to men's allegiance rested on a solid basis of authority; it was not an individual choice. Not to be a member was unthinkable. It demanded "a considerable feat of the imagination to conceive of what it would mean to be excluded, . . . to be barred from every social occasion."[16] Hence, many immigrants chose to settle in proximity to a church, preferably within an ethnic colony.

Attitudes toward religion are often a determinant of ethnic identity. Religion "reveals itself simply as man's belief in spiritual powers and his efforts to deal with them so as to have their help and not

[14] H. J. Duteil, *The Great American Parade*, trans. Fletcher Pratt, New York, Twayne Publishers, Inc., 1953, p. 153.
[15] Handlin, *The Uprooted, op. cit.*, p. 118.
[16] *Ibid.*, p. 119.

their hindrance in all the business of life."[17] Although a religion may be thus broadly defined in terms that apply to many cultural groups, nonetheless it is, in practice, colored by the particular beliefs, "attitudes and methods of devotion, the folk tales, the relics, and the symbols" peculiar to the group in which they are cherished.[18]

Every Christian nation has its patron saint or hero-saint and very often, as in the case of the French Joan of Arc, this saint expresses the peculiarities and aspirations of the local ethnic elements.[19] Within a denomination ethnic peculiarities are to be found, such as those noted by a visiting Brazilian student. He remarked that the High Mass in Chicago bore more resemblance to the service of a Brazilian Presbyterian church than to the Catholic service in Brazil. In Chicago the people sat still and listened to the sermon, whereas in Brazil people walked around and prayed at the shrines of their favorite saints or at the side altars during the Mass.[20]

When ethnic groups immigrated to the United States, they transplanted their own variety of religious practices. Lutherans, who came from several regions in Europe, established not one but several Lutheran churches, despite the essential uniformity in dogma.[21] Jews persisted in their orthodoxy, and instead of attending the beautiful temples erected by American Jews who had immigrated earlier, they constructed rude synagogues where they sought the "consoling flavor of familiar worship."[22] Catholics, too, despite the fact that the Mass was in a universal language, wanted churches where they could have sermons in the vernacular and confess their sins in the language in which they committed them.[23]

[17] Arthur L. Swift, "Religious Values," *The Family: Its Function and Destiny,* ed. Ruth Nanda Anshen, New York, Harper & Brothers, 1949, p. 396.
[18] *Ibid.*
[19] Everett C. and Helen MacGill Hughes, *Where Peoples Meet,* Glencoe, Illinois, Free Press, 1952, p. 123.
[20] *Ibid.,* pp. 23-24.
[21] Handlin, *op. cit.,* pp. 138-139.
[22] *Ibid.,* p. 141.
[23] Hughes and Hughes, *op. cit.,* p. 85.

Like most Americans, many immigrants were not well versed in dogma. Formal religious education tended to be as exceptional as formal education in general. The average European immigrant was astonished at the multiplicity of religions and did not expect to be asked why he believed as he did. Religious faith had been absorbed along with other cultural values. Among the Mexicans, for instance, religion was often imparted through such means as processions or the drama. The average Japanese had "little idea of the meaning of Buddhism" and still less any coherent notion of the religious principles behind Shinto. In fact, the Japanese have substituted the standard of correct and incorrect for the concepts of good and evil.[24] Proper relationships rather than a sense of absolute values serve as a guide.[25] A Jewish writer says that the "spiritual community of Jews lies not in creed; it lies . . . [primarily] in Jewish history and culture."[26]

Despite the lack of formal instruction, however, religion is often an important value as is illustrated by the following case of a lower-class Mexican mother and son.

Mrs. S. and her son Otto continue to be quite dependent upon each other. Mrs. S. is dependent upon her crippled son because he offers her a position of responsibility through caring for him that gives her a feeling of accomplishment and takes her out of the regular channels of everyday interaction and competition with other persons, in which role she feels she would have much difficulty. Of course, Otto is dependent upon his mother because of his badly deformed condition and because she understands his needs from years of experience and accepts him.

The main interests in life for Mrs. S. and her son continue to revolve about religion. They are extremely religious and it is believed that this

[24] Smith, *Americans from Japan*, op. cit., p. 95.

[25] *Ibid.*, p. 96. After World War II, Japan became "one of the world's most irreligious nations," but now the Japanese are rediscovering Shintoism. They are "flocking to the shrines and regaining contact with the ancient lore and cultural history of Japan." "Japanese Return to Shinto Faith," *The New York Times*, January 3, 1954, p. 20.

[26] Henry Hurwitz, "Chaos or Creation?" *Menorah Journal* (Spring, 1932), 20:11.

is a healthy type of adjustment for them since it gives them a "reason for being" which they might not have otherwise. Otto feels that he was placed on earth as a cripple by God for some kind of purpose and that his faith is being tested in this manner.

Among the Jews religion has been called the essence of cultural life, since it serves not only as a means of national self-preservation but also as a bond of unity for a dispersed people. Customs, ceremonies, and rituals can be traced directly or indirectly to the religion of the people. Expressions of culture, such as philosophy, history, music, and art, were not always religious in character, but the inspiration sprang from a single source—religion in its broader significance.[27] Religion, then, may permeate every aspect of human life.

Religion may serve either to retard or to accelerate assimilation. The Huguenots who came to the United States were quick to appreciate the fact that their Protestant faith made them more acceptable, while Buddhists and Moslems have found that their religion is just one more obstacle in the path of assimilation.[28] Catholicism is said to have "perpetuated many of the national cultures of the Old World while reconciling them with one another in the pattern of the New World" without eliminating whatever was "valid and true."[29]

Among many immigrant groups religion is a factor in keeping the foreign language "alive" among the native-born.[30] European Catholic immigrants wanted parishes set up on the basis of national origin or language, and sermons preached in the native tongue. German Lutherans, too, used their native language in religious rituals and sermons. The case of John Szabós, a Hungarian Cath-

---

[27] Judah Pilch, *Jewish Life in Our Times*, New York, Behrman's House, Inc., 1943, p. 3.

[28] Brewton Berry, *Race Relations*, New York, Houghton Mifflin Co., 1951, p. 242.

[29] John J. Wright, "The Church and American Society," *Catholicism in American Culture*, New York, College of New Rochelle, 1955, p. 42.

[30] Nelson, "Speaking of Tongues," *American Journal of Sociology, op. cit.*, 54:209.

olic, exemplifies the relation between language and religion. When he went to church in the Jersey town, he felt that a "deep peace descended upon him, he felt secure, warmed by the fellowship of God and man." He relished the familiar chants and enjoyed the words of the priest—"Hungarian words, melodious to his ears, now consciously so, the tongue that fitted into the church because it was the tongue of his childhood days." Beside him were his American-born, English-speaking children. He wanted the Hungarian words "associated with the words of Christ to percolate deep into those childish hearts so that the priest's sermon should not be alien to his children. So that he should not be an alien to them. The Hungarian language of the Hungarian church should be the link."[31]

IMPORTANCE OF RELIGIOUS PRACTICES

Attitudes which cultural groups have toward standards of conduct and which are prescribed by religion vary. To most persons, however, it is a misfortune to incur the displeasure of God. What may seem to the professional worker to be minor infractions, at most, of a code of behavior, may not be as lightly regarded by the client. Violations of dietary laws prescribed by Judaism and of laws of fast and abstinence by Roman Catholicism are often sources of concern to the client who is practical in the observance of his religion. A Jew who had married a Christian wife said: "We were married by a Christian minister. I was never married by a rabbi. . . . To this day I still do not eat pork nor do I eat lobster, both being forbidden according to Jewish ritual."[32] Some Negro sects even forbid their adherents to chew gum.[33]

[31] Emil Lengyel, *Americans from Hungary*, Philadelphia, J. B. Lippincott Co., 1948, pp. 150-151.

[32] Albert I. Gordon, *Jews in Transition*, Minneapolis, University of Minnesota Press, 1949, p. 276.

[33] Arthur H. Fauset, *Black Gods of the Metropolis*, Philadelphia, University of Pennsylvania Press, 1944, p. 74.

The strict observance of the Sabbath or of other religious holidays, with the obligation to attend services or abstain from certain activities, may also be a serious matter to some clients. To the practicing Catholic, neither birth control nor divorce can be a solution to family problems, and a civil marriage ceremony is inadequate.

The influence of early religious training, faulty as it may be, is evident in the following case:

Mrs. D., the daughter of a Presbyterian minister and a divorcee, married a Catholic who embraced Protestantism in his early twenties. Mrs. D. was well educated and she assisted her second husband in obtaining both a bachelor's and a master's degree. After he had achieved status, with his wife's assistance, Mr. D. began keeping company with a young unmarried woman who was a Catholic.

According to Mrs. D., her husband was fairly stable in his religious belief until he met the Catholic woman. Since that time Mrs. D. states that although still professing belief in the Protestant faith, during his private moments, Mr. D. reverts toward the Catholic faith, especially in moments of stress. I asked Mrs. D. how she knew this. She said that although it went against her grain of honesty, she was aware that something was wrong and had eavesdropped on her husband's private prayers. She also said that she has seen her husband reach for a rosary in time of stress. She wondered how he could reconcile Masonic teachings with those of the Catholic Church.

Mr. D. and the other woman had even gone to a priest to discuss their future marriage plans, according to a report received by Mrs. D. The priest had severely disapproved of the liaison and would not permit a marriage to take place. The other woman then told the priest that whether he approved or not, they were going to be married "in the church."

The proper religious "rite of passage," such as the marriage ceremony, tends to be a value. These rites prescribe the form that is to be used to insure safe passage to the recipient, and they generally revolve around the life cycle. Among the Jews, for instance, the following rites are observed for the occasions that generally come once in a lifetime. Rites attending birth are the circumcision of male children, the naming of babies, and the redemption of the first-born. Rites clustering about turning points in the lives of children are the beginning of religious education, and the *Bar Mitzvah* ceremonial for boys about the time they enter adolescence. Rites which adorn and sanctify wedlock are the solemnizing of the betrothal, the calling of the groom to the reading of the Torah in the synagogue on the Sabbath before his marriage, and the marriage service itself. Finally, at death, there are the rites of confession followed by a proclamation of faith, the rending of the garment in token of bereavement, the simple white shroud, the rituals of the funeral and interment, and others associated with mourning.[34]

To Roman Catholics the sacraments, or natural signs which produce supernatural effects, are equally important. Baptism is the beginning of a new life, and is absolutely necessary to attain man's final goal of eternal happiness; confirmation enables one to "function fully as a useful member of Christian society"; and the Eucharist "completes" the process of Christian initiation by uniting one with Christ. Once fully initiated, adults can enter into marriage properly only through matrimony, the sacrament by which they "dedicate themselves to God for a holy service, the extension of His kingdom among men" by bringing children into the world; or adult males may be empowered "to generate *super*natural life" through the sacrament of Holy Orders. Reconciliation with God is effected through the sacrament of penance which permits one again to participate fully in community worship; and the Christian departing this life is given extreme unction (the last of the anointings) to remove obstacles in the way of the last passage—into eternal life.[35]

Other religious groups, too, have similar rites or sacraments which are regarded as important in varying degrees, depending upon the

[34] Milton Steinberg, *Basic Judaism*, New York, Harcourt, Brace & Co., 1947, pp. 132-133.

[35] Clifford Howell, *Of Sacraments and Sacrifice*, Collegeville, Minnesota, The Liturgical Press, 1952, pp. 49-75.

particular religion as well as the fervor or strength of the adherents' convictions. To many Jews, especially the orthodox, and to practicing Catholics, however, the proper rite is highly significant.

The case of Mrs. C., a Mexican woman who is separated from her husband, illustrates attitudes toward rites of passage.

Mrs. C. does not conform to her family's concept of proper, dignified behavior. Her sisters believe that she obtained a divorce, and their feeling is that "she should not have been divorced since she is a Catholic." Moreover, Mrs. C. seems to have few inhibitions about attracting the attentions of men "in an unseemly manner." Her sisters say that she has always been one to "run after men."

When broached on the subject of her family's attitudes toward her behavior, Mrs. C. remarked that whatever her courtship was, she was "married at High Mass and with decorum."

Observance of the proper rite of passage, as Mrs. C. viewed the situation, served to exonerate her previous behavior, even though it did not explain her subsequent actions.

Another Mexican woman placed such emphasis on the little-observed Catholic ceremony of "churching" after the birth of a child that she told the social worker that she had not visited her sick father until the previous day. She knew that he had been sick, she said, but "could not visit him before because she had not been to the church."

RELIGION AMONG NEGROES

Historically, one of the chief functions of the Negro church has been to buoy up the hopes of its members in the face of adversity.[36] During slavery, Negroes had to look to the hereafter for a better life. Religion, then, gave the slaves a motive for enduring hardship.

[36] Gunnar Myrdal, *An American Dilemma,* New York, Harper & Brothers, 1944, p. 936.

They could identify themselves with God's chosen people, the Hebrews, who were also in bondage, longing for the Promised Land.[37]

The church, moreover, offered a means of self-expression and development. Since the churches were segregated, the Negro could be free and uninhibited in them. The church offered not only an opportunity for recognition and leadership but also a channel for education and social welfare. The "apparent overemphasis" by the Negro in the religious sphere is believed to be related to "his comparatively meager participation in other institutional forms of American culture."[38]

In the rural South especially the Negro church serves as a community center. There are restrictions on the use of most other buildings, including the schools, which are large enough to accommodate sizable groups. The church is usually in a central location and owned by the Negroes themselves, thus affording them freedom to do as they please.[39]

The majority of the Southern Negroes are Baptists or Methodists, except in Louisiana where Catholicism is strong.[40] In recent years the Catholic Church has made converts among the Negroes, because of the "church's firm attitude of antisegregation."[41] For many Negroes, though, religion has ceased to be as important as it was formerly. *Ebony* reported that few of the 50,000 Negro churches draw regularly more than 40 percent of their membership on Sundays, compared with 65 percent a generation ago. This decline in church attendance mirrors the pattern of the dominant group.

[37] Maurice R. Davie, *Negroes in American Society,* New York, McGraw-Hill Book Co., 1949, p. 176.
[38] *Ibid.,* p. 191.
[39] Myrdal, *op. cit.,* pp. 938-939.
[40] Davie, *op. cit.,* p. 179.
[41] "Fast-Traveling Cardinal, His Fast-Growing Church," *Newsweek* (May 24, 1954), 43:56.

It is believed, furthermore, that the Negro church has not adapted itself to the changing needs of the Negro, and that the Negro minister is inadequate. "Today's minister," says *Ebony,*

> must be informed on problems vital to labor; he must be close to the racial grievances of his flock and be a fearless fighter for Negro rights; he must be acquainted with social services and give his congregation the benefits of that knowledge. Today's man of God must be a combination of labor organizer, race leader and social worker in addition to an inspired preacher of the Gospel. . . .[42]

About three out of four Negro preachers have had no college or seminary training.[43] Religious services among rural Negroes are characterized by extreme emotionalism. The chief elements of religious expression appear to be "spontaneity, uninhibited expressiveness, excitement, rhythm, interest in the dramatic, and love of the mysterious and unusual."[44] Revivalism is, however, on the decline.[45]

Superstitions of Americans

All peoples have some superstitions or magical beliefs, and Americans are no exception. Instead of merely noting that a belief is a superstition, however, it would be better to have some familiarity with principles underlying widespread notions of magic. The principles upon which magic is based usually fall into one of two categories: first, that like produces like, or that an effect resembles its cause; and, second, that things which were once in contact with each other continue to act on each other at a distance even though the physical contact has been severed.[46] The former is referred to

---

[42] As quoted in "Backsliding," *Time* (July 24, 1950), 56:54.
[43] Davie, *op. cit.,* p. 185.
[44] *Ibid.,* p. 187.
[45] Myrdal, *op. cit.,* p. 937.
[46] Frazer, *The Golden Bough, op. cit.,* p. 11.

as "imitative" magic, and the latter as "contagious" magic. They are both forms of sympathetic magic and are very often coexistent.[47]

Perhaps one of the most universal examples of imitative magic is making an image of a person and then injuring or destroying it in the hope or belief that whatever is done to the image will also happen to the person it represents. Making effigies and burning

(Courtesy of Jerry Marcus and *The Saturday Evening Post*.)

them is not uncommon in American culture. It is a manner of releasing hostility and of obtaining satisfaction.

Red flannel has been very popular because of the belief that the red color, associated with fire, adds to the warmth of the flannel. Many Americans have also subscribed to the superstition that eating red meat makes one "red-blooded" and sipping beef extract makes one strong because bulls are strong.[48] In both these instances the superstitions are illustrations of imitative magic.

Sleep is often associated with death. A frightening belief which has no validity is that a child who has sustained a head injury must not be allowed to go to sleep. The child may have a concussion, but sleep will not alter the extent of the injury.[49]

Contagious magic is exemplified by the magical sympathy which is supposed to exist between a man and any severed portion of his person, such as his hair or nail clippings. Whoever gets possession of human hair or nails may work his will, at any distance, upon the person from whom they were cut.[50] A variety of superstitions relate to the disposition of extracted teeth. Children are often encouraged in these superstitions even though the parents have no convictions. Mutilated joints or other parts of the body removed in surgery also supply a network of superstitious beliefs. Such joints are commonly believed to be in sympathetic union with the body after the physical connection has been severed.[51]

Rusty nails often inspire terror when stepped on because of the possibility of infection. After a nail or needle has been stepped on, however, it is sometimes greased so that it "won't rust, it being assumed, apparently, that the rusting of the nail induces suppuration in the wound by sympathy."[52]

Other choice beliefs of the average man in the street include the following: thirteen is an unlucky number (some skyscrapers have no thirteenth floor); drowning people go down three times; fright turns hair white overnight; sudden fright cures hiccups; stars influ-

---

[48] Evans, *The Natural History of Nonsense, op. cit.,* p. 257.
[49] Bergen Evans, *The Spoor of Spooks and Other Nonsense,* New York, Alfred A. Knopf, Inc., 1954, p. 165.
[50] Frazer, *op. cit.,* p. 38.
[51] *Ibid.,* p. 39.
[52] Evans, *The Spoor of Spooks and Other Nonsense, op. cit.,* p. 165.

ence human events; and that unusual events or frights during pregnancy will influence the character or appearance of the child.[53]

COMMON MAGICAL BELIEFS OF ETHNICS

As noted earlier, some forms of magic are widespread, and the client who fearfully relates that an acquaintance has used magic against him should not be considered as suffering from hallucinations. One of the most universal illustrations of imitative magic, as mentioned before, is piercing the clay image of an enemy. Unless the enemy uses countermagic, he is supposed to die. A Mexican farmer, for example, was credited with saving many of the inhabitants of his village from death in an epidemic when he unearthed a pot of effigies in his field and pulled the pins from the images. This act averted the catastrophe, it was believed, and the farmer was regarded as the savior of his village.

There are negative as well as positive precepts in the system of imitative magic. The former are called taboos and the latter charms.[54] The aim of negative magic is to avoid an undesired event while the aim of positive magic is to produce a desirable one. Both consequences, desirable and undesirable, are believed to be induced in accordance with the laws of similarity and of contact.[55]

To insure a long life, the Chinese often have recourse to complicated charms. Sometimes the grave clothing is regarded as a charm. These garments are often made during the lifetime of a person by a young woman who is likely to live many years. It is believed that her capacity to live long will pass into the clothes, and thus postpone the time when they shall be put to proper use. Among the garments is a longevity robe which often has the word

[53] Evans, *The Natural History of Nonsense, op. cit.,* pp. 128, 157, 113-116, 162, 272.
[54] Frazer, *op. cit.,* p. 19.
[55] *Ibid.*

"longevity" embroidered upon it in gold. As the garment is supposed to prolong the life of its owner, he often wears it, especially on festive occasions, in order to allow the influence of the embroidered work "longevity" to have its full effect upon his person.[56]

A popular Mexican belief in negative magic is that evil can be wished upon a person by sprinkling white powder before his door. One of the first things many Mexican housewives take care of in the morning is to see that the walk in front of the home is swept in order to sweep away any possible ill effects that might have been wished upon them by an enemy sprinkling white powder. Such an action was a factor in the slaying of Mrs. Antonio Salas, a young Mexican housewife in San Antonio, and her infant son. Witnesses testified that Mrs. Salas was quarreling with her next door neighbor, Mrs. Stevens, because the latter had sprinkled white powder in the Salas' yard. One woman was "armed with a stick, the other with a chunk of concrete," and Mr. Stevens settled the scuffle which followed by shooting Mrs. Salas as well as her son. In the investigation which followed Mrs. Stevens told the police that she had sprinkled "only baking powder."[57]

The Evil Eye is another illustration of negative magic that is prevalent among the Mexicans. An American girl, Helen, who had married a Mexican, was greatly disturbed over this common superstition.

One day while Helen was wheeling [the baby] . . . in his buggy in the street, an old Mexican woman stopped her to view the boy; and, exclaiming at his beauty and glowing health, she quickly, impulsively leaned down and touched his mouth with a bony forefinger that had not recently had contact with soap and water, and then left.

Helen returned home in rare ill humor. She spent her morning sterilizing everything and preparing germless formulas; now this woman with her dirty finger—!

[56] Ibid., pp. 35-36. See account of festivity, infra. Chapter 9, pp. 169-170.
[57] "Feud Leads to Slaying of Mother, Son," San Antonio Express, September 20, 1953, pp. 1-2.

Lupe [her husband] was touched to the quick. The old woman had meant no harm, he said. She had admired the baby and touching his mouth was, in Mexican superstition, merely a bit of magic to ward off the Evil Eye. The dirt on her fingers was probably harmless "clean dirt."[58]

This is an example of negative contagious magic. Many Mexicans believe that evil will befall the person admired unless he is touched. The professional person who visits a Mexican family and admires a child without touching him may be asked by the parent to pick up the child or to touch the child on the head. If the visitor is admired by the client, invariably the latter will wish to touch him.

The Negro, too, has retained some of his beliefs in magic, but even this folklore is said to be "fast disappearing in the United States."[59] Some of the Negro sects, such as the United House of Prayer for All People founded by "bishop" Charles E. Grace, put great faith in contagious magic. "Daddy Grace" writing paper will aid the writer in composing a good letter, and the magazine distributed by "Daddy Grace" will cure a cold if placed on the chest.[60]

The following case affords another illustration of magic:

Mrs. X was referred to social service by the medical staff because they could find very little physical basis for her complaints. She was suffering with her heart, stomach, pains in the back, and severe headaches.

The patient is a tall, very thin emaciated appearing Negro woman who is thirty-three years of age. She was very reluctant to enter into the interview situation and remained quiet for the first interview, saying very few things and mumbling those in a low monotone that was difficult to hear. It was apparent, however, that she did not know why the doctors had sent her to a social worker because all of her complaints were physical. Did they think that she was going crazy? Some reassuring state-

---

[58] Louis Adamic, *From Many Lands*, New York, Harper & Brothers, 1940, p. 271. For an interesting account of Mexican superstitions see Chapter XII of De Treviño, *My Heart Lies South*, *op. cit.*, and Appendix B in Saunders, *Cultural Differences and Medical Care*, *op. cit.*

[59] Davie, *op. cit.*, p. 175.

[60] Fauset, *op. cit.*, p. 30.

ments were given and I asked her to elaborate somewhat on the difficulties that she had been having. She said that she is short of breath, just drags around the house enough to feed the children, and keeps herself locked in most of the time. She explained that her husband was overseas and that since he has gone she has progressively gotten worse and now finds that she cannot manage her home adequately. Further exploration uncovered the fact that she does not send her children to school although she has two of school age. She keeps them in the house with the shades drawn and the doors locked most of the time. In attempting to explore some of the reasons for this, I found that Mrs. X was blocked in discussing anything that had an emotional connotation and she seemed to close her lips tightly and to look fearful when I asked her why she was afraid to let her children out of the house or to go out shopping herself. She passed the questions off with a remark, "Oh, you wouldn't understand that."

Background material on Mrs. X indicates that she was born and raised in Mississippi by an aunt and that she never had brothers or sisters. She married at a very early age to get away from her aunt and family. She claims a good relationship with her husband. When he was home she depended upon him excessively. There are indications that he did all of the shopping and managing of the house and even took care of the children in addition to being the breadwinner. Now that he is gone she finds life overwhelming and cannot make any decisions or plans for herself or the children. He moved her to his own home town in Texas when he left so that she could be near his mother, feeling that this would be the wisest thing for her. However, she indicated a great deal of suspicion regarding the mother-in-law. She was reluctant for the first few interviews to talk of this, and it only emerged after many sessions of support in the area of her physical complaints.

When the material began to emerge concerning her fright and fears, there was almost a typical picture of an individual who is having a delusion of some type, along with her depression. I felt at first that I should refer this case to a psychiatrist. However, the patient had built some type of dependent relationship on me, and I had been able to help her in a few small details. Consequently, I felt that a change at this time might not be good for her.

As she gained confidence in me as a worker she began talking about some of these fears that she had: staying in the house at night, having someone under her bed, and feeling that someone would harm the children. All in all, she presented a picture of an individual who was very close to a psychotic break.

At about the fifth interview Mrs. X said that she would tell me something if I could keep it highly confidential. Although I did not promise this specifically, I told her that this information would only be shared with people who really wanted to help her. This seemed to satisfy her to some extent and she told me that she felt her mother-in-law was wishing something bad on her—perhaps wishing her to be dead. She said that she had gotten along very well until she moved to Texas, and although her husband felt that this was best for her, she finds now that she has become extremely frightened of the mother-in-law. She feels that the latter is perhaps putting an evil spell on her. This explained some of the seemingly delusional material that she presented in some of the earlier interviews. The difficulty now appears to be cultural rather than delusional. Mrs. X was oriented in all spheres and had affect after she got used to the worker. However, she continued to bring up the idea that her mother-in-law was doing something to her. She stated that white folks did not understand this idea of someone wishing something on you and that she had been advised by other Colored people in the neighborhood not to tell me about it because I would not understand. However, she stated that Colored people can very often wish something on you and it will actually happen. She stated that her mother-in-law wished one daughter-in-law to be dead and when it happened the doctors could never find the reason for it. The mother-in-law also wished another daughter-in law to be crazy and the latter ended up in an institution. Mrs. X did not want to end up like that.

Since Mrs. X talked of this situation and her deep fears that the mother-in-law was wishing something on her, it became evident that many of her fears of physical symptoms and her fright in general were caused by this feeling. At first one might think that the best way to approach a case of this type is to show the patient logically that no one can wish something on you, and that the emotional impact was really the thing that was bothering you. However, in this case it has been my experience that many Colored people in the deep South hold onto rituals and voodooism and have many magical superstitions such as hex, that they feel can be perpetrated against them. Consequently, I did not attempt to reason with the patient but rather helped her learn to "fight her fears." She stated that as long as she was cheerful and had someone with whom she could talk, the mother-in-law was unable to have any influence on her and that she might be able to fight this "hex." I gave her my support and we talked about her ability to "shake off" the mother-in-law's effect.

She had never been able to talk in a hostile manner toward her mother-in-law or even to think hostilely about her because the patient felt that this would in some way make the hex work and that she would be the victim in the long run. As she became more free and easy with the worker, she talked in an extremely hostile manner about the interference of her mother-in-law in her home and about the latter's influence over her son. The patient stated that that was one reason that her husband brought her here to live. Now that she is able to really say what she feels about the mother-in-law she does not feel that the hex will work.

My role as a social worker in this case appeared to be in the area of support—helping the patient gain enough ego-strength to express her fears and hostility toward her mother-in-law in order to break the spell that the latter apparently had on her. As the interviews progressed the patient got to the point that she could laugh about the feeble attempts that the mother-in-law put forth to make her feel bad.

Forms of contagious magic also prevail among the Indians of the Southwest. Even today, Indians will not live in a house in which someone has died, or enter it willingly. When hospitals were erected for the use of the Indians, the white man's "medicine house" was viewed with grave misgivings. After some of their number died in the hospital, the Indians flatly refused to enter the "death house" in which the spirit of the deceased still lingered or where the evil spirits that had caused his death lay in wait for another victim.[61]

These are only a few of the beliefs held by various cultural groups. The professional worker needs to bear in mind that, ridiculous as a belief may seem to some Americans, it may be very important to other peoples, for these values deal with man's deepest convictions concerning the meaning of life, and they affect not only standards of conduct but also everyday patterns of behavior.[62]

[61] Edward Everett Dale, *The Indians of the Southwest,* Norman, University of Oklahoma Press, 1949, p. 200.

[62] Cf. William E. Vickery and Stewart G. Cole, *Intercultural Education in American Schools,* New York, Harper & Brothers, 1943, p. 158.

4

Authority and Government

AMERICAN ATTITUDES

AUTHORITY, the right and power to influence others, is found in every organized group, for it insures order and the attainment of group purposes. In the primary group to which a person belongs—the family—authority is vested in the parents or parental substitutes. As one's social contacts widen, the teacher, the policeman, the clergyman, the employer, and perhaps the military, exercise legitimate authority. Political authority is, as a rule, the most remote.

The attitudes of many Americans toward legally constituted authority are in the nature of an anomaly. Law itself is venerated, yet Americans are not regarded as a particularly law-respecting people. They place their security in a "government of laws and not of men," and esteem their Constitution as the supreme law of the land. So sacred is this law that the judiciary has been empowered to declare unconstitutional any other laws which are contrary to it. Unlike the constitutions of other countries, this one has stood the test of time and has not been drastically modified since it was written by the Founding Fathers. Theoretically, every citizen is equal before the law, and no one is immune from the operation of the law.

The fact of the matter is that Americans are believed to be

relatively lawless.[1] Attitudes toward authority are instilled early in life within the family circle. The contemporary American family, it will be noted later, seems to be filiocentric or child-centered, and

"I'm back. The principal doesn't know what to do with me either." (Courtesy of Walt Goldstein and *The Saturday Evening Post*.)

American children are not renowned for discipline, either self-imposed or otherwise. Resistance to law and authority carries over into and permeates the educational system. There was a time not

[1] Myrdal, *An American Dilemma, op. cit.*, p. 14. A visiting Danish scholar remarked: "I do not see any self-control anywhere—in the children or in the old. I have not anywhere seen discipline." Marya Mannes, "The Friendliest People in the World, Fundamentally," *The Reporter* (May 25, 1954), 10:35.

too long ago, say veteran teachers, when most children were loathe to report to their parents any differences that they might have had with school authorities. To "spare the rod" was believed to "spoil the child." In 1954, however, the Pittsburgh Teachers' Association complained that sixty-six teachers had been struck by pupils and ninety-two teachers had been threatened by parents.[2] In New York

(Courtesy of *The American Magazine.*)

City hundreds of school children who were thwarted because rain ruined a school outing, "swarmed onto subway trains, . . . terrorized passengers, smashed 237 light bulbs, pulled emergency cords, ripped up seats, pummeled a guard, [and] roughed up a station elevator operator."[3]

These attitudes penetrate nearly every aspect of life. Americans tend to enjoy the embarrassment of the parents who can't work junior's algebra problem, of the teacher who is "stumped" by a

[2] "Report Card," *Time* (June 28, 1954), 63:73.
[3] *Ibid.* (May 31, 1954), 63:43.

question, and of the policeman who is outsmarted. The professional worker, too, gets "tested," and there may be secret mirth over his failure to measure up to the test of how to "figure out" a situation.

It has been observed, however, that the least respected and the most suspected professions are those of politics and, in peacetime,[4] military service, both of which by their nature involve authority over people. A man who aspires to such positions is expected to use his power for selfish purposes; if he is entirely honest and interested only in the promotion of the general welfare he is generally considered to be "a sucker."[5] The belief that the chief executive is secretly lusting after power explains to some extent the practice of alternating weak with strong presidents. Should the misuse of power become excessive, the group is expected to control such corruption through the press or the ballot box.

Certain sections of the country take pride in "rebellious exhibitions." In the South, for example, there are periodic outbursts of Confederate "fever" often characterized by a prominent display of stickers and flags of the Confederacy. The United Daughters of the Confederacy take great pride in their "lawless" heritage. Even the senators from this region traditionally filibuster to prevent the passage of legislation such as that dealing with civil rights. "We can't secede," commented one spokesman from Texas on the Supreme Court decision relating to nonsegregation in the schools. "My grandpappy did," he added, "and found out two and half years later it did no good."[6] In other states, however, there were fewer signs of conformity. Even a former justice of the Supreme

[4] Geoffrey Gorer, *The American People,* New York, W. W. Norton & Company, Inc., 1948, p. 33.

[5] Ruesch and Bateson, *Communication, op. cit.,* p. 101. For Swedish reactions toward conflicts between official and unofficial values, see Franklin D. Scott, "The Swedish Students' Image of the United States," *Annals of the American Academy of Political and Social Science* (September, 1954), 295:139.

[6] "Texans Greet Ruling With Mixed Reaction," *San Antonio Express,* May 18, 1954, p. 10A.

It's the Law!

by DICK HYMAN

Illustrated by O. Soglow

Court took a stand as state governor that definitely did not imply regard for the decision of the court.[7]

The American who observed *all* the laws would probably be subject to ridicule. Caspar Milquetoast of cartoon fame[8] is an object of mirth because he is unable to exercise discernment in observing regulations or laws. A popular magazine has a feature series entitled "It's the Law!" which is designed to stimulate laughter.

American resistance to authority is believed to be a historical phenomenon. According to one analyst, the Boston Tea Party, the Whiskey Rebellion, the industrial robber barons, and the gangsters have all exemplified this spirit.[9] Frederick Jackson Turner attributes American individualism to the frontier—a constantly shifting line which has been a social force throughout American history. The frontiersman felt that he was the equal of every other man, and Americans today have, as a consequence of this heritage, "a certain ease of manner, even a brashness, which can be extremely irritating to those who have not been bred to 'equality.'"[10] Americans do not like to be "bossed around" or "squashed." It is a basic assumption in American culture that each individual, through his own efforts, has an opportunity for distinction and economic success.[11] American culture has been compared with a "sprawling novel where every

[7] Cf. "To All on Equal Terms," *Time* (May 24, 1954), 63:22.
[8] See Part VII, "The Timid Soul," in H. T. Webster, *The Best of H. T. Webster*, New York, Simon and Schuster, Inc., 1950. See also "Beastly Rulings," *The New York Times Magazine*, August 8, 1954, p. 41.
[9] Barron, *The Juvenile in Delinquent Society, op. cit.*, p. 208.
[10] "The American Way of Life," *Fortune* (February, 1951), 43:191.
[11] Franklin J. Shaw and Robert S. Ort, *Personal Adjustment in the American Culture*, New York, Harper & Brothers, 1953, p. 31.

Upper left: It is against the law to laugh loudly in a theater in Fort Worth, Texas. *Upper right*: A Duluth, Minn., ordinance forbids you to leave your horse in bakery shops. *Lower left*: An ordinance in Normal, Ill., forbids humans to make faces at dogs. *Lower right*: It is against the law in Kentucky to sleep in a restaurant. (Courtesy of *The American Magazine*.)

page may deal with a new encounter" or with a "special choice." A great deal is demanded of individuals who have "such wide latitude and so little respected authority," but America "is built on the premise that this is possible."[12]

When Americans seek assistance from persons in the helping professions, they certainly are not then putting into practice the ideology of romantic individualism. For this reason, the client may feel that there is a stigma attached to the seeking of such services. He is no longer able to be master of his own destiny but must assume a dependent role that implies inadequacy.

Not all Americans, however, react in the same manner to professional helping services. Some want advice from family counseling agencies and child guidance clinics despite the fact that they hate "being told what to do."[13] Others are motivated by the "something for nothing" philosophy and may even be demanding. In a fictional account, one such client is reported to have said:

Here I come down to yore office to ast you all for a little hep and whadda I get? You ast me about my grandpaw and my great grandpaw and my aunts and uncles and where I went to school and how many jobs I had and how many children I got.

I'll thank you to get on with this. I ain't intendin' to set here much longer, no sirree, not when the guvner's office ain't moren three blocks away. I just doubledog dare you to keep this up much longer. By God, I'll go over there to his office and ast him what the hell he thinks this is. . . .

. . . A man comes in here hongry and you set right there in front of him with yore hair all curled and yore shoes so nice musta cost five ninety-eight if they cost a dime and a smellin' of perfume and a grinnin'. . . .[14]

---

[12] Ruth Benedict, "The Family: Genus Americanum," *The Family: Its Function and Destiny,* ed. Ruth N. Anshen, New York, Harper & Brothers, 1949, p. 167.

[13] Treudley, "American Cultural Themes and Social Work," *Social Forces, op. cit.,* 28:292.

[14] Nedra Tyre, *Red Wine First,* New York, Simon and Schuster, Inc., 1947, pp. 153-154.

Obviously, this client was not only acquainted with his "rights," but he was also ready to use threats in order to facilitate securing them.

DEMOCRACY AS A VALUE

Closely allied to the concept of individualism is that of democracy, for democracy is the value one "sets on his own full development, the condition and result of his self-realization." Within the limits allowed by society, democracy is a "function of his self-direction and self-control, of the choice and living of the life he thinks best."[15] More than this, democracy is a "form of government in which the rulers are fully responsible to the ruled in order to realize self-respect *for everybody*."[16]

The man in the street has defined democracy in various terms: "Democracy is majority rule," said one American, voicing a common assumption. "It's letting people look after their own affairs without government always butting in," declared another more individualistic spokesman. The reciprocal nature of democracy was expressed by a woman who said simply: "I—I don't know—exactly. But to me democracy is a sort of feeling I have inside me that keeps me from being as mean as I'd like to be sometimes to people I don't like."[17]

One of the problems of democracy, then, is the difference between democratic promise and democratic performance. Democracy is an official value or an ideal inscribed in American laws and public documents. In Lincoln's Gettysburg Address it is defined as "government of the people, by the people, and for the people"—an idea

[15] William H. Riker, *Democracy in the United States*, New York, The Macmillan Co., 1953, p. 19.
[16] *Ibid.*, p. 34. Italics mine.
[17] Harry and Bonaro Overstreet, "Democracy in Daily Experience," *Adult Leadership* (September, 1953), 2:24.

easy to grasp but hard, at times, to act on.[18] It is an expression of "hopes, desires, advice, or dreams" and there is nothing in legal form to distinguish the "dreams" from the "enforced reality." A Swedish analyst explains this phenomenon by the fact that the nation is young and owes its state structure to a revolution—a "revolution in the courageously rationalistic age of Enlightenment."[19]

An Englishman notes that Americans often equate democracy with equality in the sense that one man's opinion is as good as another's. Expertness may be recognized in such fields as science and technology, but "when it comes to ideas about life and love and religion and education and architecture and painting and music, indeed all forms of pleasure, there is a national conviction that an expert is a phony, or 'wants to be different,' and that what matters is you should know what you like and—this is a democracy, isn't it? —speak up and say your piece."[20]

Even the Americans who pay only lip service to democracy tend to abjure haughtiness and "putting on airs," for if they do not, they may be subject to ridicule. There is little calculated rudeness or outright condescension in social relationships whether it be between families and servants, bosses and employees, or housewives and shopkeepers. Americans may try "upstartism" and "big-shotism," but even the "worst roughnecks in power" and the "recentest beggars on horseback" learn fast that "though they can fairly safely brag, they can seldom safely bully."[21]

The open class structure of American society accounts, to a certain extent, for these attitudes toward privilege. In this society one's status is not a fixed or privileged one, but is subject to change. Many of the problems of this democratic society, then, are con-

---

[18] Cf. Charles A. Siepmann, *The Radio Listener's Bill of Rights*, New York, Anti-Defamation League of B'nai B'rith, 1948, p. 5.

[19] Myrdal, *op. cit.*, p. 14.

[20] Alistair Cooke, *One Man's America*, New York, Alfred A. Knopf, Inc., 1952, p. 257.

[21] Kronenberger, *Company Manners, op. cit.*, pp. 112-113.

nected with a system of social stratification that is still essentially fluid.[22] Some ethnics are restricted in movement and relegated to a lower status because they are *different*. "Paradoxically," says one commentator on American culture, "the strong American tendency to conform may have been fostered by our very variety of cultural backgrounds."[23] Being *different* became "a stigma rather than a mere circumstance, and being like everyone else constituted an achievement rather than an absence of one."[24] At the same time, however, others who dare to be different and exercise initiative achieve social status by virtue of their ingenuity. The fluidity and rapid mobility of American society has the effect, then, of making the attainment of social stature possible, but often at the risk of disillusionment and frustration. Even the seemingly successful never completely lose a sense of insecurity and fear, for there is no position so high that it cannot be bettered, nor any so lofty that it need not be defended.[25]

DEMOCRACY AND ETHNIC GROUPS

The concept of democracy is generally hard for ethnics to fathom. Most of them have had little or no previous experience with it. Furthermore, it is difficult to harmonize the ideal of democracy with the manner in which democracy actually functions. Such queries as the following may clamor for solution in the minds of

[22] Allison Davis, "Light from Anthropology on Intercultural Relations," *Cultural Groups and Human Relations,* New York, Columbia University, 1951, p. 82.

[23] Kronenberger, *op. cit.,* p. 173.

[24] *Ibid.,* pp. 173-174. According to a Scandinavian interpretation, the American code appears to be: "Do not be different, but if you have to, be different together." William H. Sewell, Richard T. Morris, and Oluf M. Davidsen, "Scandinavian Students' Images of the United States: A Study in Cross-Cultural Education," *Annals of the American Academy of Political and Social Science* (September, 1954), 295:129.

[25] John Sirjamaki, "A Footnote to the Anthropological Approach to the Study of American Culture," *Social Forces* (March, 1947), 25:260.

thoughtful ethnics. How can there be a fundamental political equality when experience belies the assumption? Doesn't everyone have a place within which he ought to stay? Where *was* the place for the newly arrived Oriental, barred under the quota system until recently? Where is the logic in exalting democracy with one breath and belying it with the next?

Such inconsistencies, of course, make it hard for the ethnic to become convinced of the merits of democracy. Even the Negro, who has had no other recent political experience has some reservations about endorsing American democracy without qualifications. Democracy, it has been noted, implies self-respect and equality for everybody, and the Negro has not consistently enjoyed either.

An American Negro voices the feelings of his people on this matter. The Negro's values, he says, are class-centered, but regardless of class differences the Negro wants *dignity*.

An illiterate Negro in a hovel can achieve a measure of dignity by seeing his children clothed, fed, and sheltered. A middle-class Negro achieves a standard of dignity by seeing his labors and talents well rewarded, by knowing that he is a part of his government and his community. The elite, high-brow Negro achieves dignity when he realizes that he can climb the highest hill in the land and be seen as an American capable of scaling the heights, and not as a Negro—who has reached an unusual level for a Negro.[26]

This same Negro spokesman further elaborates on dignity by stating that the Negro who says he does not want social equality is merely being expedient. What the Negro really means, he says, is this:

If social equality is sitting at the dinner table of white friends who invite me there, I want the right to be there. If it means living in a neighborhood in my economic bracket, although it be a predominantly white area, I want the right to be there. If it means worshipping God without worrying about the color of the person kneeling beside me, I want the right to do that.[27]

[26] Rowan, *South of Freedom, op. cit.,* pp. 253-254.
[27] *Ibid.,* p. 253.

Peoples whose previous democratic experience has been negligible tend to question the practical value of democracy still more than does the American Negro. The equality and individualism associated with democracy may not only be alien to them, but also undesirable. Millions of Eastern peoples today think individualism is synonymous with the American way of life and many simply do not want it. Individualism has become as distorted to them through stereotypes as collectivism has become for most people of the Western World.[28] The security of other ethnic group members is threatened by the American open class system where everyone is potentially equal and mobility is high. Under such circumstances, they ask, how can one know his place or the prescribed behavior? The comfort and security afforded by one's original culture tend to be damaged by their impact with American ways. Children question the authority of their parents and, like Americans, may strive for individualistic rather than familistic goals. Because the class structure is "open," one is never satisfied anyhow. There is always the hope of improving status, and the ever-present danger of lowering status. Are competition and selfish striving, the ethnic asks, to replace family unity and solidarity?

Social group workers can test some of the basic assumptions of the profession on members of ethnic groups who lack democratic experience. The following assumptions, for example, may not be verified: that all groups have had experience in working together for the common good; that all people have a desire for, as well as a skill in, achieving workable compromises; that a committee will operate in a familiar pattern, with the role of the chairman defined and differentiated, and all participants ready to meet the assigned tasks; that experts will serve in a consultative capacity rather than a dictatorial one; in a word, that all peoples whatever their ethnic

[28] Charles E. Hendry, *The Role of Groups in World Reconstruction*, New York, Whiteside, Inc. (Woman's Press), 1952, p. 10.

origin, education, and experience are ready to participate in the democratic process.[29]

American administrators serving in other countries have encountered many obstacles to the democratic process. In Germany one administrator stated that the main obstacle to the development of genuine group formation is the authoritarian pattern which still persists in family life, in the majority of schools, in church and state, in offices and factories. There appears to be a "sincere conviction that the individual is not ripe for any more liberal treatment" and there is a "deep-seated fear of letting go and allowing those 'below' to develop ideas and initiative."[30]

In Japan, too, the idea that the group process can be used for the growth, enrichment, and maturation of persons is alien. The Japanese understand the role of government and family, but not of country and individual. Government has traditionally been an ever-present, strong-armed reality for whom individuals were trained to sacrifice even their lives. Family is also a concept that is understood and very meaningful, as will be seen later.[31] Creative group activities are not valued by either government or family. Village headmen, town mayors, and heads of all types of organizations are suspicious of small group autonomy because it upsets the control factors. "Small groups get ideas. They ask embarrassing questions. They may act in unorthodox ways and even want to know where the money goes."[32] Small groups, furthermore, disrupt family unity in that they tend to serve age or sex groups. Group associations in Japan today still follow the formerly predominant pattern of large meetings with speakers who tell them what to do. There may be passive assent but little subsequent activity.[33]

[29] Hertha Kraus, "Identifying Professional Requirements for Social Service Abroad," *Social Casework* (April, 1954), 35:150.

[30] Hendry, *op. cit.*, p. 27.

[31] *Ibid.*, p. 5. See also below, Chapter 6, p. 121, and Chapter 9, pp. 164-171.

[32] *Ibid.*, p. 31.

[33] *Ibid.*, p. 47.

The Chinese traditionally have had similar attitudes toward democracy. Confucianism is still strong and it is often used to counteract democratic teachings. Among other things Confucianism teaches implicit obedience to authority. Hence, any experiences that would give an individual practice in democratic living would be considered unorthodox.[34]

POLITICAL HERITAGE OF ETHNICS

While Americans seem to have a regard for their political institutions and at the same time be highly critical of authority and even offer resistance to it, other peoples regard authority differently. From childhood on through adulthood dissimilar attitudes have been instilled.

The Chinese, for instance, have an explicitly submissive attitude toward authority which is largely the effect of cultural forces. A person is said to live "under the ancestor's shadow" since all "routes are, so to speak barred except one, that which follows the foot-steps of his father, his father's father, and the whole line of his more remote ancestors."[35] Ancestral authority over the individual and a pre-arrangement of circumstances for him permeate "every aspect of his life and work, including his marriage and means of livelihood."[36]

Similarly, the Japanese child according to tradition is reared to have a profound respect for authority. Even the baby is taught a "respect behavior" to his father and older brother.[37] There are meticulous rules and conventions which prescribe the proper bows

[34] Osborne, "Problems of the Chinese Family," *Marriage and Family Living, op. cit.,* 10:18.
[35] Francis L. K. Hsu, *Under the Ancestor's Shadow,* New York, Columbia University Press, 1948, p. 260.
[36] *Ibid.,* p. 258.
[37] Ruth Benedict, *The Chrysanthemum and the Sword,* Boston, Houghton Mifflin Co., 1946, p. 49.

and kneelings. The child learns to whom he bows and how much to bow, for bows range all the way from a mere inclination of the head and shoulders to kneeling with forehead lowered to the hands placed flat upon the floor.[38] There is, moreover, a respect language which indicates the degree and kind of social distance. Different words are used when speaking to inferiors and to superiors.[39] The American-born Japanese find this language very difficult to master, and often hide rather than attempt to converse with or act properly toward Japanese visitors.[40] They do, however, recognize hierarchy and for most Japanese, behavior based on this recognition is said to be "as natural . . . as breathing."[41]

In European societies, too, when persons marry they tend to define their children's probable "place in the sun." The class structure is comparatively rigid and the child's "care, his food, his shelter, his education"—all are by-products of the parents' position.[42] The tradition of nobility still prevails in many countries, even though royalty is largely becoming a thing of the past. For generations the European peasants retraced the steps of their predecessors.[43] The differences between social groups were not a cause of envy, for this was "the accepted configuration of society." Just as the lord was expected to be "proud and luxurious," so, too, the peasant was expected to be "thrifty and respectful." Not even the bitterly burdensome privileges of supporting the nobility were open to dispute.[44] The peasant order was accepted with relative docility until the population pressures and famines of the eighteenth century, and the impact of industrialization effected a change.[45]

[38] Ibid., p. 48.
[39] Ibid., p. 47.
[40] Smith, Americans from Japan, op. cit., pp. 51-52.
[41] Benedict, The Chrysanthemum and the Sword, op. cit., p. 47.
[42] Margaret Mead, And Keep Your Powder Dry, New York, William Morrow & Co., Inc., 1942, p. 40.
[43] Handlin, The Uprooted, op. cit., p. 12.
[44] Ibid., p. 23.
[45] Ibid., pp. 24-36.

Authority within the family was generally recognized and respected. Most Europeans have a patriarchal family structure and very often the father's authority is overrestrictive in nature. Harsh punishments are often inflicted, even for minor transgressions of authority. Where observance of morals is concerned, severe sanctions may be employed by parents.

The Mexican, like the European, has the same tendency toward restrictiveness. Prevailing attitudes are revealed in the following case:

Jose, a fourteen-year-old Mexican boy, was habitually playing truant from school. The stepfather was fearful of what the police might do. The mother and stepfather put pressure on the boy to force him to go to school. Both parents punish the boy by slapping him in the face. Stepfather says the thing that causes him to lose his temper is when Jose lies to him. Jose has broken his promise to go to school over and over. The stepfather has always tried to reason with the boy as he has heard of cases where fathers who treated their boys mean were later killed by the boys. Stepfather mentioned that some adult acquaintance of Jose's had told Jose that if his stepfather was ever mean to him that he should wait until his parents were asleep and stick a knife in his stepfather. Jose told this in the presence of his godparents and they were greatly shocked that the boy would have such thoughts. Mr. M., the stepfather, says that when he tries to reason with the boy the mother gets upset and cries and they all get upset.

Mr. M. just cannot understand why Jose is disobeying and staying away from school. He has tried to be very nice to the boy but Jose accuses his stepfather of taking the mother away from him. Mr. M. feels that Mrs. M. loses her temper when trying to talk to Jose. She flies into him and starts hitting him with her hands, which makes Jose very angry. That may be the reason, according to the stepfather, why Jose runs away.

The school principal had called Mr. M. and told him that they were very strict about the boys being in school and unless he had Jose in school by Wednesday of that week, they would have the police after him. Both Mr. and Mrs. M. seem to have a great fear of the police getting after them for Jose's absence. Evidently they put more pressure on Jose to conform so they will not be stigmatized by the police calling at their home.

I explained to the parents that Jose was now a teen-age boy who was naturally trying to break away from his parents; that restricting him even more at this time would likely provoke retaliation from him; that it seemed he had learned he could punish them by having the school threaten them because of his truancy. I explained that I was not trying to tell them how to discipline Jose as that was up to them, but I wondered if they couldn't work out a method of punishment that would be consistent and more in keeping with his age.

Jose complained that his mother worried about him going with girls as she felt that he was too young and would get in trouble. She further thinks the girls are carrying knives and are no good. His regular friend, a sixteen-year-old, Maria, is not attending school. Jose stated that he feels he should obey his parents but if they have to whip him he would prefer that they use a belt instead of slapping him. He feels that he is too old to be slapped around.

This case illustrates not only the overrestrictiveness of parental authority but also a fear of the law which is commonly found among ethnic groups. It further emphasizes the common practice of carrying knives or weapons on the person. Among Americans the rate of assault is about 3 percent, but among Mexicans it is 5.5 percent.[46] The child may be trained to resort to violence when molested, rather than depend upon some law-enforcing person, as was the case with Pedro.

Pedro was charged with assault and had been apprehended several times at school for threatening to knife someone. Pedro claimed that he was "only playing," but the boy who accused him had a large scratch on his back. Pedro's mother defended the boy and said he wasn't to blame; the other boys had teased and irritated him.

I asked her what they had teased the boy about and she said they had called him "wetback" and many other names. I agreed with her that Pedro had been irritated, but said that it was his duty to tell the school authorities and they would handle the situation. The mother said

[46] John H. Burma, *Spanish-Speaking Groups in the United States*, Durham, N. C., Duke University Press, 1954, p. 114.

that her boy had always been taught not to tell anybody the troubles he got into, that he was to solve them himself.

Perhaps the habit of carrying weapons and taking the law in one's own hands is a survival from simpler societies where one of the traditional family functions was to protect its members. To members of a highly organized society such an action might be viewed as lawless; to simpler peoples not to take action might be viewed as a failure to guard and preserve one's life or that of a family member.

Teachers as well as parents are, as a rule, respected and obeyed by ethnics. Among the Chinese both teachers and scholars have high social rank.[47] Confucius, it must be remembered, was primarily a teacher. Europeans, too, tend to have greater regard for the authority of the teacher than Americans have. The rules enforced in European schools are rigid in comparison with those of American schools.[48]

When authority becomes further removed from the family, however, attitudes are different. Some ethnics, for instance, who do not value education may resent school authorities and regard their intervention as unwarranted. Church authorities may be so closely identified with village and family life that this authority is acceptable, but such is not necessarily the case. Civil authorities may be regarded as still more remote and attitudes toward them may have a wide range. In American society, the social worker and the teacher will often be envisioned as a part of the network of civil authority.

[47] Daniel H. Kulp, II, "Chinese Continuity," *Annals of the American Academy of Political and Social Science* (November, 1930), 152:28.

[48] Some of the regulations mentioned in the article "New School Rules in Switzerland Smack of Oriental Strictness," *The Asian Student* (December, 1953), 2:1, are: Students must show respect to their elders, and especially to magistrates, the aged, the infirm, and women; they must not use coarse language and commit brutal acts, they must prepare their homework; they are forbidden to loiter on the streets, to smoke, to carry arms, to mistreat animals, to go out alone after 8 P.M. between November 1 and March 21, and after 9 P.M. during the other months.

Familistic societies "throughout the world . . . look with resentment upon the imposition of outside officials who try to enforce laws and local regulations alien to the folkway of rule" ordinarily exercised by older family representatives.[49] Where civil authority is strong and centralized, however, overt hostility accomplishes little. Ethnics may resort to secretiveness and deception, or perhaps to accommodation.

Among many family-minded ethnic groups, such as the Chinese and Japanese, one shares his individuality with the whole group. A brother's triumph is that of the family and a brother's need is likewise that of the family.[50] Excessively selfish or individualistic aims are sacrificed for the wider benefit of the whole family group.

Even Western Europeans, who most closely resemble Americans, have had to cajole and appeal to nobility or royalty for redress of grievances in the not too distant past. In the business of ruling, the common man did not act; he was acted upon. Government tended to be the tool of those who governed, and the latter often acted from interests that were remote from, or hostile to, those of the common man.[51] Most villagers viewed the State as an exploiter—levying taxes, exacting forced labor to build and repair roads, and conscripting young men for the army when they were ready to marry and settle down. This power was resented and yet accepted with the same passive resignation as was an unpredictable storm.[52]

It is hard to dispel the notion prevalent among some cultural groups that civil authority is very remote, somewhat sacrosanct,[53]

[49] Irwin T. Sanders, "Characteristics of Peasant Societies," *Societies Around the World*, ed. Irwin T. Sanders, New York, The Dryden Press, Inc., 1953, 2:20.

[50] Cf. Smith, *op. cit.*, p. 54.

[51] Handlin, *op. cit.*, p. 202.

[52] *Ibid.*, p. 203.

[53] In times past rulers were anointed—an indication of the sacred character of the office which they held. The Japanese regarded their emperor as divine until their defeat in World War II. The Chinese emperor was popularly known as "The Son of Heaven." Even Chiang Kai-shek wished only his official title used in newspapers, and it was always one or more notches above the rest of the text. See Francis L. K. Hsu, *Americans and Chinese*, New York, Henry Schuman, Inc., 1953, pp. 167-168.

and inviolable. That the common man has power to alter the political tide is incomprehensible to most European and Oriental immigrants, with the possible exception of the French and the English. Criticism of civil authority is futile, and may be risky; social workers and teachers might as well be accepted with passivity, many ethnics think, since nothing can be done about them anyhow.

To the newly arrived immigrant, government appears as a succession of obstacles. It sets quotas and maintains a border patrol to prevent the movement of the individual. In its name men find themselves "betagged with strange papers, herded about like cattle." They seem to be constantly encountering its "visible symbol"—"the outstretched, uniformed palm."[54]

The policeman on the beat, twirling the symbol of his authority, is not regarded as a protector or friendly informant. He is, rather, a formidable representative of the law, a law with which the average immigrant is largely unfamiliar. Entanglement with civil authority is to be avoided, if possible. To remain unnoticed by the policeman is all the immigrant asks.

Authority Vested in the Professions

Social work, compulsory education, and public health services are American cultural patterns with which most other cultural groups are wholly unfamiliar when they first come to the United States. Should a well-meaning neighbor call the attention of an agency to someone's need, a letter of inquiry from the agency might be regarded as a summons.[55] The prospective client will need reassurance that an accounting is not being demanded of his ability to be self-supporting, and that he is not under compulsion to report to the agency.

[54] Handlin, *op. cit.*, p. 204.
[55] Elizabeth W. Clark, "The Challenge of Transplanted People for Casework," *New Emphasis on Cultural Factors*, New York, Family Service Association of America, 1948, p. 16.

When unemployment, illness, or any other circumstance requiring assistance is encountered by the ethnic, he may hesitate about using professional services lest he become involved with the law. It has been said, for example, that "Mexicans shrink from contact with even those agencies of the dominant group that are intended to 'do good,'" for these agencies usually approach the Mexican client "with a questionnaire in hand."[56] Being questioned has too often been the first step toward being arrested.

Hence the reluctance of the Mexicans to ask for relief, to apply for medical assistance, or to have any truck with the formidable apparatus of any federal agency. The machinery of government, to the Mexican, has been something to avoid. It must be met only when it comes at one aggressively in the war dress of a cop. What lies across the railroad tracks can be left well enough alone.[57]

Even the Negro who is better acquainted than other ethnics with American culture patterns often prefers to handle his own affairs without the assistance of the white social worker, health official, or policeman. This attitude was revealed by the Negro who said to a social worker that he "would never have bothered to come into a place for whites" if his mother had not insisted.[58] Another Negro client who was hospitalized for tuberculosis verbalized his feelings by saying that he had "learned his own device for getting along in the white man's world." He indicated the fears pertaining to his illness by remarking that he had "less chance" because of his color. In referring to another client, he said that this man also "had to sweat out" a diagnosis, but "he was white."

If the truancy or misbehavior of a child results in apprehension by the law, the parents may be greatly distressed. A Mexican mother made the following statement to the social worker in a Juvenile Office:

[56] Ernesto Galarza, "Program for Action," *Common Ground* (Summer, 1949), 9:32.

[57] *Ibid.*, p. 33.

[58] Olga Verin, "Racial Attitudes of Negro Clients," *Smith College Studies in Social Work* (September, 1945), 16:10.

We hate to be dragged into Court. That has never happened to us or to our family in our whole life in Mexico. Juan's father gave him a real good spanking and let him know that he didn't want to hear about his family getting involved in any trouble with the law.

If possible, members of ethnic groups will tend to avoid direct contacts with law-enforcing agencies. Traditionally, the family or church or mutual aid society gave assistance when it was needed. One of the first kinds of service the average ethnic group offers its members in a new environment is that of mutual aid. When such mutual aid groups are not available, the bartender or a street-corner "fixer" is more likely to be consulted than a social worker, a policeman, or even an employment bureau. Any direct encounter with a policeman will be settled out of court, if possible. The following incident reveals the reaction common to most newly arrived immigrants.

Well, this particular Sunday when all my trouble began was in the late spring. . . .

I had my first American-bought suit on and a purple striped tie with a handkerchief to match and a real Yankee Doodle hat from straw. I felt happy and full of prance.

Five or six other fellows and me were visiting around the park. . . .

While we were making shortcut down a quiet path to get on other side of the park we came to a beautiful tree foaming over with white blossoms, how they call in English, dogswood.

"Flowers. Flowers," one Russian fellow, name of Cyrille, said. "I gonna pick. Take bouquet to my lady friend." I don't know who he was, this fellow, he joined us some place we stopped.

"Pick! Pick!" Everybody got the idea. "Pick flowers, take a bouquet to all the lady friends."

"Why spoil a tree?" I said. "Use your brains better. If you want to make friends with a nice young lady, ask her to take a walk. . . ."

No, no, won't listen. They have to break the tree down. . . .

"Personally," I said, "I would be ashamed to give a lady flowers that I got for nothing. That I stole. I prefer better to buy. Shows more respect. Or else don't give."

All of a sudden that fellow, Cyrille, who had now the biggest bunch climbed down from the top branches and said to me, "I have to tie my shoelace. Hold my bouquet for a minute, I'll be back." So I held. In that minute a policeman was there.

"Awright. Awright," he said. "Defacing public property. Awright." He asked us our names and started writing them down on a piece of paper.

"What he does?" I asked Sergei.

"Gives us a summons."

"Summons?"

"We have to go in court."

"We're arrested?"

"Something like that. If we pay the fine, everything be O.K. But if we ignore, throw away the summons, they chase us; lock us up."

"What's your name, buddy?" policeman asked me.

I explained the best I can I'm not picking, I'm only holding for the other fellow.

But he doesn't believe me. "Don't argue," he said. "Don't argue or I'll run you in right now."

So he wrote a ticket for me, too, and went away. And still tying his shoe, that fellow Cyrille wasn't back yet.

"This is an awful, awful thing," I said.

"It's nothing." Sergei could laugh.

"Nothing! I lived my whole life at home and I was never in trouble. Now I'm six months in America and I'm a crook. Nothing, you think? How my father likes to hear such kind of news? Arrested. What will our village say? The first man from Kobiankari ever comes in the U.S.A.—for what? To go in prison!"

"Look," Sergei said. "You don't even have to go in court. Send the money. Plead guilty."

"But I'm not."

"You only say you are. Saves time."

"Then the policeman's right never to believe anybody. Say first, I didn't. Then, next time, change around, say I did."

"If you won't plead guilty, you'll have to go in court and have a trial."

"Then I'll go."

"Lose a day's pay."

"I lose."

"How about we find the policeman," Arkady suggested, "and try once more?"

"No use," Sergei said. "For myself I'm gonna plead guilty, but the best thing we can do for Giorgi Ivanitch, let's we go back in New York and see a fixer."

"What means vixer?" I said. "Vixer? Kind of fox, isn't it?"

"*Ef.* Fixer. It's a man. People pays him for fixing things. He knows how to manage all kinds of permits; he fills out income tax blanks; tears up traffic tickets. Suppose you're refused a license for something, you give the Fixer money, he finds some way around to get it anyway for you."

"Still sounds like a fox."

"That's vixen," Sergei said. "Keep straight the words in your head. You get everybody mixed up. Fixers has big connections. Influences."[59]

When the immigrant becomes involved with the law, he generally prefers a "fixer" to the regular channels. The anxiety and lack of understanding evident in this adverse encounter with the law are also often present in the social worker-client and teacher-pupil relationships. Social work, compulsory education, and public health services, too, may be regarded as superimposed by the dominant authoritative group in the community. Fear may simply be a fear of the unknown. Such questions as the following may be pondered by the ethnic parents: Will the worker take a child from the home and place him in an institution? Will the mentally or physically ill be taken to the hospital or "death house"?[60]

Although the professional worker may prefer to think of his role in relation to the client as one of influence, rather than one of authority, he does have power by virtue of his position. Viewed psychologically, help given by means of the worker-client relationship depends upon the acknowledgement by the client that the worker is superior to himself for the purposes of the problem at

[59] George and Helen Papashvily, *Anything Can Happen*, New York, Harper & Brothers, pp. 14-17. Copyright, 1944, by George and Helen Papashvily. By permission.

[60] Elizabeth B. Tyler, "Casework with Negro People," *The Family* (November, 1946), 27:266.

hand.[61] Not all clients, though, are ready to make such an overt acknowledgement.

Sometimes the ethnic client is hostile. Hostility may be evident in antagonistic remarks, in a failure to keep appointments, in over-politeness, or in undue preciseness of language.[62] The professional person may be really uncomfortable with a client because of un-familiarity with the ethnic group, of preconceived ideas and unfavor-able stereotypes, or of previous unpleasant experiences with other members of the group. Under such circumstances, the client will probably sense these attitudes and may react with hostility. Even to persons who are experienced and sympathetic, the client may dis-play hostile feelings simply because he identifies the professional person with the dominant group. Negroes, for example, have been known to express their hostility openly by referring to an agency as "for whites."[63]

Aggressive feelings are also evident in a marked reserve, vague-ness, secretiveness, or even deception. Elusive or indefinite answers may be given to questions concerning income, employment, or whereabouts of family members. The following excerpt from the case record of a Negro client who came to ask for relief because she was pregnant and unable to work illustrates these attitudes:

Miss W. said she had a common-law marriage with Mr. S., the father of the coming baby. She said Mr. S. left her several months ago and she didn't know where he went or why he left. She said she has not seen her mother since she was two years old and does not know what happened to her. The last she heard about her father he was in the penitentiary. She was reared by her grandparents in another state and the grand-mother is deceased. Occasionally she hears from her grandfather who is now eighty years old. She has a brother somewhere in Germany with the army, according to her statement.

[61] Elliot Studt, "An Outline for Study of Social Authority Factors in Case-work," *Social Casework* (June, 1954), 35:233.

[62] Cf. John Caswell Smith, Jr., "Understanding the Negro Client," *The Family*, May, 1946, 27:93-94.

[63] Verin, *loc. cit.*

At a later date a phone call was received from a woman who identified herself as Mrs. W., the mother of Miss W. She heard that her daughter was receiving assistance from the agency and wished to inform the agency that Miss W. does not need it. She said, "Why, I will take care of that girl if she will just let me. I have a nice home with pigeons and everything. I am working for some white ladies and earn enough to take care of her. I don't know what is wrong with her. She will not even live with me." I asked why she supposed Miss W. did not wish to live with her and she replied, "Why, because with me she would have to leave the men alone. She likes to live away from me so that she can have her men coming and going all the time. I would not stand for that. You just send her to me and I will take care of her."

When asked by the social worker if there was some reason for denying the whereabouts of her mother, the client replied angrily: "I don't have a mother; I said so before and I still say it. I don't know anybody who lives on H. Street and I don't have any relatives who live in this town."

A visit to the girl's mother, however, confirmed the fact that the client had been deceptive. The mother had insurance policies for the client. She said, moreover, that the father of the unborn child had pleaded with Miss W. to marry him. She added that her daughter could come home, but that she never wished to do "anything but sleep, run around, and get drunk."

Another example which illustrates evasion is that of Cleone, a Negro mother. The case record contains the following comments on Cleone's reactions:

When I mentioned a subject which aroused Cleone's feelings, she always evaded the issue by saying: "How nice your hair looks," or "What a pretty dress you have on, Miss Beverly." I soon learned that she was quite clever in spite of her lack of education.

Another technique which she used to divert my attention was that of drawing Agnes and Anna, the children, into the conversation. This was a clever way to avoid being alone with me and thereby avoid discussing her real problems.

The ethnic client may also resort to accommodation. Exteriorly he plays the role expected of him in order to gain security and maximum benefits. The following advice was given to Richard Wright when he was job hunting:

When you're in front of white people, *think* before you act, *think* before you speak. Your way of doing things is all right among *our* people, but not for *white* people. They won't stand for it.[64]

One of Wright's acquaintances named "Shorty" was "hardheaded, sensible, a reader of magazines and books, . . . proud of his race and indignant about its wrongs. But in the presence of whites he would play the role of a clown of the most debased and degraded type."[65] Wright himself was accommodating in his youth. He had just taken a job as cook in a private home and was determined that the whites should like him and keep him. These thoughts ran through his head: "I would be polite, humble, saying yes sir and no sir, yes ma'am and no ma'am, but I would draw a line over which they must not step."[66] It was not long, however, before Wright tossed his resolutions overboard and was without a job. Accommodation was alien to his disposition and he could not accept white domination with passivity even though it appeared as though his economic security demanded such concessions.

[64] Richard Wright, *Black Boy*, New York, Harper & Brothers, 1945, p. 161.
[65] *Ibid.*, p. 198.
[66] *Ibid.*, p. 128.

5

Economic Values

The American Scene

Economic organization is important to all peoples, for it is through the economic institution that limited material necessities of life are provided and regulated. Unlike the values pertaining to religion, economic values are divisible, and what is consumed or appropriated by one person diminishes the amount that would otherwise be available to others. In complex and highly organized societies, values deriving from this institution may be stressed out of all proportion to those placed upon them in simpler societies. This would seem to be the case in contemporary America. The economic institution in America is believed to be in a "primary and dominant position,"[1] for security is generally related directly to the production, consumption, and distribution of material goods.

The American economy is usually pictured as a "capitalistic" one, characterized by competition, individual initiative, private property, and profit. Industrial organization is complex and formal and the working man has resorted to labor organizations to represent his interests at collective bargaining. So complex is the industrial machinery that the average laboring man does not have face-to-face relationships with his employer, but merely receives a pay check

[1] Sirjamaki, "A Footnote to the Anthropological Approach to the Study of American Culture," *Social Forces, op. cit.,* 25:257.

for his labors. The economic man in America is said to be "rational, acquisitive and egocentric in his motivations."[2] He is, moreover, "aggressive, shrewd, alert, machine-minded, [and] self-reliant."[3]

ECONOMIC SUCCESS AS AN AMERICAN GOAL

Success becomes an important goal. Its value is inculcated during childhood by both parents and teachers. When a child does inferior school work, especially if he fails to make the grade, or if he is habitually the loser in sports or games, parents tend to withdraw affection and to express disappointment. This is a punishing experience, resulting in fear or anxiety. Success, on the contrary, gives status and helps insure parental support.[4]

When the individual reaches adulthood "success is still the great American object and that success means money, power, and publicity."[5] The acquisition of material goods and the status attached thereto are measures of a man's accomplishment. Most Americans seem to have such a veneration for these material things that "the most influential group in setting the standards of our society is the big business men."[6] In this culture successful businessmen have the social status accorded statesmen, churchmen, or scholars in other cultures.

Worship of success, in the opinion of one observer, has gone further than in any known culture, with the possible exception of

[2] Ibid.
[3] Ibid., p. 258.
[4] Shaw and Ort, Personal Adjustment in the American Culture, op. cit., pp. 149-150. The major themes in American cultural life according to many Europeans are "success orientation," "materialism," and "overcompetitiveness." Arvid Brodersen, "Themes in the Interpretation of America by Prominent Visitors from Abroad," Annals of the American Academy of Political and Social Science (September, 1954), 295:31.
[5] Robert M. Hutchins, "Do Americans Want a High Culture?" St. Louis Post-Dispatch, Seventy-fifth Anniversary Supplement, December 13, 1953, p. 28.
[6] Ibid.

prewar Japan.[7] A Mexican makes the comment that Americans have one special interest in life—to work to make money.[8] Americans take for granted conveniences and comforts that are unknown to all but the wealthy of other countries. Contemporary Americans, it has been said, have "overheated their houses, insisted upon a car and a radio, consumed incredible quantities of soft drinks, ice cream, candy, and cigarettes, and spent enough annually on liquor and cosmetics to have supported the whole population of less fortunate countries."[9]

This "soft living" is the antithesis of self-denial, not to mention ascetism. The few austerities imposed by the war, such as rationing, were evaded as much as possible. Even the men in American society appear to outsiders to be self-indulgent and pampered.[10] How American culture could produce effective servicemen during the last war was an enigma to many people. An Oriental made the following critical remark: "[You Americans] haven't got enough sorrow; . . . there is something in poverty that gives a man backbone and soberness and determination, something that steadies his character and tempers his idealism."[11]

The average agency client is the individual who is unsuccessful in one way or another. He is in a situation of strain which he cannot resolve by himself and is generally humiliated by his incapacity. As a rule, the individual is conscious that his behavior deviates from the normal and that his dependency role is incompatible with the

[7] Kluckhohn, Mirror for Man, op. cit., p. 235.

[8] H. Valle, "Civilization in the United States from the Mexican Point of View," trans. Henriette R. Van de Velde, America Now, ed. Harold E. Stearns, New York, Literary Guild of America, Inc., 1938, p. 559.

[9] Commager, The American Mind, op. cit., p. 423.

[10] Ibid., p. 423. In the opinion of a visiting Dane, Americans are "so soft physically—their life is so soft—that they must be violent in other ways. They do not walk or work in the open air or exercise. . . . They eat too much and they ride everywhere and they sit in hot rooms looking at things." Mannes, "The Friendliest People in the World, Fundamentally," The Reporter, op. cit., 10:36.

[11] Lin Yutang, "Oriental: A Chinese-American Evening," America Now, ed. Harold E. Stearns, New York, Literary Guild of America, Inc., 1938, p. 554.

American success ideal. He may project the "blame" on society or someone else, but the fact remains that abnormal dependency[12] is not consonant with American cultural norms.

WORK AND WEALTH AS VALUES

The struggles and successes of business are to Americans what the battles of chivalry were to the thirteenth-century Europeans, and what the progress of empire was to nineteenth-century Britons. Business determines where a man will live and his class position. He makes both friends and enemies in business, and frequently meets his wife there.[13] An American is identified primarily by his work. One of the best ways to answer the question "Who is he?" is to say that "he is a carpenter" or "he is a banker."[14] So absorbing is business that once Americans retire, they tend to lose their zest for life. Business *is* pleasure to many Americans "as against . . . the French for whom it is business to the last centime—after which, they seek pleasure unalloyed." Making money appears to be the thing Americans do best, and it appears to be an interest as much for what it is as for what it brings.[15] The son of a successful hotel magnate gave some indication of the value of money when he petulantly exclaimed to the police: "I can buy and sell the lot of you, and I'm going to do it, too."[16]

Although many people value work for its own sake, there are others for whom it is merely a means of obtaining money. They get little satisfaction out of their jobs. Routine, mechanized jobs which

[12] Normal dependency refers to incapacity due to age, physical disability, or unemployment, while abnormal dependency implies an unwillingness to be self-supporting.

[13] Cf. "Hollywood Discovers the U.S. Business Drama," *Newsweek* (May 3, 1954), 43:90.

[14] Cf. Saunders, *Cultural Differences and Medical Care, op. cit.,* p. 125.

[15] Kronenberger, *op. cit.,* pp. 216-217.

[16] As reported in "People," *Time* (May 24, 1954), 53:48.

are bereft of creativeness leave man "little or none of the deep and lasting pleasure that comes from a job well done." Hence the battle for shorter work hours and the physician's advice: "Do something to forget your work." After work hours, time is spent in enjoyable

"Pearson, for years I've noticed you admiring this clock, so I thought it fitting to present it to you upon your retirement."
(Courtesy of Leo Garel and *The Saturday Evening Post*.)

activities in the basement workshop or at such hobbies as photography and sports.[17]

Because money is an index of status, Americans tend to live beyond their means and spend much energy in "keeping up with the Joneses." Advertising creates demands for material goods that are often superfluous, and installment-plan buying is widespread. Excessive demands for material things may threaten family unity, as was the case with the family of Ina, a young wife and mother. Ina expressed her feelings in the following words:

. . . Unless I feel well dressed, as well dressed and pretty as the other girls, a wave of cold embarrassment sweeps over me. I clutch for Nick's hand and fight my desire to run away. . . .

. . . Our place is a ranch-type rambler—it's the first real house either one of us has ever lived in—and I wish we'd had the sense to choose a split-level model. The people across the street have a split-level house and it's much nicer. I haven't met the people yet, but they must have lovely furnishing. Yesterday I saw a spinet piano arrive. . . .

There is nothing in our den except a television set, a table-model sewing machine I was talked into buying—I can't sew—and three wrought-iron chairs originally intended for the patio. . . .

. . . The other day, out of sheer spite, [the grocery boy] . . . told me the woman next door had received a fur coat as a birthday present from her husband. I've never had a fur coat in my life. . . .[18]

Many Americans, then, see work as a means of attaining material goods—things which affect status and emotional security.

Among other groups there are also prevailing attitudes and cultural patterns. Indigenous peoples like the Indians and their Spanish-speaking descendants do not identify a man by the kind of work he does, for specialized occupations are practically nonexistent. The rural village offers few opportunities for "doing," and

[17] "What They Think . . .," *Newsweek* (May 24, 1954), 43:76.
[18] "Can This Marriage Be Saved?" *Ladies' Home Journal* (June, 1954), 71: 55, 78.

the best way of differentiating one man from another is in terms of personal characteristics.[19]

Work is seen as a necessary means to an *observable* end—to food, clothing, or shelter that is to be immediately utilized—and not as something which must be done for a specified number of hours a day. To have money in the bank is utterly foreign to many persons.[20] Why work for more money, they argue, "when it would only result in more food than one could eat or more clothes than one could wear or more houses than one could live in?"[21] A Southern Negro probably had the same viewpoint when he is reported to have said when asked if he would like to earn a quarter, "No, boss, I already has a quarter."[22] Those who engage, at times, in selling or exchanging goods tend to be more interested in the social contacts involved than in profits. This was evident in the response received by a traveler who desired to buy all an Indian's handiwork in a marketplace. "I couldn't do that," protested the Indian, "because then I'd have nothing left for the rest of the day." To the Indian, such a "clearance sale" would have resulted in social deprivation. Another American was surprised at the response he received when he asked a native who was presenting a gift, "What do you do with that?" "That" happened to be a piece of native handiwork. The creator of the handiwork answered, "You enjoy it!"

Because of prevailing attitudes toward work, many persons prefer intermittent work, like harvesting crops, to regular day-by-day labor. Attitudes toward work and money explain, moreover, why these persons fail to appear regularly for work, and also why, if pressure

[19] Saunders, *op. cit.*, p. 126.
[20] See Charles T. Loram, "The Fundamentals of Indian-White Contact in the United States and Canada," *The North American Indian Today*, eds. C. T. Loram and T. F. McIlwraith, Toronto, University of Toronto Press, 1943, p. 7.
[21] Saunders, *op. cit.*, p. 127.
[22] Vannevar Bush, "Today's Research and Tomorrow's World," *Congressional Record* (March 24, 1954), 100:A2246.

is put upon them to be "dependable," they may send a brother, cousin, or friend to take their places, whether or not the substitute has the same ability or skill. Since these attitudes undoubtedly complicate the procurement of steady work, it is important that professional persons be acquainted with them.

The following case of a Mexican, who lived in a midwestern city where meat packing is an important industry, illustrates the conflicting attitudes of Americans and some ethnics toward dependability.

An unemployed Mexican man came to the agency for relief. He said that he liked to work in the meat packing plant, had experience, and considered himself a good worker. He didn't seem to understand why the employer simply ignored him when selecting men from the line waiting for work.

The social worker contacted the plant and was told that this laborer wasn't dependable. When the work was heavy and they needed him most, he wasn't on the job. He was a good worker when he was there, but the company preferred men on whom they could depend.

The social worker discussed with the client the reasons for his absenteeism from work. The man said that very often his wife didn't feel well and she wanted him to stay home and help her with the children. Questioning revealed, however, that there were relatives in the neighborhood who visited the family frequently and who could be depended upon to care for the children when his wife was ill. The client eventually admitted that he wasn't too eager to work as long as necessity didn't require it. When he needed money, though, he expected to find work at once and to stay on the job only as long as he wished.

The attitudes of this Mexican are a reflection of the traditional concepts of work. In the comparatively simple economy of Mexico, the villager is able to set his own pace when working. He works according to natural units of labor such as "building a fence, plowing a field, [or] plastering an adobe house."[23] As a rule, he not only works at his own rate of speed, but also selects the job which he wishes to do at a certain time.

[23] Burma, *Spanish-Speaking Groups in the United States, op. cit.,* p. 63.

Many Chinese, too, are puzzled by the zeal of Americans for excessive wealth, although the average Chinese also values success and material comforts. Elaborate homes, exhibitionistic funerals and weddings, and excesses in other forms of ceremonialism give evidence that value is placed on material goods.[24] But once sufficient material goods have been acquired to meet needs that can be anticipated—including a certain amount of ostentation—the Chinese tend to retire from economic enterprises even at an early age. This attitude is summed up in the saying, "When currents are swift, bravely stop at the suitable moment."[25]

Among the Chinese, moral and spiritual values generally transcend material ones. Chinese contributions have been in the fields of art and philosophy. They have preferred to produce beautiful porcelain, exquisite paintings, a "contented philosophy of life," and advanced social and political theories rather than to construct great industries, highways, and cities.[26]

This "contented philosophy of life" is often associated with a resignation or kind of fatalism that is attributed to many peoples. The Mexicans, for instance, say "Al cabo Dios es muy grande," which, freely translated, means "After all, God is very great," with the implication that God will provide. When an agency grant is inadequate or if there are relatives who are able but unwilling to give assistance, the Mexican tends to accept the situation philosophically. The Italians, too, accept disappointments with the unprotesting word "pazienza" (patience).[27] Resignation or acceptance extends also to the area of health. While an American tends to "do something" about an illness, the Mexican may be indifferent. A dis-

[24] Hsu, *Under the Ancestor's Shadow, op. cit.,* p. 262.

[25] Francis L. K. Hsu, *Americans and Chinese,* New York, Henry Schuman & Company, 1953, p. 297.

[26] Theodore H. E. Chen, "Racial Characteristics of the Chinese," *Sociology and Social Research* (January-February, 1940), 24:228.

[27] Phyllis H. Williams, *South Italian Folkways in Europe and America,* New Haven, Yale University Press, 1938, p. 8.

ease which causes no great discomfort may not be reason for alarm. If treatment is given, it may be abandoned if it is expensive, extends over a long period of time, or produces no immediate observable results.[28]

One form of economic security which peoples with a peasant heritage tend to value is land. This is true of most European immigrants and their descendants.[29] The success of communism today is undoubtedly due, in some measure, to the promise to restore the land to the masses of the people. Chinese peasants, too, value land. "Land is there," a peasant remarked. "You can see it every day. Robbers cannot take it away." Another Chinese peasant called land "living property." "Money will be used up," he said, "but land never."[30] A reformer in India taught the value of land by saying: "The land is like your mother," and adding, "Would you evaluate how much your mother is worth in money?"[31] The American Indian is also said to be "rooted in the land." Money lacks the value it does for the dominant group. An Indian who received an offer of a good salary could not convince his wife of the value of money. "We belong here," she replied. "I married you to live with you, not your money."[32]

The Jews seem to follow the American pattern. The good things of the world are regarded as "infinite and acquirable."[33] Poverty has never been regarded as desirable, and it is not accepted passively. A poor man is advised to work on the Sabbath rather than become dependent upon charity. Even the ancient rabbis engaged in economic activities as a form of security. The man with means may give only a certain percentage of his property away, according

[28] Saunders, op. cit., p. 130.
[29] Cf. Handlin, The Uprooted, op. cit., p. 20.
[30] Hsiao-T'ung Fei, "Land as a Social Value," Societies Around the World, ed. Irwin T. Sanders, New York, The Dryden Press, Inc., 1953, 2:52.
[31] "The Land Beggar," Jubilee (June, 1954), 2:14.
[32] Anibal and Barbara Buitron, "What About Our Indians?" Americas (March, 1954), 2:3.
[33] Natalie F. Joffe, "The Dynamics of Benefice Among East European Jews," Social Forces (March, 1949), 27:239.

to law, in order that he himself may not become dependent.[34] The economically secure, however, are expected to share with the less fortunate. "Giving," it is said, "is both a duty and a joy; it is a source of heavenly approval and also a source of earthly prestige."[35]

Jews, for the most part, tend to be white-collar workers. Their forebears in Eastern and Central Europe were denied an opportunity to work creatively with their hands since medieval trade guilds would not accept them, nor was agriculture possible because of the prohibitions against Jews owning land. As intellectual life became glorified, manual labor was deprecated; Jews became laborers unwillingly, under the lash of necessity.[36] Hence, the Jews have traditionally engaged in commerce or the professions and automatically fall into the white-collar group. So many of them have won renown in professional fields that it is popularly believed that Jews have a predilection for the professions.

Some European and Oriental immigrants, on the other hand, tend to place a high value on hard work, and sometimes on manual labor. They work long hours at arduous occupations in order to become financially secure. When illness or age forces them to restrict their hours of work, they may resent the financial loss and imperil their physical as well as their mental health. Some persons gain status by physical prowess and value work which requires great physical strength. To engage in less strenuous or white-collar work is to be "less a man" in their estimation. If the professional worker wishes to make realistic suggestions regarding rehabilitation, knowledge of these attitudes is indispensable.[37]

[34] Eva Cohen and Helen Witmer, "The Diagnostic Significance of Russian Jewish Clients' Attitudes Toward Relief," *Smith College Studies in Social Work* (June, 1940), 10:289-290.

[35] Joffe, *op. cit.,* p. 238.

[36] Steinberg, *The Making of the Modern Jew, op. cit.,* p. 240; Cf. Gabriel Davidson, *Our Jewish Farmers,* New York, L. B. Fischer Co., 1943.

[37] Dorothy T. Pearse, *Social Information Report in the Administration of Aid to the Permanently and Totally Disabled,* Washington, Department of Health, Education and Welfare, 1953, p. 11. See also Caroline F. Ware, *Greenwich Village,* Boston, Houghton Mifflin Co., 1935, p. 173.

Apart from enforced absence from or curtailment of work, illness has other repercussions. There are numerous superstitions concerning the cure of illness, ranging from the use of a good luck piece or an article of clothing to highly questionable medicinal remedies. Even the suggestion of hospital care may have a traumatic effect. In other countries where there are few hospitals, they are used as a last resort; hence, the hopeless cases referred there seldom emerge alive. To be sent to a hospital, then, is to many persons the end of hope.[38] Despite the fact that a family member has a communicable disease and that the fears of hospitalization are based on lack of knowledge and experience, these fears must not be minimized or ignored by the professional worker. They are real to these people, and they do have psychological effects. In time, through contact with American culture, especially the educational institutions, many of these problems may become less common.

TIME AS A VALUE

Time is worth money, hence, Americans place a high value on punctuality and speed. Calendars and clocks are commonplace. In the American culture, one rises by the clock, dashes to work at a certain hour, punches a timeclock, eats lunch at a specified time, and stops work at the stroke of a clock. The housewife makes appointments by the clock, cooks with the aid of a clock, sends the children to school by the clock, and expects the family members to return home at specific times. Even amusement is time-centered. Radio and television programs are interspersed with advertisements at a rapid tempo. To outsiders, Americans appear to do things with great speed. The French have the general impression that "Americans get out of bed running and don't stop till they have spent the

[38] Cf. Chapter 3, p. 65.

evening rushing from spot to spot, climbing in and out of autos with crowds of other people."[39]

The value placed on speed is evident in the behavioral processes. Among Americans, human relations "are quickly initiated and easily dissolved; industrial enterprises mushroom up out of nowhere, and if they do not produce a satisfactory return, are quickly abandoned."[40] At a social gathering individuals are called by their first names almost immediately, but they may be abruptly disregarded shortly thereafter. The same thing occurs in a business transaction. The prospective buyer is "showered with courtesy and friendliness," but as soon as the business is completed he is "immediately relegated again to the status of a complete stranger."[41]

To people of many other cultures our hurried way of life is neither comprehensible nor appreciated. Life is to be lived leisurely and enjoyed, not spent, as a Hawaiian remarked, "trying to get somewhere else."[42] It is not the past or the future that is paramount, but the present. Of the Mexicans, one authority notes that the past was not carefully recorded, since the Mexican came from a folk culture with no tradition of writing. There was, moreover, "little that was sufficiently out of the ordinary to justify recording." Hence, the past "has been almost forgotten." The future, too, "offers no particular promise and is neither to be anticipated with joy nor feared," since for hundreds of years it brought almost nothing different from what he already had. But the present is not

---

[39] Ann Hightower, "French Myths About America," *The New York Times Magazine*, February 27, 1949, p. 15. Similarly, Scandinavian analysts remark that "the intense drive of the businessman" and the "bustling sales personality" are part of the American personality syndrome. Sewell *et al.*, "Scandinavian Students' Images of the United States," *Annals of the American Academy of Political and Social Science, op. cit.*, 295:128.

[40] Ruesch and Bateson, *Communication, op. cit.*, p. 143.

[41] *Ibid.*

[42] Blackey, *Some Cultural Aspects of Social Casework in Hawaii, op. cit.*, p. 41. European observers also remark that the American is "so impatient to live that life passes him right by." Freymond, "America in European Eyes," *Annals of the American Academy of Political and Social Science, op. cit.*, 295:38.

to be ignored; its demands must be coped with—now![43] Whatever the present brings should be accepted with equanimity, for the praiseworthy person is not the successful one nor the one who breaks time records, but rather the one who "obediently and graciously plays out the role defined for him."[44] This is the attitude of the typical Oriental and Latin, many Indians, and some Europeans.

Regard for the feelings of others and for one's own dignity often precludes bluntness in speech or hasty ill-timed actions. Among the Chinese, the practice of "saving face" or preserving one's self-esteem has led some observers to call the Chinese incorrigible liars who are incapable of sincerity. Instead of answering a question immediately—especially if a truthful answer means an acknowledgment of something "dishonorable"—the Chinese tend to evade the issue. Sharp questions or accusations may receive an indirect, gracious response.[45]

The Japanese, too, tend to be more concerned about their honor than about giving an immediate, entirely truthful response to a query.[46] A Japanese war-bride found that her long-cultivated habit of graciousness did not blend very well into her American environment. Making apologies, for instance, was a habit which she decided she had better "outgrow." "When I took my leave after a pleasant visit," she related, "I would say, 'I'm so—oops!'" Then she would stop, and instead of apologizing for overstaying her welcome, she would simply say, "Thank you so much. I had a lovely time."[47]

Like the Japanese, the Navaho Indian may also be concerned with being courteous and saving face. The Navaho is not too

[43] Saunders, *op. cit.*, p. 119.
[44] Florence R. Kluckhohn, "Cultural Factors in Social Work Practice and Education," *Social Service Review* (March, 1951), 25:40.
[45] Chen, *op. cit.*, p. 227.
[46] Benedict, *The Chrysanthemum and the Sword*, *op. cit.*, p. 171.
[47] J. P. McEvoy, "America Through the Eyes of a Japanese War-Bride," *The Reader's Digest* (April, 1955), 66:97.

bothered about lying or theft—unless he is found out. If he is caught, though, he experiences considerable shame. The Navahos stress affectionate duty to relatives, pleasant manners, generosity, and self-control, as well as a courteous, nonaggressive approach to others.[48] Physical injury to others and acts of violence are highly disapproved, but not a little stealing or lying.

Most Mexicans also place a high value on courtesy. A little exaggeration or flattery may be resorted to, or even outright lying. "My house is yours," the Mexican may say to a visitor, but this statement is not to be taken literally. Life is meant to be lived graciously and at an easy pace, according to the Latin.

Unhurriedness is the hallmark of most rural peoples.[49] Italian workmen commonly greet each other with the remark, "Take it easy." In Italy this same remark would evoke scorn or horror, but in America it reflects the Italians' deep-seated resistance to the speed of American industry.[50]

Although these ethnic groups set their own schedules for transportation, work, and even amusement, the schedules are not adhered to rigidly. Latins, for instance, almost never keep an appointment on the stroke of the hour scheduled. It is taken for granted that the time set is just approximate. Hence, if a client comes late for an appointment it does not necessarily indicate shiftlessness, ambivalence, or hostility. In emphasizing the importance of being on time, the professional worker must be careful not to give the client the impression of being rejected. Time has a different significance to other cultural groups. A Navaho Indian who was told emphatically to report for work at a certain time arrived an hour early in order to take no chances with a system which, from his point of

---

[48] Clyde Kluckhohn and Dorothea Leighton, *The Navaho,* Cambridge, Harvard University Press, 1946, pp. 219-220.

[49] Dorothea Leighton and Clyde Kluckhohn, *Children of the People,* Cambridge, Harvard University Press, 1947, p. 108.

[50] Williams, *South Italian Folkways in Europe and America, op. cit.,* p. 33.

view, was arbitrary because it was not geared to observable natural phenomena as was his "sun time."[51]

These clients may, over a period of time, give contradictory information when asked about their ages or the ages of their children. A mother may know which of her children is older and younger, but actual years of age may be unimportant. This is true of the Navahos[52] as well as of other Indians. The average Indian refuses to be a slave to the calendar or to the clock.[53]

COMPETITION

Americans are both individualistic and competitive. They seem to have a zest for winning that permeates nearly all activities from childhood to senescence. Early in life sibling rivalry for the affection of parents tends to occur. When the child reaches school age he competes with his classmates for good grades and may indulge in "apple-polishing" to secure the favor of the teachers. On the playground he engages in many competitive games, and if the games are played in true American fashion, he strives to win.

During adolescence and early adulthood rivalry often extends to the emotional realm. The love triangle is a typical American theme, which is not unknown even after marriage is supposed to have determined the victor. Competition is quite evident, of course, in business. Not only the male breadwinner but also the housewife engages in the economic struggle. She competes for bargains and attempts to balance the budget while at the same time "keeping up with the Joneses."

The competitive spirit penetrates even into the sphere of leisure-

[51] Leighton and Kluckhohn, op. cit., p. 109.
[52] Ibid.
[53] Federal schools on some Indian reservations which were scheduled to open in September were not filled to capacity until November. See Dale, The Indians of the Southwest, op. cit., p. 183.

time activities. Money acquired primarily in competitive business is a prerequisite for admission into certain clubs, for entertainment of one's acquaintances, and for commercialized recreation. Compe-

"Darned if I know. I saw another woman rushing for it and it was the last one left . . ." (Courtesy of Chon Day and *The Saturday Evening Post*.)

tition for status is marked in the way leisure time is used. Americans enjoy a variety of competitive games and sports ranging from card parties to all kinds of racing—boat, car, horse, dog, and even turtle.

While Americans tend to be individualistic and competitive, many other peoples are group-minded. For the Navaho Indian to take initiative in any obvious manner would have the psychological effect of separating him from his social group. By training and experience he works best as a "member of a familiar group where authority is diffuse, informal, and shared, and where adequate performance is enforced by the subtle sanction of 'shaming.' "[54]

In a certain Indian tribe where language and brown skin seemed to be the only vestiges of the past, a young man recently became so successful at farming that he earned ten thousand dollars in a single year. His success was partially due to his industry and the use of modern machinery and farming methods. Instead of being congratulated or envied, the young man was censured by his kinsmen and neighbors. Only a stingy man or one helped by witches, they said, would accumulate so much wealth. Group pressure became so strong that the young man had to make a choice between deserting his people and curbing his ambitions.[55]

Most American Indians see no value in competition. To strive to excel others in games or compete in school work is to them impolite, to say the least. Some Hopi school children evidenced embarrassment and resisted the injunction to turn around from the blackboard just as soon as they had finished a problem. Distinction of this sort was not a part of their culture.[56]

Chinese children, also, apparently have no pattern of individualistic competition. Siblings may engage in a form of rivalry by trying to excel each other in the care and attention they give to their parents. For the most part, though, this competitiveness results in group cohesion rather than in its opposite.[57]

[54] Leighton and Kluckhohn, *op. cit.*, p. 107.
[55] McNickle, "A U.S. Indian Speaks," *Americas, op. cit.*, 6:10-11.
[56] Shaw and Ort, *op. cit.*, p. 33. Mexican students are often shocked, too, at the competitiveness engendered by grading systems, especially in the universities. Ralph L. Beals, "The Mexican Student Views the United States," *Annals of the American Academy of Political and Social Science* (September, 1954), 295:111.
[57] Hsu, *Americans and Chinese, op. cit.*, p. 311.

Japanese schools devise ways of avoiding direct competition. Children are not allowed to compare their records with each other, but are merely urged to do better. Elementary school children in Japan begin and go through school together, without fear of losing status by being forced to repeat a grade.[58] The Japanese, like the Chinese, employ an intermediary or go-between in competitive situations such as negotiating marriage and offering one's services for hire where a man might feel shame if he is rejected.[59]

When the Japanese do engage in competitive sports, the losing team does not act like "good sports" according to the American standards of good losers. To lose even in a game is to "lose face," and the defeated team often weeps and bewails loudly and publicly. A losing baseball team might gather in a huddle and cry aloud.[60] Even when engaging in competitive games during leisure-time activities, cultural values influence reactions of various ethnic groups.

[58] Benedict, *The Chrysanthemum and the Sword, op. cit.*, p. 155.
[59] *Ibid.*, p. 156.
[60] *Ibid.*, p. 154.

6

Recreation

Development of American Recreational Institutions

RECREATION is usually considered as a relatively important social institution in contemporary American society. Its present importance is, however, closely associated with mechanization and urbanization. Authorities on American urban life believe that the "way city people spend their leisure time is one of the most important criteria of the values they cherish."[1] If family relationships have high priority, leisure time will be spent with family members. The same holds true for religious, educational, economic, or any other values.

In earlier times recreation was more informal, for as long as Americans were occupied primarily with land settlement and exploiting natural resources "there was neither opportunity nor great necessity for an elaborate system of leisure-time pursuits."[2] Work was varied and small intimate groups enjoyed picnics, card parties, dances, church socials, weddings, and even funerals.[3] Much of the fun was family-centered—dancing to the fiddler's music, singing in

[1] Noel P. Gist and L. A. Halbert, *Urban Society,* 3d ed., New York, Thomas Y. Crowell Co., 1948, p. 434.

[2] Jesse F. Steiner, "Recreation in an Urban Society," T. Lynn Smith and C. A. McMahan, *The Sociology of Urban Life,* New York, The Dryden Press, Inc., 1951, p. 558.

[3] Stuart A. Queen and David B. Carpenter, *The American City,* New York, McGraw-Hill Book Co., 1953, p. 344.

the parlor to the music of the upright piano, story-telling on the porch, or games in the yard. Families were large, and there were often nearby neighbors or friends to join in the fun. Although vaudeville, circuit road shows, and the circus did come to town, their visits were infrequent and the cost of such recreation was beyond the means of many families. Fairs, too, were generally annual events.

As industry developed, however, cities expanded and American society became more and more urbanized. Primary, intimate social relationships were replaced by casual and formal ones. The individuals who had previously done creative, outdoor work were now employed in factories, stores, and offices in congested urban centers. Speed and output were emphasized to the extent that little time or initiative was left to mingle pleasure with work. Hence, shorter work hours were demanded in order to provide relief from a monotonous job.[4] Little relief could be found in the cramped and dismal dwelling places in which urban people lived. These circumstances began to make city people self-conscious about recreational needs.[5]

The commercial recreation agencies that had developed in the nineteenth century such as the theater, public dance hall, bowling alley, billiard parlor, and saloon had hitherto been frowned upon by substantial citizens and even aligned with gambling and prostitution.[6] With increasing industrialization and dissatisfaction with factory jobs, however, many of these forms of commercial recreation began to assume an air of respectability.

Semiphilanthropic recreational agencies such as the Y.M.C.A. and the Boy Scouts began to function in the last quarter of the nineteenth century. The settlement house movement, too, lent an aura of respectability to organized recreation. These groups at-

[4] Cf. Steiner, loc. cit.
[5] Wilbur C. Hallenbeck, American Urban Communities, New York, Harper & Brothers, 1951, p. 463.
[6] Queen and Carpenter, loc. cit.

tempted to offset the rapidly expanding commercial recreational enterprises as well as to provide recreation for people who had none.[7]

Rising standards of living and the accumulation of wealth gave further impetus to the growth of such forms of commercialized recreation as the movies, amusement parks, pool halls, sports, and dancing.[8] People had the money and the time to spend on recreational pursuits which eventually became recognized as necessary in American urban life. So essential did the recreational institution become in modern life that the twentieth century has witnessed the development of public, tax-supported recreational facilities.

Entertainment has permeated even certain heretofore purely business transactions. Some businessmen regard entertainment as a legitimate business function, and the government recognizes the relationship between business and entertainment by allowing tax exemptions. The wage earner today often takes into consideration the recreational facilities offered by respective employers.[9]

Within a century, then, there has been a considerable change in attitudes toward recreation. From being regarded as a waste of time and energy, recreation has become an important social institution. Where formerly the young person who spent time regularly having fun was censured, young people today are expected to spend time in pleasurable activities. The person who is not asked for dates is apt to feel "inadequate, impotent, and also unwanted."[10]

For the most part, however, this recreation is not family-centered but is enjoyed with others of one's own age or sex. Young people date other young people and they do not appreciate involvements

[7] *Ibid.*

[8] Cf. Steiner, *op. cit.*, p. 559.

[9] Cf. S. R. Slavson, *Recreation and the Total Personality*, New York, Association Press, 1946, p. 183; Joseph Nolan, "Play as You Work," *The New York Times Magazine*, January 30, 1955, p. 50; Jackson M. Anderson, *Industrial Recreation*, New York, McGraw-Hill Book Co., 1955.

[10] Martha Wolfenstein, "The Emergence of Fun Morality," *Journal of Social Issues* (1951), 7:22.

either with older relatives or with younger siblings while they are dating. Baby-sitters are brought in to care for the children while the parents go outside the home for an evening of relaxation. Although married couples frequently recreate with other couples, there are many clubs which offer relaxation or entertainment to sex groups.[11] Americans tend to be great joiners and many of these organizations restrict membership according to age or sex.

It has been assumed that Americans join organizations not so much for sociality as to obtain security and status in a group.[12] The preponderance of formal group associations in American life is believed to be closely related to the decrease in family size and functions. Americans seem to become uneasy when left alone; "girls accompany each other to the rest rooms or for coffee in the afternoon, and boys and girls have roommates, rarely live alone, and practice double-dating."[13] Houses are built close together even where there is adequate space for isolation. In public parks and beaches one group of picnickers will join another, or will set up camp in the vicinity of others. Foreigners are often amazed at the number of meeting places Americans have established. The popular person is one who belongs to many groups and has many associates. In Europe, friends who can be depended upon in time of hardship are valued more than the sheer number of associates.[14]

[11] Grace L. Coyle lists three motivating forces in the use of leisure time: "the American habit of organizing voluntary associations for all kinds of civic and social purposes," the search for enjoyment, and the desire for learning. *Group Work with American Youth*, New York, Harper & Brothers, 1948, pp. 2-3.

[12] Sirjamaki, "A Footnote to the Anthropological Approach to the Study of American Culture," *Social Forces, op. cit.*, 25:261.

[13] Ruesch and Bateson, *Communication, op. cit.*, p. 110.

[14] *Ibid.*, p. 111. Scandinavian analysts remark that Americans "have hundreds of acquaintances but no true friends," and Swedish students have observed that American relationships "lack the depth of true understanding and mutual regard that Swedes feel for one or two close friends." Sewell *et al.*, "Scandinavian Students' Images of the United States," *Annals of the American Academy of Political and Social Science, op. cit.*, 295:127; Scott, "The Swedish Students' Image of the United States," *Annals of the American Academy of Political and Social Science, op. cit.*, 295:138.

Even the school child in America is encouraged to belong to formal organizations such as the Boy or Girl Scouts, the Glee Club, Dramatics Club, and the like. He is told that affiliation with such groups and the responsibilities connected with them will develop qualities of leadership. In addition to school-connected organizations, the child may also be expected to belong to church groups, neighborhood clubs, or civic organizations. As the young American matures, the network of formal organizations tends to spread to business groups.

Americans have become so much in earnest over recreation that other peoples question the amount of energy expended in leisure-time pursuits.

For Americans not only work hard, they play hard; simple gaiety, as the Italians know it, for example, seems not to be in their make-up. All the energy that the American saves from toil by the smart application of technology is freely expended on his most conspicuous passion, the great American outdoors. In every section of the country, even the industrial East, Americans pour out an incredible amount of energy whacking golf balls, playing tennis, baseball, hiking, camping, sailing, fishing, hunting —everything but just "walking." Most foreigners fail to understand—let alone enjoy—all this dashing around. The strenuous life is bad enough at the factory; why double it during leisure time? This reaction is a matter of temperament, and Americans must be prepared to accept the criticism that they are just too damn energetic.[15]

Closely allied with these active forms of recreation, however, is a corresponding amount of spectatorism in leisure-time activities. The more congested urban centers become, the more important mass recreation becomes. Only a limited number of persons can actively participate on a ball field or a golf course, but the grandstand and theater can accommodate large numbers. Much of American recreation in urban centers is perforce, then, of the spectator commercialized variety.

[15] "The American Way of Life," *Fortune, op. cit.,* 43:192.

COMMERCIALIZED RECREATION

In contemporary American society recreation tends to be commercial about one third of the time, if not oftener.[16] Commercialized recreation has a variety of offerings—motion pictures, amusement parks, pool halls and bowling alleys, racing, baseball, dancing, motoring, television, and radio. After making a selection one pays so much per hour, per reel, per ride, per dance, or what not.[17] The manager or owner, of course, operates his establishment for profit, not merely for fun. Profits are made by large scale production which requires a capital investment. Consequently, recreation is big business in America. The film *Gone With the Wind*, for instance, has made twenty-six million dollars and is still in demand.[18] Baseball, however, is believed to be a favorite sport and to give insight into "the heart and mind of America" because of the American "virtues" it reveals—"accuracy and speed, the practiced eye and hefty arm, the mind to take in and readjust to the unexpected, the possession of more than one talent and the willingness to work in harness without special orders."[19] In order to enjoy these commercialized forms of recreation, though, one must generally go to the fun factory, pay a certain price, and enjoy the product on the site.

Much of commercialized recreation, it has been noted, is of the spectator type. There are several factors which account for the popularity of spectatorism. As previously mentioned, city living is congested and there is a premium on space. Huge crowds can be accommodated as spectators, but not as participants in sports or

[16] Cf. Gist and Halbert, *op. cit.*, p. 436.
[17] Ray E. Baber, *Marriage and the Family*, 2d ed., New York, McGraw-Hill Book Co., 1953, p. 263.
[18] "Newsmakers," *Newsweek* (May 31, 1954), 43:44.
[19] Jacques Barzun, *God's Country and Mine*, Boston, Little, Brown & Co., 1954, pp. 159, 161.

games. The larger the crowd, the more there are to share the costs and, hence, the less expensive the amusement—as a rule. Another factor which plays an important role in the prevalence of spectatorism is the increasing number of older people in the population. Old people generally prefer to observe rather than to exert themselves physically. Where skills or talents are involved, there will be fewer qualified participants and consequently more spectators. Since Americans tend to demand professional rather than amateur performances, there has been a corresponding increase in spectatorism.

Commercialized recreation is further characterized by the inclusion of those forms of amusement which are considered illegal or unconventional, such as poker games and the betting associated with horse racing. Very often these activities receive protection from the political machine and they are sources of huge profit. Frank Costello, for example, estimated that he made $2,500,000 during 1936-37 in New Orleans alone on the slot machine business. The nationwide slot machine business is believed to gross between two and three billions a year.[20]

THE ORGANIZED RECREATION MOVEMENT

Organized community recreation is a product of the twentieth century. Play space was set aside for children and public parks were developed with tax funds in the early 1900's. Recreation came to be recognized as a medium for "creativity, self-expression, and self-discovery." It was seen as a means of promoting mental and physical health, as a teacher of the ways of democratic living, as a method of fostering good citizenship and lessening delinquency and crime, and as an economic factor in making communities more attractive.[21]

[20] "Kingpin Costello, Gamblers' Gambler," Newsweek (November 21, 1949), 34:31.
[21] Charles K. Brightbill, "Recreation," Social Work Year Book 1954, p. 440.

The social group worker's role is to assist in the attainment of these goals. He is to "affect the group process so that decisions come about as the result of . . . the sharing and integration of ideas, experiences, and knowledge rather than as the result of domination from within or without the group."[22] He is supposedly aware of the interplay of personalities within a group and is to assist each group member to get from the experience "the satisfaction provided by the program activities, the enjoyment and personal growth available through the social relations and the opportunity to participate as a responsible citizen."[23]

Activities are sponsored by nongovernmental voluntary agencies or by public, tax-supported authorities. The former include community recreational associations, settlements, boys' and girls' clubs, scouts, hostels, and similar groups, while the latter comprise park commissions, school boards, welfare divisions, and the like. So widespread is this organized recreational movement that there are 863 known settlements alone—with one in nearly every city of 250,000 or over.[24]

The range of activities is very broad. Figures supplied by the National Recreation Association report a large number of facilities such as tennis courts, softball diamonds, horseshoe courts, picnic areas, baseball diamonds, ice skating areas, shuffleboard courts, and handball courts.[25] Attendance is exceptionally heavy at bathing beaches, outdoor swimming pools, wading pools, stadiums, golf courses, and theaters.[26]

When working with ethnic group members, the professional worker can assist them to develop a healthy identification with their

[22] Grace Longwell Coyle, "Social Group Work," *Social Work Year Book 1954,* p. 481.
[23] *Ibid.*
[24] Francis Bosworth, "Settlements and Neighborhood Centers," *Social Work Year Book 1954,* p. 471.
[25] There were more than 1,000 of each of these facilities available according to "Community Recreation in 1948," *Recreation* (June, 1949), 43:107.
[26] *Ibid.*

group by fostering pride in its history and cultural values. Heavy reliance can be placed upon past and present ethnic group contributions in such program areas as arts and crafts, music, drama, discussions, and social action. As a consequence, these activities may produce positive intragroup associations resulting in a sense of emotional satisfaction in identification with the group, afford opportunities for creative expression, and provide an outlet for negative feelings connected with membership in the ethnic group.[27]

At the same time, settlement houses and community centers are often influential in interpreting American culture to the ethnic member and in bridging the gap between two cultures. Sometimes there is encouragement to adopt American cultural values by virtue of the fact that leaders talk to ethnic members about American ideals in connection with group activities and because these leaders are often persons with status in the community. There may be subtle rewards of approval by these admired leaders when the ethnic members conform to American culture.[28] The social group worker should, then, be acquainted with the relative merits of the two value systems and try to avoid pressures upon the ethnic member to sacrifice those cultural values which are basic to psychic security.

ETHNIC RECREATIONAL PATTERNS

Recreation which is formally organized and commercialized to satisfy individualistic needs is alien to most ethnic groups. In underdeveloped regions and rural areas so much attention is given to

[27] Sanford Solender, "Comments on Helen Green's Paper," on "Cultural Factors in Social Group Work," *Toward Professional Standards*, New York, American Association of Group Workers, 1947, p. 81.
[28] Cf. Child, *Italian or American? op. cit.*, p. 41.

meeting the basic human needs of food, clothing, and shelter that there is little energy or few resources left for leisure-time pursuits.[29] Just as early Americans regarded certain recreational activities a waste of time, so, too, many ethnic groups fail to see the utility of the types of recreation common in American society. They could see no sense, for instance, "in the athletics, the infantile antics of grown men playing at ball."[30] A young Polish Jewess expressed her reactions as follows when she heard her high school classmates discuss sports: " 'Tennis' was a curious word to me. And when they spoke of their *fathers* 'playing' *golf*! I did not know their simplest standards, the simplest forms of their daily life."[31]

More important, though, than the seemingly useless loss of energy is the danger which many ethnic groups perceive in individualistic recreational activities. For most ethnic peoples the family tends to be the group around which all others revolve, and the welfare of the family group supersedes that of the individual family members. It is through the family that the necessities of life are provided for all group members. Actual physical survival, the right to work and to protect property, are immediate goals. Japanese youth who have retained the traditional patterns do not, then, feel their importance or strength as individuals; it is the family that matters.[32] The Chinese, too, place great emphasis on the family. It is said that in China an individual appears to have little concern for another individual, unless he be identified with a family unit.[33]

Small diverse groups are not part of most ethnic cultures. In addition to the basic family group, the Japanese have tended to form mass control groups with all the farmers in one coöperative and all the teachers in another, and so forth. Europeans with a

[29] Cf. Hendry, *The Role of Groups in World Reconstruction, op. cit.*, p. 4.
[30] Handlin, *The Uprooted, op. cit.*, p. 253.
[31] E. G. Stern, *My Mother and I*, New York, The Macmillan Co., 1917, p. 89.
[32] Hendry, *op. cit.*, p. 5.
[33] *Ibid.*, p. 28.

traditionally paternal structure are inclined to be authoritarian and are unwilling to allow small groups to experiment.[34]

Wherever size permits, the whole village may operate as a unit. In Mexican villages, for example, this pattern tends to prevail, and opportunities for achieving leadership are practically nonexistent. There are few formal organizations, and the range of community activities and interests is limited to those in which "every member of the community could, at some stage in his development, be expected to share." One is a leader, then, only in the sense that he heads a procession of individuals, all of whom know exactly where they are going. Even this role of leadership is usually reserved for those with "requisite institutional rather than personal qualities."[35]

That the group process can be used for the enrichment of personality except within the primary group is foreign to Chinese or Japanese culture. A Japanese is said to feel his personality most fully when acting as a member of his group rather than as a separate individual.[36] Emphasis has traditionally been placed upon nationalistic goals by the Japanese, and individuals were taught to sacrifice themselves for nationalistic as well as familistic ends.[37] As the rule, then, there are tremendous obstacles to the introduction of a new type of group organization that does not fit naturally into the prevailing pattern.[38]

Since the family group is the pattern, the ethnic child tends to be at a loss when he encounters the age groupings of American children. The school group, for example, which begins as a group of age mates who are strangers, may be a frightening experience for the ethnic child who has no techniques for entering a school group. School teachers often notice the isolation of the ethnic child

[34] *Ibid.*, pp. 11, 20, 24.
[35] Saunders, *Cultural Differences and Medical Care*, *op. cit.*, p. 137.
[36] Smith, *Americans from Japan*, *op. cit.*, p. 54.
[37] Hendry, *op. cit.*, p. 5.
[38] *Ibid.*, p. 16.

and may urge the parents to have the child visit classmates and play with them. Among Chinese and Japanese, however, children are not sent out to play with just any other children, and children's parties are alien to these cultures. Children of a given family may play with those of another family, usually when the families are related or are visiting. Teachers, group workers, and recreation leaders who are forming groups ought to be aware of these cultural patterns.[39] They should, moreover, bear in mind that recreation as such is not regarded as a basic need in most ethnic group cultures. Even small children in Italy, for instance, are traditionally trained to do useful tasks at any early age.[40] Orientals in America tend to exact much work of their children; and Mexicans who may appear anything but industrious may protest if children have nothing useful to show for the time spent in a settlement house. A Polish Jewess of first-generation parents tells how recreation was viewed among her group:

Playing was forbidden. It was in the eyes of the wise adults in our courtyard a waste of time. Our neighbours permitted their children to play only on suffrance, and most of my companions understood that any child of seven or eight caught frolicking merited punishment from a tired and harassed mother.[41]

Many ethnic groups prefer to keep adolescents in sex groupings in school, in work, and in play. The Italians, for instance, have separate schools for boys and girls in the mother country and they may be uneasy about coeducation.[42] Even supervised play of mixed groupings may be unacceptable. The Mexicans have the same attitudes toward mingling of the sexes during adolescence. A group worker in a Mexican district reported that she had had repeated failures in trying to form teen-age groups with both sexes. In spite of

---

[39] Lee, "Some Implications of Culture for Interpersonal Relations," *Social Casework, op. cit.,* 31:360.

[40] Williams, *South Italian Folkways in Europe and America, op. cit.,* p. 20.

[41] Stern, *op. cit.,* pp. 27-28.

[42] Williams, *South Italian Folkways in Europe and America, op. cit.,* p. 128.

home visits and assurances to the parents that activities would be supervised, the teen-aged mixed groups never were successful.[43] The Mexican is said to consider sex "a fire that only experts can play with, and a kind of gasoline that should not be allowed around loose where children can get into it." Hence, it is "considered foolhardy to bring these essential elements [male and female] . . . together before it is okay to let Nature take its course."[44]

Where ethnic patterns are strong, adults will prefer family activities to those sponsored by recreation centers and settlements. Italians in New Haven gave as an additional reason for nonparticipation the fact that refreshments were not typically Italian and wine was not permitted. A relatively high standard of dress prevailing in settlements also deterred many Italians from participation.[45]

The recreational activity of adults tends to be closely associated with family hospitality and with holiday or feast-day celebrations.[46] A client may take offense if the visiting professional person refuses refreshment. Very often a client will be insistent that the professional worker accept some gift as well as the offer of refreshments. Italian culture, for instance, dictates reciprocity, and the client who has received financial or other assistance from a professional worker may feel obliged to make some return.[47] The Mexican and Chinese clients often react in a similar manner. Pardee Lowe tells of his initiation into this phase of culture as follows:

At Christmas and Chinese New Year, the volume of money and energy Father and Mother spent for presents astounded me. I learned that the Chinese, even the poorest, were a gift-bearing and gift-giving folk. Soon I became a part of that system. The giving of presents as a visible expression of gratitude became an integral part of my own life.[48]

---

[43] This situation did not prevail among the Mexicans in the same community who had become more assimilated.

[44] De Treviño, My Heart Lies South, op. cit., p. 49.

[45] Williams, South Italian Folkways in Europe and America, op. cit., p. 121.

[46] Ibid., p. 107.

[47] Ibid., p. 123.

[48] Lowe, Father and Glorious Descendant, op. cit., p. 78.

When Pardee's Aunt Lillian went to school with him to offer presents to the "Barbarians" who were his teachers, the principal protested that the Board would not allow them to accept such expensive gifts. Aunt Lillian insisted that Pardee's parents would feel "highly insulted" if the gifts were not accepted. She said that in China the teachers stood next to the parents, and since they "cherished as well as instructed their pupils, nothing was too good for them." After such an explanation, Aunt Lillian had her way.[49]

Just as the gifts were often beyond the financial means of the family, so too the activities of Lowe's family were often a financial burden. In less than two months his family had celebrated seven major holidays, and on each occasion

. . . the entire family had gathered for a huge banquet, exchanged presents or money gifts, visited the family tombs, and worshiped the ancestors. The burden of servicing this expanding Chinese-American standard of living was proving ruinous. Vast outlays of time, effort, and money were made solely for face-saving purposes.

Yet when the celebrations were over, the family members always said, "This feast was worth it."[50]

A young Mexican wife describes the kinds of celebration enjoyed by her family in the following words:

To us, of Mexican descent, the family is very important. Although we have taken up many modern methods and fads, there are many old Mexican customs we would never give up. For instance, the christening of a baby is a big day. The ceremony will be in the morning or early in the afternoon and it is followed by a big meal and then dancing until late in the afternoon—even though the honoree has long since been put to bed. It is a gala affair. Uncles, aunts, grandmothers, grandfathers, and children have a good time. The children are especially excited because the godparents by custom have a "bolo" for them. A "bolo" is a gift given to all children immediately after the ceremony, and it usually consists of pennies or nickels.

[49] *Ibid.*, p. 79.
[50] *Ibid.*, pp. 296, 321.

Baptismal celebrations are only one type of family get-together. We have many more. As might be expected, a wedding is also an occasion for an all-day celebration. Since my family is rather large, we are not able to get together at the homestead all at one time. However, without fail we unite on Christmas, in time of illness or crisis, baptisms, weddings, funerals, birthdays, graduation parties, picnics, etc. No club, theatre, or nightclub can provide us with more enjoyment than these family affairs even though some of us might be all tired out after preparing a big meal consisting of *gallina en mole,* rice, beans, salad, tortillas, or a strictly American meal of fried chicken, French fried potatoes, peas and carrots, salad, rolls and iced tea.

Religious festivals, wherever possible, have been transplanted to America,[51] and the whole ethnic community tends to participate in them. Some festivals last only one day, but others, such as those associated with Christmas, are of longer duration. The Italians in New Haven have religious processions with floats, a profusion of flowers, and ornate vestments.[52] Mexicans in the Southwest often have dancers performing in the religious procession. Streets are blocked off for the occasion and those who are not actively participating in the procession line the sides of the streets. During the Christmas season, especially, religious dramas are enacted in the churchyard or parish hall. *Los Pastores,* for instance, is the story of the shepherds who came to worship the Christ Child. There are several versions, and parts are generally handed down (sometimes by word of mouth) from one generation to another after the manner of the Oberammergau Passion Play. The performance is a distinctly ethnic one with an all male cast and is sufficiently spectacular to attract the ethnic community.[53] The Italians, too, have brought to America certain plays of a religious or historical nature, but there is not the same continuity from one year to another as

[51] Williams, *South Italian Folkways in Europe and America, op. cit.,* p. 109.
[52] *Ibid.*
[53] William Eugene Carter, "The Religious Drama of Mexico: Its Use in Program Planning in a Group Work Agency," Master's thesis, Worden School of Social Service, Our Lady of the Lake College, 1951.

there is with the Mexicans. Japanese plays, like those of the Mexicans, often have men assuming the female as well as the male parts.[54] The opera is a chief feature of religious thanksgiving among the Chinese.[55] In many instances the festival has a carnival as well as a religious tone. There are banners, costumes, and games, as well as wining and dining for an entire day or longer. Dancing may or may not be associated with the festival. Folk dancing and the solemn Indian dances performed by the Mexicans at religious processions are often an integral part of a festival, but not the ballroom type of dancing popular among Americans.

Movies in the mother language are a source of entertainment for most ethnics. Older Italians look upon attendance at American films by the younger people as a "waste of money" and time, but they enjoy Italian movies themselves.[56] In the Southwest Spanish-language films are popular among Mexicans of all ages. Unless the ethnic group is sufficiently numerous, however, to make the foreign-language film business profitable, this form of recreation will not be widespread.

Radio and television are popular even among the poor ethnic group members. They tend to have a great love for music and song, and the Italians' knowledge of outstanding compositions is greater than that of Americans of the same social status.[57] Newspapers and books are less common, especially among the older people, unless they are printed in the mother tongue. English publications may be available for the younger generations. With the Italians in New Haven the "funnies," along with motion-picture, Wild West, and detective story periodicals, were most prevalent.[58]

[54] Smith, *Americans from Japan, op. cit.*, pp. 56-57.
[55] Martin C. Yang, *A Chinese Village*, New York, Columbia University Press, 1945, p. 197.
[56] Williams, *South Italian Folkways in Europe and America, op. cit.*, pp. 118-119.
[57] *Ibid.*, p. 121.
[58] *Ibid.*, pp. 120-121.

Each ethnic group, of course, has other specific forms of entertainment. The Japanese have traditionally enjoyed the bath which was not merely a cleansing process, but "a ritual, a medicine, a social club, a physical and mental pick-me-up, and occasionally a side show."[59] Distinctive Italian games are *bocce,* a bowling game, and *morra,* a finger-guessing game.[60] The Mexicans enjoy breaking the *piñata,* a clay container which is brightly decorated and contains goodies and small trinkets. Every group has its own legends, stories, games, and songs which are passed on from one generation to another and which are an integral part of the culture.

The Negro, too, has recreational patterns, but they are largely adaptations of those of the dominant group. Negroes are often barred from using public facilities and have inadequate facilities of their own. Since they are concentrated in the rural South, their patterns follow those of that region. Unorganized, informal recreation predominates. Hunting, fishing, and swimming are popular. There are also considerable loafing, talking, boasting, telling tall stories, and singing. Sometimes there are good-natured "bantering," boisterous laughing, and perhaps obscenity.[61] These activities serve as a relief from monotonous labor or help to fill the dull, empty days when there is no work.

Rural Negroes do not have many opportunities to travel, but "going to town" on Saturdays or in the evenings is generally considered fun. Time is spent shopping, watching the trains come and go, and visiting on the street corner or in the stores. Going to church is also a form of recreation. The Negroes put on their best clothes, meet their friends, and experience some emotional relief in the kind of singing and music which tends to prevail among rural Negro sects.[62]

[59] Smith, *Americans from Japan, op. cit.,* p. 50.
[60] Child, *op. cit.,* p. 25.
[61] Myrdal, *An American Dilemma, op. cit.,* p. 982.
[62] *Ibid.,* p. 983.

ETHNIC YOUTH LEISURE-TIME ACTIVITIES

In a study of the leisure-time activities of teen-age youth, there were some significant findings in regard to ethnic groups. "Leisure time" included all of a youth's waking hours not spent in school.[63] According to this definition, work would be a leisure-time activity, although work is not commonly associated with recreation. Oriental youth spent more time working—probably in the family business— than any other group. The Negroes and Mexicans had the lowest employment rate, a fact which may be attributable to the scarcity of jobs for them. Jobs for which teen-agers were paid included delivering papers, working in stores, and baby-sitting.

Apart from work, the leisure-time activities which had a high rate of frequency for all youth were watching television, attending church, going to the soda fountain and drive-ins, social dancing, movies, talking on the telephone, pleasure reading, and attending sports events.[64]

Negro youth rated higher than any other in frequency of resort to parks and playgrounds, Y.M.- and Y.W.C.A., and church attendance. In frequency of movie-going they were exceeded only by the Mexicans. Rate of participation was high, but not in organized groups.[65] These Negro youth are hardly typical, though, because they reside in a West Coast urban community.

Mexican youth were also relatively high in their use of "parks and playgrounds, Y.M.- and Y.W.C.A., church attendance, 'walking around town,' automobile pleasure riding, movie attendance, house parties, and television watching."[66] They were the lowest

[63] Davis McEntire, *Leisure Activities of Youth in Berkeley, California,* Berkeley, Council of Social Welfare and University of California, 1952, p. 10.

[64] *Ibid.*, pp. 10-11.

[65] *Ibid.*, p. 13.

[66] *Ibid.*

of any group in organized group participation and school home-work. They appeared to have a "disinclination toward activities involving social participation." Sports events, social dancing, and music or art lessons were relatively unimportant to them.[67]

Oriental youth, too, seemed to withdraw from the forms of social participation represented in organized group meetings, social and folk dancing, and attendance at sports events. In addition, there was a deëmphasis of movies, television, house parties, and telephone talking that was probably a reflection of culture. Since a great deal of leisure time was spent in study and part-time jobs, there was a limitation on participation in many other activities.[68]

Study generally ranks relatively high as a leisure-time activity among adolescents.[69] Among adults, too, there appears to be a widespread interest in recreation that has educative value.[70] Classics and scholarly works have been reprinted in cheap pocket editions for wide distribution. Radio and television programs are a further index of the trend toward purposeful, informative recreation. They often feature a panel of experts or educators; they may bring a symphony or opera into America's homes; and they also serve to enlighten the public on the manner in which government operates by having programs depicting events of national importance such as political conventions and congressional hearings. In a lighter vein, there are numerous quiz programs which promise financial returns to the educated Americans who have some familiarity with American history, geography, or government.

[67] Ibid.
[68] Ibid., p. 14.
[69] Cf. McEntire, op. cit., pp. 10-14.
[70] Coyle, Group Work with American Youth, op. cit., pp. 2-3.

7

Education

ONE social institution which clearly reflects cultural values is education. "It is," in the words of Robert M. Hutchins, "a means of perpetuating the prevailing hierarchy of values."[1] Culture is learned rather than biologically transmitted, and it is through education that cultural values are imparted to succeeding generations. American culture regards education "primarily as a means of getting ahead in life," that is, of achieving success in terms of money, power, and publicity. In a highly specialized society professional or vocational training is important if one is to be successful. Consequently, vocational interests seem to be paramount in the American educational system.[2] Social interests also rank high, for education is one of the important rungs on the social ladder. Some young people go to college chiefly for social contacts and social advantages. College gives them an opportunity to make contacts with prominent families, and it is hoped that these contacts will be stepping stones to success.

Purely aesthetic works of art or thought, which in common par-

[1] Hutchins, "Do Americans Want High Culture?" *St. Louis Post-Dispatch, op. cit.,* p. 28. See the same author's *Education for Freedom,* Baton Rouge, Louisiana State University Press, 1943.

[2] *Ibid.* For an analysis of official educational values see *The Purposes of Education in American Democracy,* Washington, National Educational Association, 1938.

lance are called "cultural," are not seriously pursued in American society. A century ago most men would not be seen at an opera or art gallery unless they were reluctantly escorting their spouses, and even today the realm of the "cultural" is primarily a woman's world, a leisure-time activity. The successful American businessman probably would oppose his son's choice of a career in poetry, music, or sculpture. In recent years, however, there has been some change in attitudes toward a man's interest in such pursuits, especially if they be avocations. Winston Churchill and Dwight Eisenhower indulge in painting, and college boys may engage in such pastimes as "part-singing or violin-playing—sissy occupations both" thirty years ago. Nonetheless, in an "environment that is not on the lookout for brains" or "in a family that feels they're unmanly or undemocratic," "young talent" is believed to "go to waste."[3] George Mikes, a European intellectual, makes the following cynical observation on American culture:

Jazz is their music, comic strips their most admired pictures, magazine stories their literature, Hollywood films their most popular entertainment, skyscrapers their architecture and their newest ball-point pens can write under water. . . . We know, too, that God could make America a wonderful country if he only had the money.[4]

Philosophy, too, is not highly esteemed for which reason Americans are thought to be "intellectually immature." It is too often regarded as "the resort of the unhappy and the bewildered," and Americans consider themselves neither.[5] "Wooly-headed theories or impractical idealism" are not for Americans; "instead, down-to-earth, hard-rock facts: the miles of cement, the telephones, the cars laid end to end—all the things . . . our friends have envied and our

[3] Barzun, God's Country and Mine, op. cit., pp. 213-214.
[4] As quoted in "Have We Any Friends?" Fortune (February, 1951), 43:118.
[5] Sewell et al., "Scandinavian Students' Images of the United States," Annals of the American Academy of Political and Social Science, op. cit., 295:128; Commager, The American Mind, op. cit., p. 9.

enemies have conceded."[6] The Japanese have said that what Americans seem to lack is an explicit ideology that they could communicate with the same effectiveness as the Russians explain theirs.[7] A Chinese gentleman remarked of the American: "He is always getting educated—for what, he doesn't know. . . . He makes a better engineer than a philosopher."[8]

Despite the fact that many Americans seek higher degrees, nowhere else are "intellectuals held in such contempt or relegated to so inferior a position."[9] The professor, caricatured as long-haired and absent-minded, is an object of humor. Young people are sent to college because it is "the thing to do," or, perhaps, for the same motive that prompts people to buy a larger television screen than that of their neighbors. Many parents believe college to be a waste of time, yet are somehow afraid not to send their children.[10]

FOREIGN-LANGUAGE AND CHURCH-RELATED SCHOOLS

Since a democracy presupposes an educated electorate, America has free, tax-supported, compulsory education in nonsectarian schools. This compulsory education is often a threat to members of other cultural groups. Their children are forced to go to a school where they are "taught alien ways in an alien language, generally by teachers of an alien religion."[11] Hence, many cultural groups support private schools, often church-related, where the mother

[6] "Have We Any Friends?" op. cit., p. 117.

[7] Clyde Kluckhohn, Mirror for Man, op. cit., p. 231.

[8] Yutang, "Oriental: A Chinese-American Evening," op. cit., p. 553. European observers say that "the fundamental thoughts all come from France or England or Germany, anyway, from Europe." Freymond, "America in European Eyes," Annals of the American Academy of Political and Social Science, op. cit., 295:38.

[9] Commager, op. cit., p. 10.

[10] Ernest Havemann and Patricia S. West, They Went to College, New York, Harcourt, Brace & Co., 1952, p. 4.

[11] Handlin, The Uprooted, op. cit., p. 177.

tongue is understood, if not taught. Other groups, such as the Chinese, Japanese, and Jewish people send their children to special schools after the regular school hours or on week ends where the native language is taught and other important cultural values are reinforced.

The foreign-language or special schools often prevented a sudden rift between generations which might have occurred if the acculturation process had been too rapid. Attendance at two different kinds of schools, however, also tended to prove confusing. If Japanese children, for instance, applied in the Japanese school what they were taught in the public school about asking questions and using initiative, they were apt to receive a good lecturing and sometimes punishment. If they asked questions in the public school, they were often badgered about their incorrect speech. The standard Japanese which they learned in school could not be spoken at home, nor did they dare speak the standard English which they were learning in the public school lest they suffer ridicule from the rest of the family.[12]

An American-born Chinese reveals his attitudes toward the Chinese school by remarking that Tutor Chun

paid chief attention to our Chinese diction and to the finer abstruse points of Chinese philosophy. He was not particularly interested in making Chinese simple. He prided himself that he had learned it the hard way and, over his dead body, he declared, it was the only way he would teach it.[13]

Apparently the tutor did not appreciate the bewilderment of his charges for he continued to drill them in the classical Chinese characters which required a dictionary to decipher.

The words could not be used in daily conversation, and each variation of a sound had a disconcerting meaning all its own. The simple sound

---

[12] Cf. Smith, *Americans from Japan, op. cit.*, p. 122. See also the account of a Chinese school in San Francisco, "Hard Work at Hip Wo," *Life* (April 25, 1955), 38:71.

[13] Lowe, *Father and Glorious Descendant, op. cit.*, p. 111.

"C," for instance, possessed a myriad of different meanings. It could stand for silk or fiber, a corpse, twigs, food, animal excrement, a commissioner, a company or office, a year, contraband . . .

This laborious method of learning formal Chinese, I very soon concluded was . . . an unmitigated nuisance for me. Even at the age of ten I wondered if it wasn't a waste of time. I wrote no Chinese letters to our relatives in China. Only the simplest phrases were used in Chinatown. In our home I spoke mostly pidgin Chinese or English. . . .[14]

Like the Chinese, Jewish children often go to Hebrew school after regular hours. Classes may be held in rooms adjoining the synagogue, or at a private home. A Jewish girl gives the following description of the school which she attended:

Each day after school hours I went to Hebrew school; Hebrew school was in the kitchen of a friend of father's. We would sit, fourteen of us, about the table, I the only girl. In unison we read the Hebrew, in unison translated it. Our teacher was a gentle old man whom we sorely tried, we children with our strange American disrespect. "Oh, you American children," he would say when we refused to remain in longer on hot summer days. . . .[15]

Church-related or parochial schools were believed to prevent estrangement between generations by inculcating respect for traditional values, although the chief purpose of this school system was to include religion in general education for democratic life.[16]

[14] *Ibid.*, p. 112.

[15] Stern, *My Mother and I, op. cit.*, pp. 51-52.

[16] The pastoral letter of the archbishops and bishops of the United States assembled in the Third Plenary Council of Baltimore, December 7, 1884 states: "Now the three great educational agencies are the home, the Church, and the school [and] . . . each of them, to do its part well, must foster religion. . . . To shut religion out of the school, and keep it for home and the Church, is, logically, to train up a generation that will consider religion good for home and the Church, but not for the practical business of real life. . . . Therefore the school, which principally gives the knowledge fitting for practical life, ought to be pre-eminently under the holy influence of religion." Some recognition is given ethnic factors, however, in the following excerpt from the address of Archbishop Francesco Satolli given in Pottsville, Pennsylvania on April 25, 1895: "Here in America the Catholics . . . consider [their] . . . customs and usages, inherited from their fathers along with their language, as an important and effective means of maintaining

There was a controversy over the relative merits of the parochial and the public school systems, and it was often believed that the public school introduced into the child's life a rival source of authority. Before long the child in the public school came home to tell his parents, *"They say in school that . . ."*[17] Public school teachers were usually unacquainted with the traditions of the various ethnic groups, and often had little sympathy for alien customs. Contacts with the public school system, then, often led ethnic children to question traditional patterns which their parents were striving to instill in them.

In one study of attitudes of ethnic groups toward the parochial schools, it was found that the Irish placed a high value on the schools chiefly because of religious education available in these schools. The French Canadians, on the other hand, who had no parochial school of their own, were less insistent that their children attend the parochial school on the high school level. For one thing, the French Canadians did not place too much value on a high school education. More important, however, was the fact that it meant identifying themselves with the Irish since they lacked a school of their own. They had some sympathy with the public high school, moreover, since French was offered as a language there. The Italians were still less insistent on the need for parochial school education. Many Italians were trying to identify themselves with American culture and they maintained that they could teach religion in the home. The Jews, too, regarded the public school as

intact religious and domestic virtues as much as possible. They see them rightly as a strong aid to education. This does not prevent such education from being truly American and genuinely national since religion is the best and most certain foundation of all civic virtues. Thus youths learn in our parish schools the virtues which are the treasures of every good citizen." Colman J. Barry, *The Catholic Church and German Americans,* Milwaukee, Bruce Publishing Company, 1953, pp. 321-322. See the last named work for an account of the controversy over the relative merits of the parochial and the public school system. See also John J. Kane, *Catholic-Protestant Conflicts in America,* Chicago, Henry Regnery Company, 1955, Chapter 7, "The School Question."

[17] Handlin, *op. cit.,* p. 244.

a means of transition into the cultural stream of American life. Many of the latter, however, did want their children to attend the Hebrew school after regular public school hours.[18]

ATTITUDES OF ETHNICS TOWARD FORMAL EDUCATION

Some Europeans were lured by tales of the educational opportunities in America. To many of them education appeared as a magic wand that prepared everyone for pleasant and profitable positions. First-generation Italians, for instance, made sacrifices to get the oldest child through elementary school and this child was to help finance the education of the younger siblings. Few immigrants attempted to jump the illiteracy hurdles themselves, but they did encourage their children to receive an education.[19]

Very many European immigrants, however, could not see the value of a formal education. "We have grown old and we cannot read nor write, . . . yet we live," they said to their children. "So you too may live without knowledge."[20] Children were expected to contribute to the family earnings when they reached their teens, if not earlier. Compulsory education was looked upon as undue interference of the State in family affairs. The children, too, tended to share these attitudes.

[Very] . . . often, as they sat in the torpid classrooms, their attention wandered from the drone of recitations. Through the windows . . . they could see the bustle of purposeful men. By contrast, the school seemed empty of achievements, empty of the possibility of achievement. For what reason were they thus confined? What could they hope to gain from all this?[21]

[18] Elin L. Anderson, *We Americans,* Cambridge, Harvard University Press, 1938, pp. 97-123.

[19] Williams, *South Italian Folkways in Europe and America, op. cit.,* pp. 125-130.

[20] Handlin, *op. cit.,* p. 179. In italics.

[21] *Ibid.,* p. 245.

Other ethnic groups experience the same feelings in regard to formal education. The federal government once withdrew rations on an Indian reservation to force Indian parents to send their children to school.[22] Mexican parents, too, very often need to be coerced to send their children to school. The following case of a Mexican mother who complied with the compulsory education only under duress illustrates the attitude prevalent[23] among many Mexicans.

A Mexican mother of a twelve-year-old boy apparently kept the child from school because she attached no importance to his attendance. She had defied the authority of the school and also of the visiting teacher. The case was referred to the Juvenile Office.

When questioned by the social worker from that Office, the mother appeared to be willing to coöperate. She informed the worker that the reason Rudy had been absent was because her mother had been ill and it was necessary for her to keep the boy at home to help her out with some work around the house and to go to the drug store for medicine. The worker answered that the boy had been missing school for a long period of time. The mother then complained that the school had always been sending messages to her, but little attention was paid to her reasons for keeping the boy at home. When the worker asked if the illness in the family was the only reason for keeping the boy at home, the mother replied that the child did not have a pair of shoes. She was told that if she had been interested in securing shoes for the boy, arrangements could have been made. According to the school report the boy had had prolonged absences from school for the past four years. To this the mother responded that she had tried to get the boy to school "as often as she could." She denied the possibility of the child's going elsewhere when he had been sent to school.

[22] Dale, *The Indians of the Southwest*, op. cit., p. 182.

[23] High illiteracy rates prevail among the Mexicans of California and Texas. About 75 percent of the Mexicans of school age actually attend school, but the most serious problem is withdrawal from school before completing high school, rather than failure to attend school at all. Over 69 percent of the Mexican children as compared with 25 percent of other children were below average for their grade. Cf. Burma, *Spanish-Speaking Groups in the United States*, op. cit., pp. 72-73. See also Wilson Little, *Spanish-Speaking Children in Texas*, Austin, The University of Texas Press, 1944.

A few weeks later the school reported that Rudy was again missing. When the social worker from the Juvenile Office visited the home, a neighbor was with the mother. Mrs. R. explained that this neighbor was the man she had previously referred to as "the friend who brought up her family." Mr. O. asked the purpose of the worker's visit and it was explained to him. He said that he had been telling Mrs. R. all along that she had to see that the boy got to school every day and on time. She hadn't paid any attention and he knew that sooner or later "they would be after her." He looked at Mrs. R. and said, "Woman, you don't blame me for saying the truth, because it is the truth!" Mr. O. asked Mrs. R. why the boy had not gone to school the day before and she said that earlier in the morning she had sent him to school but when he came home at noon he didn't find anything to eat and decided to stay home.

Mrs. R. stated that she had never felt the same after having had to come to Court. Her attitude was anything but indifferent or aggressive— the attitudes she had shown to the school authorities and to the visiting teacher. She was respectful and tried to give the impression of coöperativeness, probably because she identified the worker from the Juvenile Office with the Court.

Not all Mexican parents, of course, have such attitudes. As a rule, education is deemed to be more necessary for a boy, but the following case excerpt reveals a Mexican father's solicitude over his daughter's education.

Mr. F. is quite anxious that his daughter continue her education. She decided to quit high school and try to supplement the family income, but she does attend classes at night school. Mr. F. said that he can see himself that he would be qualified for many more jobs if he had gone further in his own education. He would hate to think that his daughter had to spend all her life washing dishes. A person without an education always has to do a harder job.

This same attitude is evidenced by Pedro, a sixteen-year-old Mexican immigrant.

Pedro said that the school made arrangements for him to spend part of the time in the sixth grade class and part of the time with the second graders where he can do a lot of reading. This way he is learning to understand English much better, and he likes this arrangement.

I asked him if he was bothered by the fact that he had to be among very small children. He said that he wasn't because his interest was to learn English. His father had scolded him for not learning English fast enough.

The American concept of advancement through education has parallels in the attitudes of some ethnic group members toward education. Chinese culture also stresses self-improvement and the cultivation of mind and character through study.[24] Both the Chinese and Japanese[25] have traditionally valued education. Scholarship was, until very recent times, the most important criterion for membership in the Chinese upper classes.[26] One of the important aims of the Chinese village was to produce scholars who could successfully compete in the civil service examinations and become eligible to enter officialdom.[27] A recent study of leisure-time activities among young people in a California community revealed that the Oriental youth were more studious than any others, while the least studious were the youth of Mexican parentage.[28]

' It seems to be the consensus that the "pursuit of knowledge has always formed a cardinal ideal in Jewish life."[29] For centuries the Jews emphasized the study of the Torah and the Talmud. An American Jew says that the "most precious possession" in his childhood home was his father's many-volumed edition of the Talmud, and when his father was "buried in his religious books," his mother "recognized it as her function to keep this communion undisturbed; she was like the wife of an artist who is engaged in creating a masterpiece and whose concentration she must incessantly strive to

[24] Al-Li S. Chin, "Some Problems of Chinese Youth in Transition," *American Journal of Sociology* (July, 1948), 54:7.

[25] Smith, *Americans from Japan, op. cit.*, p. 119.

[26] Hsu, *Americans and Chinese, op. cit.*, p. 135.

[27] Kulp, "Chinese Continuity," *Annals of the American Academy of Political and Social Science, op. cit.*, 152:27.

[28] McEntire, *Leisure Activities of Youth in Berkeley, op. cit.*, p. 10.

[29] Ruth Tennenbaum, "Jewish Parents in a Child Guidance Clinic: A Study of Culture and Personality," *Smith College Studies in Social Work* (September, 1939), 10:69.

protect."[30] Traditionally, the Jews valued knowledge for its own sake. It was believed, moreover, that the solidarity of the Jewish community was dependent upon the diffusion of knowledge, especially of religious lore. Until a century ago the emphasis was placed on religious knowledge. In recent times, however, secular learning has been recognized as a valuable goal.[31] The Jews are not a rural people, and since they tend to encounter discrimination, they must be prepared by a formal and possibly a professional education to compete. One of their contemporary problems is coping with the barriers to admission to institutions of higher learning.

The Negro has the lowest level of educational attainment. The median years of school completed is 7.8 for urban Negroes and 4.8 for rural Negroes, in contrast to 10.5 for urban native-born whites and 8.6 for rural native-born whites.[32] It would seem as though the Negro might be expected to place the same value on education as do other Americans. Education does act as a social elevator, and in this one respect, at least, the Negro can become the equal of everyone else. There are, however, several factors which impede the free operation of this elevator.

In the rural South, particularly, the educational system does not measure up to that of other regions. Negroes in the South have had segregated schools which were usually inferior to other Southern schools. Hence, there were fewer opportunities available to the ambitious Negro, and little stimulus to the less ambitious. There has been, moreover, a controversy over the value of "classical" education for the Negro. Stress is often placed upon "industrial" education to train the Negro to do better the jobs open to him. Although Negro leaders regard the emphasis upon "industrial" education as an attempt to keep the Negro "in his place," even those leaders

[30] S. N. Behrman, *The Worcester Account*, New York, Random House, 1954, pp. 13, 223.
[31] Tennenbaum, *op. cit.*, p. 69.
[32] Paul B. Horton and Gerald R. Leslie, *The Sociology of Social Problems*, New York, Appleton-Century-Crofts, Inc., 1955, p. 278.

who advocate "classical" education are of the opinion that the Negro needs to be taught Negro history and Negro problems in order that he be better able to champion the rights of the group.[33]

Negroes who obtain a "classical" education are often frustrated in their attempts to secure a living. Reid E. Jackson relates a few of his experiences in the following words:

After a hard struggle deciding upon my life's vocation, I finally went into teaching, and it was not because of the money. I was making four and five times as much playing the piano in a professional dance band as I could teaching. . . .
. . . I would . . . go to work on my master's degree. This decision seemed foolish to my father and mother. Anyway, I went on to the . . . white state university. . . .

I spent my first months . . . trying to convince the university examiner that I should be admitted into the graduate school of education without "condition." This was very necessary because my Negro undergraduate college had not then secured regional accreditation.

My studious habits finally got me into an embarrassing situation. One afternoon I was cornered by members of the leading men's honor society. . . . Whispering . . . they told me that I was "likely timber" for their organization and asked if I would be interested in joining their fraternity. Shortly afterwards, I was notified that I had been chosen . . . and enthusiastically I performed the initiation chores. . . .

It never occurred to me, though, that the other two candidates were white and that I, alone, was colored—not until the usual fate overtook me. Without explanation I was suddenly informed that my name had been dropped from the candidates' list. My perplexity was cleared up . . . when a staunch white friend, . . . a member of the organization, . . . told me . . . a clause in the national constitution . . . forbade initiation of a Negro. I tried to appear nonchalant; . . . nevertheless, in the pit of my stomach, there was a sickening feeling of despair. . . .

To forget my wounded pride, I plunged more deeply into my work towards the Ph.D. degree. By that time I had made many friends, . . . gained the respect of others, and knew my way around the campus pretty well. . . .

[33] Myrdal, *An American Dilemma, op. cit.,* p. 901.

After I received my coveted doctor of philosophy degree, I made another discovery. Immediately, my white classmates, who had also received Ph.D.'s, were shipped off to lucrative positions which came through the Appointments Office. While my record was just as good or better, I was not offered a chance even to consider a job. It was not because the . . . Bureau felt that I was not qualified; the bare fact was that the jobs were for "whites only." [So] . . . I accepted a job as dean of education in a small southern church college for Negroes. I soon found . . . the title was worth more than the salary. In fact, . . . I was making twenty-five dollars less a month than I did *before* I had started working on my Ph.D. degree.[34]

INFORMAL AND AESTHETIC EDUCATION

Although formal education tends to be less important to many ethnic group members than it is to the average American, in many respects these groups place a higher value upon certain aesthetic or philosophical pursuits. Even the unlettered immigrant may value an opera or a work of art. Material comforts will often be sacrificed by the Italian or other Southern European in order to enjoy aesthetic pleasures such as attendance at an opera or symphony or a visit to an art exhibition.[35] Professional workers are undoubtedly familiar with families who lack the necessities of life, but have a radio or television set bought on the installment plan. If these families lack bread, they will nonetheless enjoy music, classical or otherwise.

At times, a television set is actually preferred to bread, as was the case in the following Mexican family.

[34] Reid E. Jackson, "Education in Black," *The Crisis* (October, 1945), 52:289-290. By permission.

[35] Sol Hurok achieved renown by bringing good music to the masses, especially the immigrants. His audience was reached largely through the medium of the foreign-language papers. S. Hurok and Ruth Goode, *Impresario*, New York, Random House, 1946, p. 31.

The police went to notify Mrs. G. that her husband was in the hospital in a critical condition. They found six children, ranging in age from eight years to nine months. All of them appeared to be undernourished and they were covered with scabby infections. The mother was eventually located and she excused her absence from the home by saying that she had been out all day having the car repaired. She had left nothing for the children to eat except garlic cloves, and according to the police the apartment was completely unfurnished except for a new television set.

The Koreans are great lovers of music, as the Americans discovered when stationed there in the early 1950's. When the city of Seoul was about to be captured by the Communists in December, 1950, the city officials had a momentous decision to make. Only a few minutes remained to salvage a last precious cargo, and the government chose to rescue the Seoul Symphony Orchestra. To the officials who made this decision for their people, there could be no Korea without music.[36]

Love of the aesthetic is also revealed in the pictures or decorations found even in unpapered shacks. The Mexicans, for example, will have a shrine to Our Lady of Guadalupe profusely decorated with flowers and a bright backdrop of colored paper if nothing more elaborate is available. Instead of a vegetable patch in the yard, one is more likely to find a flower garden.

Orientals, too, cherish works of art even though they may lack many necessities. These people are of a more philosophic bent than are Americans, due in part to their heritage of Buddhism and Confucianism. Study of the classics is considered essential. Pardee Lowe, or "Glorious Descendant" as he was known to his family, relates what happened when his aunt discovered that his classical education had been neglected. "Glorious Descendant's a dolt!" she said, urging his mother to send him to Tutor Chun at the Chinese school before it was too late.

[36] James Michener, "One Must Respect Korean Culture," *The Reader's Digest* (April, 1954), 64:15.

"There he will obtain," she said, "a generous old-style classical Chinese education. He will meditate upon the sayings of Confucius and Mencius, and peruse the Four Books and the Five Classics. This will neutralize his excessive Americanism."[37]

Glorious Descendant could, of course, have learned some of these classical "gems" within the family. Informal education is always valued as a channel of communicating culture to the young child or the neophyte. Culture, it must be remembered, is learned rather than inherited and much of this learning is informal in nature. Within the confines of the family circle the small child learns his first and most enduring lessons in culture. The family, then, deserves special emphasis in any analysis of cultural values.

[37] Lowe, *op. cit.*, p. 110.

Part III

FAMILY ROLES AS VALUES

8

Family Solidarity:
The American Family

INTRODUCTION

THE value approach to cultural factors in social work relationships affords insight into the important means which ethnic
groups have institutionalized to meet basic needs. Of all social
institutions, the family is most basic, for on it all others rest. Its
cultural forms and practices regulate behavior between the sexes
and provide for the perpetuation of the human species. Man's
cultural as well as biological heritage is transmitted through the
family. Unlike biological drives, however, cultural values are not
common to all people. The newborn child is potentially capable
of learning to speak any language and to foster any attitudes toward
authority, work, education, religion, and other lesser values such as
food preferences. It is in the family that the child's attitudes toward
values are learned.

In the family, too, the child forms his first social relationships.
Through the interaction of personalities he learns whom he must
obey and what he must do, that is, he defines familial statuses and
roles. A social role is the part played by a person in response to
the expectation of a group in a specific social situation. Family roles

149

concern the organization of behavior patterns on the part of family members, whatever their position—father, mother, son, daughter, uncle, and so forth. Conforming roles are valued and deviant roles are censured in order to maintain some degree of equilibrium within the social group. There are, then, relatively uniform expectations about the behavior of persons in these various positions, and the behavior of these persons is interpreted in terms of such expectations.[1]

Generalizations made about ethnic family patterns need to be qualified in the same manner as those made about other values. In Chapter 1 the following qualifications were noted: gradations in class structure, extent of acculturation, the hierarchical arrangement of values, official and unofficial values, age and sex differences, as well as variations according to the life cycle. In addition, allowances must be made for traditional and developmental roles.

Traditional roles might be equated with the conservative patterns which have persisted over a long period of time. Hence, the traditional conception of parenthood includes keeping house, caring for the children, training and disciplining the young, and the father's supporting the family.[2] Developmental roles, on the other hand, take account of changes in the expectations of the parents, such as the "modern" view that they are to help the children develop socially and mentally as well as to guide them with understanding and love.[3] Both the traditional and the conservative roles are utilized in this analysis and, at times, it is difficult to draw a clear line of distinction.

In viewing ethnic family patterns, the traditional form will ordi-

[1] Irwin T. Sanders, ed., *Societies Around the World, op. cit.,* 2:11; Eugene Jacobson, W. W. Charters, Jr., and Seymour Lieberman, "The Use of the Role Concept in the Study of Complex Organizations," *Journal of Social Issues* (1951), 7:18.

[2] Rachel Ann Elder, "Traditional and Developmental Conceptions of Fatherhood," *Marriage and Family Living* (Summer, 1949), 11:98.

[3] *Ibid.*

narily be presented as a cultural norm against which modifications can be noted. Setting up family types presents several methodological difficulties apart from those already mentioned. The majority family—that is, the category which embraces the largest number of families and is generally recognized as most representative—will, whenever possible, be considered typical. In some instances, however, there are few available data upon which to base a generalization.

The Negro family presents analytical problems inasmuch as it is set apart by biological differences. Racial characteristics coupled with a background of slavery have influenced the Negro family, but they have been wholly or partially inoperative in other ethnic family types. The Negro, moreover, has been exposed to American culture for approximately three centuries, whereas other ethnic families have had less exposure to the dominant culture. Hence, the traditional Negro family is not the family as it is found in Africa, but rather as it is found in earlier American history. Although rural lower-class Negroes are reviewed as representative of the group, in the Southern plantation economy they appear to rely primarily upon the plantation owner rather than upon the urban professional person for services. Consequently, there is a dearth of case illustrations on the rural Negro.

Some Jewish families have also been exposed to American cultural patterns over a long period of time, but there are many first-generation Jews who came to America around the turn of the century or even at the mid-century. The latter have retained traditional patterns, while the former have become largely acculturated. Variations in Jewish family forms will also depend, to some extent, upon whether the family is classified as orthodox, conservative, or reform. Orthodox Judaism is the historical form which links ancient and modern times. It is based on the belief in the Torah (which came to mean the sum total of Jewish religious teachings of all ages), and it implies fulfillment of all religious observances.[4] Orthodoxy was undermined by the rationalism of the eighteenth century and also by the social forces which caused the ghetto to disintegrate. Reform Judaism was a movement to adjust to the modern world. Only those parts of the original religion which were of a general religious nature and of ethnical value were deemed essential.[5] Traditions which made for a typically Jewish life were eliminated. Dietary laws were disregarded and Sabbath services held on Sunday.[6] Conservative Judaism represents the middle path between orthodoxy and reform. It refuses to throw aside the traditions and does not wish to reduce Judaisim to a creed.[7] All three forms, then, have different positions regarding customs and rituals.

The Chinese family presents still other problems since the very term "family" should be defined according to the meaning it has in an agricultural, semifeudal society.[8] Distinctions must be made between "family," "kin," and "clan." The "family" is an economic unit comprised of members related by ties of blood, marriage, and adoption, having a common budget and common property. "Kin" extends to relatives outside the family for whom mourning is worn. "Clan" embraces all those who have the same surname and claim descent from common ancestors.[9] The term "family," when used in reference to the Chinese, often refers to "clan" rather than to the smaller economic unit. Chinese scholars decry this confusion in terminology, stating that the "clan" is forceful especially in Southern China and among the upper classes.[10] It must be recognized,

[4] Pilch, *Jewish Life in Our Times, op. cit.,* p. 8.
[5] *Ibid.,* p. 12.
[6] *Ibid.,* p. 13.
[7] *Ibid.,* p. 16. For a more complete analysis of these forms of Judaism and for figures on the numbers affiliating with each, see "Judaism," *Life* (June 13, 1955), 38:107-110.
[8] Rose Hum Lee, "Research on the Chinese Family," *American Journal of Sociology* (May, 1949), 54:498.
[9] Olga Lang, *Chinese Family and Society,* New Haven, Yale University Press, 1946, pp. 13, 19-20.
[10] Lee, *op. cit.,* p. 499.

however, that Chinese immigration to America was, in large part, from Southern China and that the lower classes tended to emulate upper-class values and roles. These were the values extolled in the classics and by the rulers. Among Chinese immigrants of the lower classes, the attainment of these values would probably be a goal.[11]

The term "family" as used in American society applies chiefly to the conjugal family composed of parents and siblings. Among other groups, such as the Italians and Mexicans, "family" refers to consanguinal or blood ties which extend beyond the conjugal family of procreation.

Class structure will also have a bearing upon the typical family of other ethnic groups. Again, the majority family—that is, the category which embraces the largest number of families—will be considered typical. It will be the type that is generally recognized as representative of the group. For the most part, other ethnic family types tend to fall into a lower social class status than the typical middle-class family of the dominant group, classified as "American."

Since the Oriental family types offer the strongest contrast to the American family, they will be viewed immediately after the American family. The order of presentation of other family types will approximate the degree of similarity to the Oriental or to the extended family.

SMALL CONJUGAL UNIT

The American family is one in which monogamy is prevalent. Its solidarity hinges upon a small, open, multilineal, somewhat unstable conjugal unit. By way of comparison, the dominant American family is small inasmuch as it is made up exclusively of interlocking conjugal families, each consisting of parents and children.

[11] See Chapter 1, page 23.

Ordinarily, a person is a member of two conjugal families—the family of orientation into which he is born and the family of procreation which he establishes at marriage. He is the only common member of the two families.[12] Kinsmen who are not a part of these two conjugal families are called "relatives" to distinguish them from the "family." Only one conjugal family consisting of husband, wife, and children ordinarily comprises a household, and the presence of relatives within the household is not considered desirable. Once the children reach adulthood and marry, sons as well as daughters are expected to leave the paternal home and establish their own households.

The "openness" of the American system is symbolized by the "in-law" family to which one has affinity only by virtue of marriage. Preferential mating which takes into account the interlocking of kinship roles and gives a kind of institutionalized support to the role of the marriage partner does not influence the choice of a spouse in American culture. Being "in love" might be regarded as an institutional sanction, but the range of persons with whom one might fall in love is sufficiently broad to make the American system an "open" one.

Descent is not confined to such kin groupings as the patrilineal or matrilineal class, but relatives are recognized in both categories. Evidence of the multilineal pattern is apparent in the custom of allowing all children to share in the inheritance of the family estate.[13] The eldest male child is preferred in many societies, and he may inherit the whole estate and the title of nobility, if there be any. The kinship system is a factor which accounts, in large part, for the status of women in American society, since "it does not, as do so many kinship systems, place a structural premium on the role

[12] Talcott Parsons, "The Kinship System of the Contemporary United States," *American Anthropologist* (January-March, 1943), 45:24-25.
[13] *Ibid.*, p. 28.

of either sex in the maintenance of the continuity of kinship relations."[14]

DIVORCE AND DESERTION AS INDEXES OF INSTABILITY

As a system, the American family appears to be lacking in security. Divorce is one indication of family instability. The rates for divorce have steadily increased—with some fluctuations during depression and war—until by 1946 the rate was fourteen times what it had been in 1867 when divorce statistics were first collected.[15]

Another index of family disorganization is desertion, or the irresponsible departure from the home of either husband or wife. It is difficult to estimate the extent of desertion, which has been called "the poor man's divorce." Social workers report a high incidence of temporary desertion on the part of husbands when their wives are confined at childbirth.[16] Although the initiating problem called to the social worker's attention may be of an economic nature, there are usually more deeply rooted causes for the lack of integrated family functioning and harmony.[17]

CHILDREN

Among the factors contributing to family unity and strength, obviously one of the most important is that the family is a functional unit for the procreation and rearing of children. Children

[14] *Ibid.*, p. 33.
[15] Mabel A. Elliott and Francis E. Merrill, *Social Disorganization,* 3d ed., New York, Harper & Brothers, 1950, p. 437. Divorce rates for each year since 1867 are given in a table in this source, p. 440.
[16] *Ibid.*, p. 413.
[17] *Ibid.*, p. 415.

themselves seem to act as a unifying force, for they are the ones who will perpetuate the family.

Families with children are less likely to end in the divorce courts than are those without offspring.[18] Some American families are, however, childless by choice and others limit the size of the family to one or two children. The average size of the American family in 1952 was 3.5 persons.[19] A society which highly values material things will take into consideration the distribution of limited economic goods when planning family size. Instead of viewing them as "helping hands" as was once the rule, children are seen as "hungry mouths" in an urbanized society that has laws against child labor. Moreover, children usually limit or prevent the full-time employment of a wife who has economic potential. Urban living conditions are, furthermore, inhospitable to children in that housing is often inadequate for large families, play areas are scarce, and there are traffic and accident hazards. Hence, it would seem that American society penalizes parenthood, a traditional source of family strength.[20]

Although family solidarity is usually stronger when there are children, the mere presence of children does not necessarily promote unity. American culture is conducive to individualism inasmuch as it insures certain rights to individual family members. One of the "basic contributions of Christian thought" is that "the child, even while in its mother's womb, has intrinsic rights which are not dependent on either the parents or the group, but are

[18] Although childlessness is not necessarily associated with divorce, an analysis of divorce statistics for 1948 reveals that the divorce rate for childless couples is almost double the rate for families with children, but the differential between childless and parent couples varies with the number of years married. Paul H. Jacobson, "Differentials in Divorce by Duration of Marriage and Size of Family," *American Sociological Review* (April, 1950), 15:244.

[19] "160,000,000 and Bigger by the Minute," *The New York Times Magazine*, August 23, 1953, p. 21. For a good analysis of the effect in the postwar baby boom, see Kingsley Davis, "Small Families Are Still the Fashion," *The New York Times Magazine*, July 11, 1954, p. 17.

[20] Winch, *The Modern Family, op. cit.*, pp. 190-191.

founded in his dignity as a person."[21] Abortion, infanticide, and the failure to nurture the child are contrary to Christian practices. Democracy, too, espouses the principle that all persons—regardless

"I reasoned with him about it, and he convinced me it was O.K."
(Courtesy of Glenn R. Bernhardt and *The Saturday Evening Post*.)

of age, sex, color, or creed—have inherent dignity and worth and should have an opportunity for self-development. Personality development, then, definitely has a place in American culture, and at times may take precedence over family demands.

[21] Clement S. Mihanovich, Gerald J. Schnepp, and John L. Thomas, *Marriage and the Family*, Milwaukee, Bruce Publishing Co., 1952, p. 273.

Unless this individualism is tempered with group responsibilities, family solidarity will be impaired by the selfishness of its constituent members. Sometimes the efforts made by Americans to respect the individuality of the child appear a bit ridiculous to Europeans and Orientals. American cartoonists seem to have in this theme a reservoir of material, and advertisers are quick to take advantage of the child's influence. Food containers are decorated with cutouts for the child, and the sponsors of radio and television programs offer atomic submarines or space ships for a box top and a coin. Even the manufacturers of shoe polish have taken advantage of the child's influence, although one would expect the American child to be about as much interested in shoe polish as in his bath. By means of movie parties, jingle contests, and the distribution of more than a million party hats one brand of shoe polish greatly increased its sales.[22]

Rampant individualism not only hampers family unity but it also may place serious burdens upon the American; namely, "to fashion his own life, to make his own decisions, to pluck his own happiness, in a constantly shifting culture and in a precarious world."[23] Under such circumstances, an individual may experience emotional insecurity, especially if expectations are too high. In cultures where the strong extended family prevails, however, the family acts as a shock absorber.

Preserving Family Honor

Maintaining the family "honor" likewise makes for family solidarity. Keeping the name of a delinquent child out of the press,

[22] "Feature 'X'," *America* (March 13, 1954), 90:627.
[23] Sirjamaki, "A Footnote to the Anthropological Approach to the Study of American Culture," *Social Forces, op. cit.,* 25:261.

preserving a united front before outsiders, and concealing anything that might reflect on family integrity strengthen family ties.

An elderly couple who had temporary custody of two of their daughter's children resented the fact that the children's father did not make support payments. The grandparents were in comfortable financial circumstances, but they felt that if the father did not keep his word, he should let them adopt the children. One child broke his arm and since the grandparents did not happen to have cash on hand temporarily, they had to borrow money. This increased the resentment of the grandparents but they said that they would rather not press any charges by the court to enforce payments in order to avoid stigmatizing the children with a jailbird for a father. They were of the opinion that the father might not pay even if the district attorney so ordered and as a consequence the children would have a jailbird for a father.

An illegitimate child is generally considered a stain on family honor, and the strong family may take precautions to prevent the fact from being known. In the following case the strain was so great upon the mother of the illegitimate child that she isolated herself and the child and began losing contact with reality.

The agency received a call from a man who described himself as a neighbor of Mrs. A. at V. Courts. He requested that someone look into the care being given a four-year-old boy who was kept locked up in the apartment all day and whom they believed might be ill.

In an attempt at verification, the worker called the offices of the Housing Authority and Mrs. T. said that the family was well known to her. The Housing Authority, too, wished an investigation. Mrs. A. has not worked since she came to the Courts about a year ago, and has shown unnatural concern for her son. She claims to have a husband but he has never been seen or contacted by anyone.

Mrs. A.'s sister, Mrs. C., pays the rent at the office, takes care of medical bills, and leaves food for her sister and child every few days. Sometimes the food is left on the doorsteps to spoil. When Mrs. C. attempts to visit her sister, there is usually an outburst of violence.

No one is allowed in the apartment and vague answers are given about the child's father. At one time he is in Derry and at another time in Tayor. Again, Mrs. A. says that her husband is afraid to come to town for fear of her sister.

The agency tried to encourage Mrs. A. to work. She has had two years of college and held a responsible job before the birth of the child. She has accepted financial aid, but made no effort to find work or improve herself. When foster home care was arranged for the child in order that she could work, Mrs. A. interfered and the plan had to be abandoned.

Consensus on Values

Consensus on values and goals is important to family unity. Solidarity is strongest when husband and wife have common values, that is, when they share confidences and communicate ideas in an intimate, informal manner; have joint interests in religion, in work, and in recreation; and combine as a unit to preserve status in the community. Consensus on goals presupposes an interdependence of family roles. The wife and mother may, for example, conceive her own role to be one of housekeeper, disciplinarian, and budget balancer. If her husband has the same conception of the maternal role and sees his own role as a supporting and complementary one, family objectives will be more readily attained and conflicts minimized. Should the father, however, envision his role to be an authoritarian one, lack of consensus might imperil family unity.

Mutual affection appears to be one of the principal bonds which unites the contemporary American family. A marriage is deemed successful if it contributes to the personal happiness and individual development of family members. A century ago, marital success was judged on the basis of its endurance, of its fertility, or its good repute.[24] Now, however, the American family is said to be approaching the companionship type, with its unity based primarily upon companionship and affectional ties, which imply compati-

[24] John Sirjamaki, *The American Family in the Twentieth Century*, Cambridge, Harvard University Press, 1953, pp. 79-80.

bility, sustained mutuality of interests, and frequent demonstrations of devotion.[25]

The prevailing attitude is exemplified in the case of Enid, mother of two young children, who expressed her ideas in these words:

"Maybe, as Clay insists, most wives don't expect romance," Enid added bitterly. "But he can't convince me that wives whose husbands love them get along without companionship. I have no companionship. Except for Janice and Susie, I might as well be living on a desert island."

Enid expected not only companionship but also attention, as is evident from the remark:

"In twelve years I doubt Clay has paid me twelve compliments. Like every other woman, I'd sometimes like to look pretty for my husband. I want Clay to *notice* me. When I break loose and buy a new becoming dress, his sole interest is in the price."

Family unity is intensified by participation of all the members in celebrating Christmas, Easter, Fourth of July, and in other family events such as picnics, vacations, and birthday or anniversary commemorations. Most Americans expect the family to remember certain occasions, as did the young woman in the aforementioned case when she exclaimed: "Four different times in twelve years, Clay has forgotten *my* birthday. I refuse to remind him of my own birthday. There's no romance or meaning for me in receiving a present I've asked for."[26]

TRADITIONAL FAMILY FUNCTIONS

The solidarity of the American family has been further jeopardized by the loss or modification of traditional family functions,

[25] Hypothesis of the study by Earnest W. Burgess and Harvey J. Locke, *The Family*, New York, American Book Company, 1950.

[26] Case taken from records of American Institute of Family Relations for series on "Can This Marriage Be Saved?" *Ladies' Home Journal* (December, 1953), 70:88.

or the activities which the family characteristically performs. One of the most obvious changes has been in the economic function. Three fourths of American family members have departed from the traditional pattern of economic production and the accompanying social relationships. Now they work for wages or salaries outside the home and make their economic contribution in ways other than directly through the family.[27] The money income is not derived from the coöperative efforts of the family as a unit. The father is out of the home most of the day, a fact partially responsible for the alteration in his role as family head. Moreover, the mother frequently works in an office, factory, store, or classroom. Instead of being a coöperative producing unit, the family has increasingly become a unit of consumption—purchasing goods and services with money. Occupational status is no longer associated with kinship status, for a person holds a job as an individual, not by virtue of his status in a family.[28]

The teacher has assumed many of the educational functions formerly performed by parents and older children. Mechanical and practical skills formerly taught in the home are now imparted along with conventional subject matter in the schools. Young people aspire to occupations requiring special training which their parents are unable to impart. Moreover, children start school younger, spend a larger proportion of every day in school, and attend school later in life than ever before.[29]

Even the religious function of the family has been modified, especially among Protestants in urban areas.[30] Seventy-two percent of adult Americans of all creeds polled in a recent survey said that they had received their religious training at Sunday School.[31]

[27] Andrew G. Truxal and Francis E. Merrill, *The Family in American Culture,* New York, Prentice-Hall, Inc., 1947, p. 330.

[28] Parsons, *op. cit.,* p. 33.

[29] Truxal and Merrill, *op. cit.,* pp. 351-353.

[30] Cf. Truxal and Merrill, *op. cit.,* p. 356.

[31] "Do Americans Want Their Children to Receive Religious Instructions?" *Catholic Digest* (September, 1953), 17:9. See also Ben Bradford, "Rebirth of

Family prayers before meals and in the evenings have become less common in the urbanized American family than in former times. Meals are less regularly taken with the family unit at the table, and frequent evening recreation outside the home precludes family night prayers. Religion is more than ritual, however. Even in families which ostensibly ignore it, religion is believed to be a force which accounts for the ways in which "choices and goals and self-appraisals" are made.[32] Just how forceful religion is in this respect is a matter of conjecture.

In earlier times nearly all recreation centered around the home and the family. Quilting parties, husking bees, and barn raisings are, however, things of the past, as are the milder diversions such as popping corn, pulling taffy, and singing to the accompaniment of the family "fiddler." Recreation has become commercialized, and individual family members often go their separate ways to the movie theater, ball park, dance hall, or other places of amusement.[33] The automobile, of course, is largely responsible for this trend, and whereas distance was once a barrier it has now become an inducement. With the advent of the automobile, remarks one commentator, it "was no longer necessary to eat at home, and hence to keep servants, or even to sleep at home or, with the coming of the trailer, even to have a home."[34]

All these changes in family functions are indicative of the fluidity of American society. If this mobility and its concomitant individualism are disconcerting to many contemporary Americans, they are even more so to those members of less mobile cultures that temper individualism with family-mindedness.

---

the Sunday School," *The New York Times Magazine*, September 19, 1954, pp. 30, 60.

[32] Swift, "Religious Values," *op. cit.*, p. 395.

[33] Baber, *op. cit.*, p. 263.

[34] Kronenberger, *Company Manners, op. cit.*, p. 79.

9

Family Solidarity:
Ethnic Family Types

ORIENTAL FAMILY

ONE recognized family-minded culture is that of the Chinese. In China, the family has been cultivated perhaps more than in any other country in the world.[1] It has usurped the roles which Western religious, economic, political, and social institutions have developed, and has dominated all areas of human activities and relationships.[2] The Chinese family offers the strongest contrast to the American family. In its traditional form[3] it is an extended or joint family characterized by several generations living in the same household, subject to parental authority, with familial control of customary family functions.

The extended family system persists, but in varying degrees, among the Orientals in America. Traditionally, the sons bring their wives to their parental home which shelters the unmarried siblings, grandparents, and others dependent upon the family head.[4] The

[1] Lang, *Chinese Family and Society, op. cit.,* p. 9.
[2] Lee, "Research on the Chinese Family," *op. cit.,* p. 504.
[3] This traditional form is believed to be predominantly an upper-class phenomenon because the poor have fewer children and they die at an earlier age. Cf. Lang, *op. cit.,* p. 332.
[4] Kazuya Matsumiya, "Family Organization in Present-Day Japan," *American Journal of Sociology* (September, 1947), 53:109. An ancient law forbade Japanese children to live independently of their parents and the custom persists to this day.

domicile is expanded if necessary, or is gradually adapted to the needs of the family as it becomes increasingly extended. This housing arrangement tends to lead to difficulties in the urban American setting. Among the newly married, in America, then, it is not customary to reside with the husband's parents unless the home is in a rural environment.[5]

Sometimes, however, tradition is followed out of respect for parental wishes, as is illustrated by the following case:

The client, a twenty-five-year-old patient of Chinese extraction with pulmonary tuberculosis, was born in China, but is an American citizen because his paternal grandfather and his father are citizens. He came to the United States when he was twelve years of age and later returned to China. There he married a girl his own age and they now have a three-year-old daughter. His parents assumed the financial responsibility for his wedding and when it was time for him to return to this country with his father, the patient's wife remained in China with his mother because his parents wanted her to do so. This separation of patient from his wife has not been satisfactory to either of them, but both have felt obligated to his parents and have tolerated the arrangements. He planned to save money and send for her, but before he was able to carry out this plan he became ill.

It seemed apparent in talking with the patient that it was not just because of financial reasons that he had never sent for his wife and child but because of his parents' feeling about her staying in China. He pointed out that if his wife came to the United States his mother would be left alone and that in the small village where she lives, it has long been customary for a man to bring his wife and children home to live with his parents. He and his wife have modern ideas about marriage and family life but his mother feels very strongly about the Chinese tradition, and he has been reluctant to go against her wishes.

Children are highly valued by both the Chinese and the Japanese. Not to have offspring is regarded as a tragic failure and modern influences have not changed this attitude.[6] Children are needed

[5] LaViolette, *Americans of Japanese Ancestry*, *op. cit.*, p. 128.
[6] Cf. Lang, *op. cit.*, p. 162.

not merely for emotional satisfaction but to carry on the family line. A man needs a son to do daily homage to his memory after death at the living-room shrine, to preserve the family honor and possessions, to be trustee of the "house," and, in short, to carry on in his father's place.[7] If a family is childless, a child may be adopted or the husband may take a concubine. John C. H. Wu, noted Chinese teacher and diplomat now resident in this country, was born of his father's concubine, since there were no children by his father's wife.[8]

Concubinage was so widely accepted in China that all government regulations of the system were carefully qualified so that those without male offspring would not be unduly affected. According to the laws of the Ming Dynasty, for example, the eldest son of a family was allowed a maximum of three concubines. If he was without a male heir when he reached thirty years of age, he might take a first concubine. If at thirty-five he still lacked a male heir, he might take his quota of concubines.[9]

The family head is usually the eldest male, and his wife rules over domestic affairs. The sons' wives are subordinate to her and they may be subjected to trying circumstances in learning their roles as members of the family into which they have married. The eldest son, if physically and mentally competent, is destined to become ultimate family head.

Family welfare supersedes that of its individual members, and it is the role of the family head to promote this welfare. This is evident in the demands made upon the eldest son who is destined to replace the father as head of the family, in the sacrifices required of the daughters-in-law who must take subordinate positions in a

[7] Benedict, *The Chrysanthemum and the Sword, op. cit.,* p. 255.

[8] J. C. H. Wu, *Beyond East and West,* New York, Sheed & Ward, 1951, pp. 26-27.

[9] Cheng Ch'eng-K'un, "Familism the Foundation of Chinese Social Organization," *Social Forces* (October, 1944), 23:53-54.

large household, and in the arrangement of marriages for daughters into families with whom an alliance is desirable.

So important is the family that there is no respectable place for the unmarried adult or the illegitimate child in these strongly familistic societies.[10] It is the duty of the family head to preserve status by arranging suitable matches for the marriageable womenfolk and to see that the family name is carried on by his own sons and those of his brothers. Commenting on the importance of family status for the Japanese child, a commentator writes:

Every aspect of life [in Japan] . . . is governed by the family unit. Not to belong to a family who will find you a job, secure you a wife, care for you in illness and protect you against a hostile world is to invite despair.[11]

Divorce and desertion are rare.[12] Concubinage has traditionally been a solution to childlessness and to the amorous tendencies of the male. The wife, however, retains her position within the family. Among the Chinese a concubine is brought into the household where her children are reared with those of the wife.[13] The Japanese, however, rarely bring the other women into their homes, unless they have children whom the father wishes to rear with those of his wife. In that event, the women are classified as servants rather than concubines, and the children acknowledge the lawful wife as their mother. As a rule, the Japanese restrict their extramarital affairs to prostitutes or perhaps to geisha girls. The girls are ordinarily protected from abandonment and assured financial security by means of a contract which is signed with the house where they

[10] See Natalie Siao-sieu Mao, "Ceremonies and Rites of Chinese Marriage Before the Republic," unpublished Master's thesis, Washington, Catholic University of America, 1948, Chapter VI.

[11] James A. Michener, "The Facts About the GI Babies," *Reader's Digest* (March, 1954), 64:7.

[12] Burgess and Locke, *The Family, op. cit.*, p. 38.

[13] Concubines may be not only tolerated by the wife, but even accepted. See Pearl S. Buck's novel, *Pavilion of Women*, New York, The John Day Co., 1946.

are employed. Sometimes the men set up separate establishments for their mistresses.[14]

The extended family is a vast social structure in which the members tend to find security and strength, for it functions as an economic and social unit.[15] Whatever is earned by any family member goes into the family funds and whatever is spent is drawn from these funds, chiefly at the discretion of the family head. As an economic unit, then, the family provides for its young, sick, aged, and less gifted members. It also makes provision for such exigencies as depressions, epidemics, and other crises. The young man is not torn by indecision as to choice of employment when he reaches adulthood, nor is the young woman afraid that she will be left stranded on the matrimonial market. An exceptionally talented youth would not be expected to finance his own education, nor would the son who desired professional training have to rely on individual resources. These are all family matters.

Chinatowns in America have been patterned upon the extended kinship structure which prevailed in the home village from which the ethnic group emigrated. Like the original pattern, the transplanted one was intended to be a help in all the vicissitudes of life and it served the additional function of giving support in adjusting to a new, hostile, and impersonal environment.[16] Both the clan and the family associations have been established—members of the former being recognized as "blood brothers," while the latter is usually restricted to those bearing the same surname.[17] The Chinese still take care of their own family members when they are in trouble. During the last depression when the relief rolls were crowded

[14] Benedict, The Chrysanthemum and the Sword, op. cit., p. 185.

[15] In China, for example, anyone who bears the same surname is a clan member —part of a vast coöperative enterprise. There are 450 million inhabitants but only 470 family names. Stuart A. Queen and John B. Adams, The Family in Various Cultures, Philadelphia, J. B. Lippincott Co., 1952, p. 88.

[16] Rose Hum Lee, "The Decline of Chinatowns in the United States," American Journal of Sociology (March, 1949), 54:429-430.

[17] Ibid., p. 430.

in New York City, the names of every ethnic group except the Chinese appeared frequently.[18]

Recreation among the Chinese is a family affair centered around festivals, births, marriages, funerals, and birthdays at which times an assemblage of the family and kinsmen is expected. Pardee Lowe gives an account of his father's Great Birthday—his sixty-sixth—and the occasion when he was invested with longevity robes.[19] All the relatives and kinsmen were summoned by telegram.

They came in a hurry. Two kinsmen, one at Portland and the other at Los Angeles, hopped planes and flew. All in order to fulfill properly their duties as members of the Greater Family.[20]

Long before the appointed day kinsmen filled the Lowe home. They formed the reception committee, recorded names of donors and descriptions of gifts, displayed the gifts, and acknowledged them.[21]

When the eve of the Great Birthday arrived, there were not enough beds to accommodate the guests. Young and old stayed up all night, and the household waxed merry, as befitted the joyous character of the occasion.

Stepmother started games to make the watch through the night pass quickly. The young and old women played Swallows; the young men, stud poker; and the old men gathered in the Great Hall and reminisced with pleasant sighs of the days when they were young and Chinatown was un-Americanized. When the lottery agent made his appearance, Stepmother invited each member of the Greater Family to mark a ticket at her expense. . . .

For those uninterested in games, Stepmother found tasks, such as stacking paper spirit offerings, revising banquet seating arrangements and invitational lists, cataloguing and displaying gifts, and preparing

[18] "America's Chinese," *Life* (January 8, 1951), 30:76.
[19] See Chapter 3, pp. 60-61.
[20] Lowe, *Father and Glorious Descendant, op. cit.*, p. 298.
[21] *Ibid.*, pp. 299-300.

the meals to be eaten on the morrow. . . . She sighed with weariness and sheer pleasure as she served the midnight repast.[22]

Like recreation, religion is also family-centered. One of the main family functions has been the observance of ancestor worship. This practice has prevailed from the beginning of Chinese history[23] and it is still found in the homes of America's Chinese and Japanese. Ancestor worship is based on the belief that an ancestor continues to watch over his descendants and to intercede for them after death with the supernatural powers.[24] The practice gave status to the aged, since they would shortly be in a position of power in the next world and would be an object of worship. It also had the effect of increasing the birth rate and gave some justification for polygyny. The more sons a couple had the more frequently the rites would be performed and the better their chances of eternal life.[25] Both the Chinese and the Japanese tend to have living-room shrines where food is set out for parents, grandparents, and other family members who are represented by pictures or miniature gravestones.[26] Only the third- or fourth-generation ancestors are usually honored, and even in the Japanese cemetery the markers on the graves of great-grandparents are no longer relettered and their identity sinks into oblivion.[27]

Through the strong, extended family, then, the Chinese tend to satisfy their needs. "Family feeling is the most important thing" in life for this ethnic group.[28] Without doubt, there are certain drawbacks to this family system: initiative may be stifled in order

[22] Ibid., p. 306.
[23] Lang, op. cit., p. 18.
[24] Ibid.
[25] Ibid., p. 19.
[26] Benedict, The Chrysanthemum and the Sword, op. cit., p. 51. There is a story to the effect that a Westerner scoffed at the idea of putting food before the shrine of the deceased, and he is supposed to have said, "You don't expect the dead to eat that food, do you?" His Chinese guide replied, "Do you expect your dead to smell the flowers which you put on their graves?"
[27] Ibid.
[28] "America's Chinese," op. cit., 30:76.

to carry out traditional roles, especially in the case of the eldest son; debts of the extended family may prove to be a burden to certain members; and the indolent members may easily become parasites. On the whole, however, traditional family roles are carried out in spite of obstacles that would be considered unendurable to many American families.

MEXICAN FAMILY

The Mexican family has many characteristics of the joint family system. Married sons and their wives do not always live under the paternal roof, but there is a strong tendency for them to do so, if they can be accommodated. In many Southwestern communities the newly formed families live in a small abode adjoining that of the boy's parents. The courtyard of the original home may become crowded with the dwellings of the sons.

The daughter-in-law is generally expected to be a part of her husband's family, and should the husband die, she may still be expected to fulfill her obligations toward his family. A young Mexican woman was made aware of this tendency when she attempted to return to her childhood home.

Mrs. D., six months pregnant, applied to the agency for financial assistance and medical referral. She was married in August of 1953 and her husband was killed in an automobile accident a few weeks later. She lived with her mother-in-law and went out in the fields cotton-picking with the family. Two months after her marriage date, Mrs. D. discovered her pregnancy, but she continued to work until the fifth month when she no longer felt able to continue. She decided that she wanted to return to the home of her aunt who had raised her and where her two younger brothers lived. Her mother-in-law, however, strongly resisted this suggestion and was emphatic in her refusal to give any support or assistance if Mrs. D. left the home of her husband's family.

Among the Mexicans the joint family extends beyond the con-jugal and consanguinal ties even to the spiritual. According to a Christian custom observed in varying degrees by some other ethnic groups, when a child is baptized, a relationship is formed between the parents, the godparents, and the child. The godparents assume responsibility for the child's religious upbringing and among the Mexicans they very often contribute financially toward the support of their godchild. To show the close relationship which is formed, the godparents are called compadres of the parents. The godmother is a comadre to the child and the godfather is a compadre.

First-generation Mexicans, who are numerically important, value the extended family system highly. They believe it gives a feeling of security and is good for the children. The second and third gen-erations also have friendship groups formed in the church or com-munity, but they have, in addition, the attitude that the happiness and welfare of the individual should be subordinated to that of the family.[29]

Children are generally cherished and an orphan is usually cared for by other relatives as a matter of course and without legal pro-visions. In urban areas, however, the Mexicans are becoming in-creasingly aware of the importance of the legal process of adoption. The necessity for legal adoption was apparent to the residents of a Mexican neighborhood when a fifteen-year-old orphan needed an operation. The doctor would not perform the operation without the consent of her guardian. In this instance the girl had lived with eight or ten families in the neighborhood, but none of them had assumed legal guardianship. Apparently all the families were fond of the girl and there was little difficulty in getting one of them to assume temporary guardianship, but until this incident none had given the matter any thought.

Preserving the good name and honor of the family is most impor-tant. Two Mexican women seeking treatment for a brother who

[29] Burma, *Spanish-Speaking Groups in the United States, op. cit.,* p. 85.

was mentally ill experienced great difficulty in telling the social worker about the situation. Concerning the case, the worker recorded this observation: "To maintain the honor and dignity of their family seems one of their main goals, and for this reason they are reluctant to give details which they believe will take away 'honor.'"

Another Mexican woman remarked that one reason for the strictness found among Mexicans was to preserve family honor. "We believe," she says, "that strictness prevents delinquency." Elaborating on this point, she added:

Like most people, we place the blame for delinquency on the family. None of us in the family would ever steal, be vagrants, or destroy public property, if for no other reason than that we would not want to bring shame to the family name. This same strictness and chaperoning is a good protection against an unsuccessful marriage, desertion, and divorce. We have been taught that if a marriage is not successful it is our duty to do the best we can but never to desert the family or resort to divorce.

Since the Mexicans are predominantly Catholic, their culture makes little provision for divorce. Desertion is not prevalent among these simple rural people in their homeland; it is inconsistent with the ideology of the large family system. Like the Oriental, however, Mexican culture tolerates a form of concubinage. Some men establish a "little house" apart from that of the legal family, and they usually support both establishments. The conventional wife and family reside in a so-called *casa grande*, or big house, and a mistress with her family in a *casa chica*, or little house.[30]

Although family ties are generally strong, divorce and desertion are becoming more common among the Mexicans. The village controls are not operative in an urban environment and the American patterns are making an impact upon the bulwark of the strong extended family system. One study of Mexican families in Texas

[30] Cf. Norman S. Hayner, "Notes on the Changing Mexican Family," *American Sociological Review* (August, 1942), 7:489.

revealed that more than 80 percent were classified as normal—husband and wife, with or without children. In the urban community of San Antonio, however, only 57 percent were normal.[31]

There is excessive mobility among the Mexicans, but it has had the general effect of strengthening rather than weakening familial and cultural bonds. Until very recently, when migratory farm labor was to be done, the entire family went along. They remained only a short while in any place, and depended upon each other for social satisfactions. Another factor in strengthening traditional cultural patterns has been the frequent contacts with the mother country. Mexico is in close proximity to the Southwest where the bulk of the Mexican population is harbored. Even long-time residents of this country make periodic trips to Mexico, visiting relatives and reinforcing cultural ties.

Accompanying this mobility is a tendency to buy a home where the elders reside more or less permanently while the younger people migrate. Mexicans seem to place a great value on having their own homes, humble as they may be. A shack constructed of salvaged tin cans and a tar paper roof may be preferable to public housing where sanitary facilities are provided. Health and sanitation appear to be less important to the average Mexican ethnic than owning his own home. This attitude is exemplified in the following case:

Mrs. H. applied to the agency for financial help because Mr. H. was ill and unable to work. After a home visit an emergency food allotment was made pending a case study. It was difficult to get the coöperation of the couple in going to the clinic for testing and diagnosis—tuberculosis was suspect in several members of the family—because they did not want to leave home, giving as an excuse that their duties at home and care of the children were more "important" than seeing a doctor.

After pressure was put upon them by withholding assistance because of the agency policy of not rendering prolonged aid without a medical investigation, Mr. H. attended the clinic. The family was certified for ADC on the basis of his inability to work because of progressive arthritis.

[31] Burma, *op. cit.,* pp. 84-85.

The family, with six children, lives in a dilapidated one-room structure with very poor facilities. In his contacts, the caseworker discussed low-cost housing with the family, but Mr. H. would not follow up on a referral to a housing unit. His home had "sentimental values," and he intended to stay there. He had been born there and had resumed residence there after his marriage.

Traditional family functions are largely retained by the Spanish-speaking groups. The family head is a male who expects all earnings to be turned over to him and they are disposed of largely at his discretion, presumably for the best interests of the entire family. As previously noted, the migrant Mexican in this country took the entire family along to work as a unit. The father was paid for the family's work and made provision for their needs. In an urban setting, too, the unmarried child who has a job is ordinarily expected to deposit the pay check with the family head. Even the married person may be expected to continue this practice, as is illustrated by the following case:

Mrs. M. applied to the agency for relief because her twenty-five-year-old husband was ill and unable to work. Mr. M. was referred first to a chest clinic as his rapid loss of weight and chronic fatigue suggested tuberculosis. The x-rays were negative. He was next suspect as a cardiac patient and sent to an out-patient clinic for diagnosis. An EKG indicated no heart malfunction. He continued to lose weight, had marked shortness of breath, difficulty in sleeping, and complained of lack of appetite and pain when he did eat. He was given a series of laboratory tests and physical examinations with no organic disease being proved.

Finally, in one of the interviews with a caseworker, he told that he had worked with his father since childhood—sometimes as a construction laborer or with the family in the fields—and had always turned over his pay check to his father, even since marrying and having a family of four children of his own. On the one occasion when he and his wife decided to withhold the check, his father and brothers sought him out and beat him unmercifully. Mr. M. since had been treated like an outcast by his family and evidenced great emotion in telling of his rejection, especially since the family called him "T.B." and "walking corpse."

The physical and mental cruelty of his family following his unsuccessful attempt to break from the patriarchal pattern was apparently the basis of his many psychosomatic symptoms. Mr. M. was subsequently sent to the neuropsychiatric clinic. Later, his father was accidentally shot while investigating a neighborhood fight and the resulting emergency led to Mr. M.'s reacceptance by the family group. This promoted his recovery, though he still manifested various symptoms and continued to need some medical assistance.

The educative function is still retained to some extent by the traditional Mexican family. Formal education is not deemed important, especially for the girls. They learn how to perform domestic duties in the home, and those who receive an education outside the home are expected to become proficient in homemaking or in the fine arts. Boys learn a trade or handicraft, or perhaps how to farm, from their fathers. Learning such skills as how to make pottery or to weave is traditionally a part of normal childhood development. In the Mexican way of life, it has been said, "education was lived, not imposed from without."[32] Mexicans who reside in an urban environment in America tend to rely on the school system for an education as they become more and more acculturated.

Recreational functions were traditionally family- and village-centered, rather than adapted to age or sex groups. Entertainment was enjoyed in the home with one's family. Relatives and friends frequently visited with each other, and there was seldom a lack of companionship. The practice of having "all the uncles, aunts, cousins and other relatives to a home dinner celebrating the saint's day of each member of the family" still prevails.[33] The traditional pattern is, however, being altered in the urban American environment, for commercialized recreation is competing with family-centered fun.

[32] Stuart Chase, *Mexico: A Study of Two Americas,* New York, The Macmillan Co., 1931, p. 50.
[33] Felix Fraga and John J. Kennedy, "A Study of the Recreational Needs of the Senior Latin-American in San Antonio, Texas," unpublished Master's thesis, San Antonio, Our Lady of the Lake College, 1954, p. 54.

Religious festivals provide an occasion for recreation as well as for devotion, both in Mexico and in this country. The entire community or ethnic colony may celebrate such an occasion with processions, dances, and prayers. In Southwestern centers, for example, streets in the Mexican quarter are blocked off for processions on such feasts as Our Lady of Guadalupe on December 12. Religious dances are performed around the image of Our Lady as she is carried in procession.[34] On the feast of All Souls, November 2, the entire family usually goes to the cemetery where the day is spent at the graves of family members. Lunch is packed for the occasion and such equipment as may contribute to the comfort of the group is often taken. The latter often includes stools, umbrellas, and blankets. Although it is a sombre occasion, there is some visiting and admiration of floral arrangements. One family group, for instance, took great pleasure in relating to a group of school children the life story of their deceased daughter whose tomb they were decorating.

The religious function, as has been indicated, was closely interwoven with the activities of the whole community, and the family participated as a unit. In instances where the ethnic group in America is clustered in colonies and where village practices persist, religious functions are still important. Religion usually proves to be a bulwark of the family system, and Catholicism has tended to preserve the folk culture.[35] Many Mexican ethnics, however, associate religion with these festivals to the extent that religion is less meaningful to them when divorced from such occasions.

On the whole, the Mexicans more closely approximate the Chinese familistic system than any other ethnic group. The Mexican family is generally a large one extending to blood relatives and spiritual compadres, and it has retained many of the traditional family functions.

[34] See Chapter 6, p. 126.
[35] Sanders, *Societies Around the World*, *op. cit.*, 2:20.

EUROPEAN FAMILIES

Generalizations about diverse European groups who have become assimilated in varying degrees will not have much validity. It would seem, however, that the Southern Europeans who came around the turn of the last century approximate more closely the patterns of the extended family type than do the Northern Europeans who came in large numbers at an earlier time. Migration disrupts the operation of the extended family system, but the pattern is retained in the memory of the immigrants. First-generation immigrant families tend to be large—ten children is not unusual among Italians[36]—and as the family grows in size the old extended patterns are reëstablished. This is especially true when grandchildren are born. The family structure may extend to godparents as it does with first-generation Italian immigrants with a Catholic heritage.[37]

The degree to which the family exercises traditional functions depends upon the extent to which it has become assimilated. Among first-generation Italian immigrants from Southern Italy (about two million Italians came from Southern Italy between 1900 and 1910), family functions include the semirecreational, social, and affectional.[38] These functions are depicted in the activities of the La Falce family, portrayed in *Life*. All nine sons play in the family band and they had been accompanied by one of their sisters before she left home. The third generation likewise carries on the family's musical tastes. The eleven children with their offspring enjoy the family gatherings where a huge table is set with

[36] Paul J. Campisi, "Ethnic Family Patterns: The Italian Family in the United States," *American Journal of Sociology*, 53:444.

[37] Ruth Shonle Cavan, *The American Family*, New York, Thomas Y. Crowell Co., 1953, p. 204.

[38] Campisi, *loc. cit.*

favorite dishes. The youngest son, aged twenty-six, is greeted with a kiss from his mother when he comes home. Religious functions are evidenced in the family's participation in the church choir and in the prevalence of sacred images and pictures in the home.[39]

Many South Italian families function as an economic unit and as long as a child lives at home, regardless of his age, he is expected to turn over all his wages to his parents. In return, he is supplied with an allowance and all the comforts of home. If he becomes ill or unemployed the family will support him, and when he is married he will be provided for from the family fund.[40] Although many of the younger people are reluctant to conform to this custom, others express no objection.[41] Respect for parental wishes is generally a strong factor in maintaining the practice. One youth remarked that his father would think the home had been transformed into a boarding house if any changes were made.[42]

An overt display of affection between the Italian husband and wife, parents and children, or between children is not customary. Kissing and other signs of affection between husband and wife in the presence of others is nearly always taboo, but other forms may occur.[43] Absence of such expressions does not imply weak affectional ties, for a husband who never engages in such overt expressions may be very considerate of his wife and have a deep respect and affection for her.

Southern Europeans are, for the most part, Catholic and their religion forbids divorce. Among the second and third generations, however, there are occasional divorces. Desertion is rare among Italians,[44] as it is among all those groups whose family ties are strong. Northern Europeans, who are Protestant, such as the Lu-

---

[39] "An Italian Family in America," *Life* (October 5, 1953), 35:134-148.

[40] Child, *Italian or American?, op. cit.*, p. 27.

[41] *Ibid.*, p. 144.

[42] *Ibid.*, p. 107.

[43] *Ibid.*, p. 28; Williams, *South Italian Folkways in Europe and America, op. cit.*, p. 77.

[44] Campisi, *op. cit.*, p. 446.

theran Finns, make provision for divorce. A stigma is, nevertheless, attached to divorce by those who value family unity.[45] Since, however, the bulk of Northern European immigration antedated that of the Southern Europeans, the former have become more completely assimilated, except in rural ethnic islands. Rural Norwegians in Iowa and South Dakota, for example, have preserved much of their culture and their children are expected to marry within the Norwegian group and the Lutheran church, and to pass the culture on to their offspring.[46]

JEWISH FAMILY

Although the traditional Jewish family in Biblical times was an extended one, this is no longer the case. Family solidarity seems to be affected by the same forces that imperil that of the majority American family, namely, the weakening of religious and parental authority, transfer of functions from the home to institutions, and a large number of mixed marriages.[47] Study of the Talmud, or Jewish law, has decreased, and consequently many modern Jewish families are in ignorance of the traditional form of Jewish family life.[48] Jews to whom religion is a value, however, will endeavor to observe the precepts of the law in regard to family life. That law prescribes a strong patriarchal family which provides the setting for many religious ceremonies.[49] In fact, it has been said that the "ob-

[45] Cavan, op. cit., p. 210.

[46] John and Ruth Hill Useen, "Minority-Group Pattern in Prairie Society," American Journal of Sociology (March, 1945), 50:384-385.

[47] "Family and Family Life," The Universal Jewish Encyclopedia, ed. Isaac Landman, Patrons ed., 1941, p. 244. This statement refers to Jews who have been in the United States for generations rather than to recent immigrants.

[48] Ibid.

[49] Trude Weiss-Rosmarin lists some of the ceremonial practices inseparably bound up with the home and family life as follows: The kiddush, on the Sabbath and the holidays, the zemiroth, which grace the Sabbath meal with charm and

servances of the faith are so entwined with the everyday customs of
the home as to make the Jewish religion and the family life one, a
bond of sanctity."[50] A young Jewish girl describes the observance
of the Sabbath in her parental home in these words:

> What I liked was to have mother entrust to me the important task of
> the Sabbath cleaning. Once every week all the furniture was moved,
> each corner meticulously cleaned and scrubbed, every window-pane
> polished. . . . At night we all sat tired and happy about the Sabbath
> table. The candle-sticks held tall white candles. Mother brought the
> loaves she had baked that day. Then she sat down beside father at the
> head of the table. Her eyes would beam upon us, her voice rose with
> ours to join father's baritone in singing the Sabbath songs, and there
> would be such a deep peace in our kitchen. The Sabbath evenings were
> evenings to which one looked forward all the week long. Then mother
> and father were happy; and no plans were discussed.[51]

Among many Jews, however, religion is primarily a symbol of
their identity. Just as the kilt became a precious sign of common
nationality for the Scot, so, too, Judaism with its precepts and practices is a sign of ethnicity. Commenting on one practice, a Jew
says: "The Jew, by covering his head, expresses his bond to his
fellow Jews and his religion, the Jewishness that he refuses to hide
or ignore."[52]

The closely knit family will attempt to preserve family honor,
sometimes at great sacrifice. A second-generation Polish Jewess relates the efforts of her family to maintain status and honor, even
though the family was in need of assistance.

> . . . We children knew that whatever happened in our home not one
> word might we disclose to our neighbours. For if we did, mother assured
> us with the greatest solemnity, grandfather and grandmother in Poland

---

festiveness, the *seder,* the *sukkah,* and the Purim *seudah. Jewish Survival,* New
York, Philosophical Library, Inc., 1949, p. 342.

[50] "Family and Family Life," *The Jewish Encyclopedia* (1910), 5:338.

[51] Stern, *My Mother and I, op. cit.,* pp. 74-75.

[52] R. Brasch, "Why Jews Cover the Head," *Commentary* (January, 1954),
17:39.

might hear of it. And that would be dreadful, we comprehended, though we did not know why. No one who came down to our kitchen knew whether there was black bread in the cupboard, and milk for us children.[53]

Like the Americans, the Jews rely upon the school system to educate their children. White-collar and professional jobs generally require a specialized education which the school is best equipped to impart. Jewish culture places a marked emphasis on education,[54] for it is often upon education—with the security and status derived therefrom—that group survival depends. Jewish culture is not interested, however, in the education that emphasizes mechanical things and gadgets, but rather upon personality and interpersonal response. "Argument, controversy, debate—the eliciting of response —rather than impersonal discussion, in intellectual contacts" are stressed. Medicine and law are preferred to engineering, buying and selling to manufacturing, and the manipulation of people rather than of things.[55]

Children have traditionally been regarded as a blessing. The Talmud says: "Children are builders; they not only build the future of the family, but likewise of the community."[56] Intentional childlessness is denounced as sinful and the "childless person is accounted as dead."[57]

Jews who retain their identity tend to value the religious precept of charity, one of the "three highest duties of the Jew."[58] Jews, then, have traditionally cared for their own poor and have not been

[53] Stern, op. cit., p. 23.
[54] Anon., "An Analysis of Jewish Culture," Jews in a Gentile World, eds. Isacque Graeber and Steuart H. Britt, New York, The Macmillan Co., 1942, p. 252.
[55] Ibid., p. 251.
[56] Tennenbaum, "Jewish Parents in a Child Guidance Clinic," Smith College Studies in Social Work, op. cit., 10:55.
[57] Ibid.
[58] Charity ranks next to worship and the study of the law. Cohen and Witmer, "The Diagnostic Significance of Russian Jewish Clients' Attitudes Toward Relief," Smith College Studies in Social Work, op. cit., 10:287.

permitted to accept support from Gentiles, although they might include Gentiles in their own acts of mercy.[59] In a sense, then, there is a Jewish solidarity that resembles that of the extended family system, even among those Jews who have become largely assimilated.

Although Jewish law permits divorce,[60] marriage is considered sacred and binding. Orthodox and conservative Jews often insist upon a Jewish divorce or *Get*.[61] American cultural patterns seem to be prevalent among many Jewish groups, however. In a study of the Jewish community in Minneapolis, it was found that the divorce rate was definitely increasing.[62]

NEGRO FAMILY

Of all ethnic family types the Negro is perhaps the most unstable. To some extent this instability is rooted in the history of the American Negro family. During slavery husbands and wives were often separated and new relationships formed without legal sanction. Negro family unity was no more thought of as a necessity than that of the animals on the slave plantation.[63] Emancipation further confused matters. Some of the freedmen interpreted their freedom broadly, and promptly fled family and other responsibilities. One former slave rejected marriage proposals by saying that she meant to enjoy her liberty, and did not intend to accept any offers.[64] When

[59] *Ibid.*

[60] For an explanation of the ways of dissolving marriage see Sidney E. Goldstein, *The Meaning of Marriage and Foundations of the Family: A Jewish Interpretation*, New York, Bloch Publishing Co., Inc., 1942, p. 179.

[61] *Ibid.*, p. 181.

[62] Gordon, *Jews in Transition, op. cit.*, p. 200.

[63] Charles E. King, "The Negro Maternal Family: A Product of an Economic and a Culture System," *Social Forces* (October, 1945), 24:101.

[64] E. Franklin Frazier, *The Negro Family in the United States*, rev. and abr. ed., New York, The Dryden Press, Inc., 1948, p. 80.

formal unions were about to be sanctioned, it sometimes happened that someone at the ceremony protested that he was already spouse to the bride.[65] Not all Negro families had such experiences, but slavery and subsequent emancipation were hardly conducive to strong family bonds.

Children had stronger ties to the mother than to the father and among many lower-class Negro families today this tendency persists. Since the Negro is still a subordinate group, identified by racial characteristics, status is difficult to attain. There is an emerging middle class (estimated to constitute from 25 to 30 percent of the Negro population) which has a more stable family.[66] Negroes are largely in the rural South, however, and fall into the lower social strata.

The Negro family today is culturally akin to the American family. There are, of course, folk culture patterns and perhaps some African cultural survivals[67] but, for the most part, the Negro family bears close cultural resemblance to the American family. The Negro family functions in much the same way as the American family in the economic, educational, recreational, and religious spheres.[68]

Negro family disorganization is seen in the large number of desertions, especially in Northern urban areas. In 1930-1931 nearly 15 percent of the relief in Chicago went to deserted Negro fami-

[65] *Ibid.*, p. 81.

[66] E. Franklin Frazier, "Ethnic Family Patterns: The Negro Family in the United States," *American Journal of Sociology* (May, 1948), 53:438. It must be remembered that Negro family types vary according to class status, geographical location, and historical period.

[67] There are two conflicting points of view regarding the persistence of African culture among the American Negroes. Robert E. Park, E. F. Frazier, and Charles S. Johnson are of the opinion that the amount of African tradition which the Negro brought to the United States was very small and that it did not survive. Melville J. Herskovits, however, gives evidence to support his assumption that African folkways have survived among the American Negroes in *The Myth of the Negro Past*, New York, Harper & Brothers, 1941.

[68] Cf. Frazier, "Ethnic Family Patterns: The Negro Family in the United States," *op. cit.*, p. 438.

lies.[69] Separations are frequent. Since many marriages are common-law—unlicensed and unrecorded—they may be broken as unceremoniously as they are contracted.[70] As in the American family, women seem to play a more important role than they do in other family types. In 1940 women were heads of Negro families in from 21 to 34 percent of the cases.[71] A larger proportion of Negro than white women are gainfully employed, which means that the children are deprived of their mother's care and training. It is difficult for Negro men to find jobs with adequate salaries, hence the family tends to rely primarily on the mother for support while the father exercises little authority.[72] Most Negro women place a high value on large families. Among the plantation Negroes the women consider it an insult to infer that they cannot have children. Interest in large families may be a survival from slavery when emphasis was placed on the fertility of Negro slave women.[73] Family membership often extends beyond the limits of the small conjugal group. Grandparents, grandchildren, and illegitimate children often reside under the same roof.

IMPLICATIONS FOR THE PROFESSIONS

Attitudes which ethnic group members have toward professional services may depend, to some extent, on the degree to which the family approaches the strong extended familistic type. When responsibility and authority have been traditionally vested in the family system, the individual may be distrustful of the professional person and enlist the support of family and kinsmen in facing the new situation. If a Chinese or Mexican is called "on the carpet," the

---

[69] Elliott and Merrill, *Social Disorganization, op. cit.*, p. 412.
[70] Davie, *Negroes in American Society, op. cit.*, pp. 213-214.
[71] Elliott and Merrill, *op. cit.*, p. 412.
[72] Davie, *op. cit.*, p. 215.
[73] Burgess and Locke, *op. cit.*, p. 171.

professional worker may be astonished at the number of kinsmen who insist upon sharing the carpet during the interview. As a rule, these ethnics who are unacquainted with social work or with other professional services are prone to rely upon familial ties for assistance and solution of their problems.[74] Rather than go to an employment office, they will depend upon the primary contacts of family and friends for a job. The Chinese or Mexican herb dealer will be resorted to during an illness in preference to the impersonal medical attendants at a clinic. Death at home may be preferable to prolonged life in a sanitarium.

On the other hand, ethnic persons from an extended family may react to such professional services in much the same way as they react toward assistance from the family. After a certain amount of experience they may regard these services as their due; assistance is, to them, the function of the professional helping person. Hence, they may exhibit an attitude of passivity and express neither anxiety nor shame in seeking assistance, and give no display of initiative. Should the social worker, for example, attempt to curtail assistance, they even may be demanding. The family has traditionally cared for them; in this new setting it is the social worker's function to do likewise.

Jewish clients may experience a strong sense of shame in applying for assistance. Those who know and value their religious teaching will be embarrassed at receiving rather than giving. Although the dispenser of charity is admonished by the Talmud not to hurt the feelings of the poor in giving them assistance, the actual status of the poor is very low.[75] Assistance from their own

---

[74] Cf. Lee, "Research on the Chinese Family," *American Journal of Sociology, op. cit.,* 54:503.

[75] Cohen and Witmer, *op. cit.,* 10:289; Joffe, "The Dynamics of Benefice Among East European Jews," *Social Forces, op. cit.,* 27:241. See also the opinion of Otto Pollak who states that Jews coming from an Orthodox background "are demanding when they need social services and extend their attitude in this respect also to social welfare services in this country." "Cultural Factors in Medical Social Work Practice—Part II," *Medical Social Work* (October, 1954), 3:146.

ethnic group is generally easier to accept than is help from outsiders. Jews tend to apply for assistance to Jewish agencies wherever
such agencies are available.

Extended families that value a large number of children will
seldom be amenable to limiting family size, regardless of the circumstances in which the children are being reared. "Have . . .
people ever stopped to think," says a young woman in commenting
about her own people, "that Puerto Ricans have big families because they feel that material possessions cannot make up for the
affection of a family?"[76] Prevalent attitudes of extended families
toward offspring have been succinctly expressed by Gardner
Murphy in writing of India. He says that children are regarded
as "the stuff of one's being" and it is "warmth and closeness to
them that makes life important, meaningful, and continuous."
Continuity of life is "conceived naturally in terms of fruitfulness,
in terms of health, welfare, reproductive capacity, long life of all
the individuals who issue from one's own body."[77]

Although divorce or desertion tend to be crisis situations, they
are much more so in the family systems that make little or no provision for them. Anxiety reactions will generally be much more
intense; marital failure and loss of status in the ethnic community
are difficult to accept. Among family systems where divorce or
desertion is relatively frequent, the situation may not engender as
much anxiety. Some Negroes may experience little or no trauma
over desertion or divorce. Inconveniences or economic difficulties
may loom larger than family disintegration. In the case of the Negro
there is another interrelated problem. Family and child welfare
agencies center their philosophy around the importance of stable,
satisfying relations and the significance of this kind of environment
for the child. Can the Negro client whose cultural heritage permits

[76] Sylvia Martinez, "How It Feels to Be a Puerto Rican," *Integrity* (July, 1955),
9:8.
[77] Gardner Murphy, *In the Minds of Men,* New York, Basic Books, Inc., 1953,
p. 32.

weak or loose family relationships be treated in the same manner as the client whose culture sanctions a strong family?[78]

There are, then, many problems involved in treating clients having varying degrees of family unity. The primary value may be preserving this unity at all costs, even at the risk of spreading tuberculosis, or shortening life, or living in crowded unsanitary conditions. At the other extreme there is the problem of treating those ethnics who place little value on the family unit, which most American professional workers believe is the basic unit of society.

[78] Cf. Patricia Knapp and Sophie T. Cambria, "The Attitudes of Negro Unmarried Mothers Toward Illegitimacy," *Smith College Studies in Social Work* (March, 1947), 17:203.

10

Establishing the Family: Mate Selection and Marriage

MARRIAGE AS A GOAL IN LIFE

SINCE the family is the basic unit of society, all other societies are organized on the assumption that people will mate and have children. Marriage, then, is a social expectancy among all ethnic groups. There are, however, variations in the degrees of expectancy, and the status of the unmarried adult differs from one society to another.

Marriage is regarded by Americans as one of the major goals of life, and nine out of ten Americans marry at some time in their lives.[1] Marrying is recognized as the normal thing to do, and it seems to contribute toward one's status. Husbands and fathers are usually considered more stable and trustworthy than are single men, and marriage may be a prerequisite for some positions involving great responsibility or the handling of huge sums of money.[2] Marriage implies that a man is settled and dependable.

[1] Sirjamaki, *The American Family in the Twentieth Century, op. cit.,* p. 55.
[2] John J. Kane, *Marriage and the Family,* New York, The Dryden Press, Inc., 1952, p. 102.

If a man is not married by the time he reaches thirty or thirty-five, people begin to seek reasons for his bachelorhood. Among other things it may be believed that he is bound to his mother's apron strings, or that he has a distorted attitude toward marriage, or that he is too selfish to marry.

The unmarried woman, however, is generally dealt with even more critically. She is called a "spinster" or an "old maid," perhaps in tones of mild opprobrium. It is popularly believed that all women want to get married and the unmarried women are those who have not had the opportunity.[3] The unmarried woman is thought to be too "homely" to attract a man or perhaps she is thought to be too aggressive or too efficient. Although American society has a place for the career woman, the unmarried business or professional woman is generally aware of the fact that she is competing in a man's world.

In Chinese society where the family system pervades every aspect of life, marriage is almost obligatory. As noted previously, outside the family there is no respectable place. Even concubines are brought under the family roof. Marriages are traditionally arranged by the family and it is the duty of the married couple to have progeny to carry on the family name. As a rule, marriages are arranged for the children in the order of age. A Chinese student, Lin, who was studying in an American university, decided to work toward a higher degree after completing the studies which she had originally intended to pursue. She was notified by her family in China, however, that her younger sister at home was ready to marry. This marriage could not be conducted properly, she was reminded, before her own marriage. Before pursuing further studies, Lin was instructed to spend a semester with relatives in a large urban community with a Chinese colony. At the end of that semes-

---

[3] Judson T. and Mary G. Landis, *Building a Successful Marriage,* New York, Prentice-Hall, Inc., 1948, p. 45.

ter she was expected to be married in order that arrangements could proceed for her younger sister's wedding.

Traditionally, marriage is regarded of such importance that until the present century a form of posthumous marriage was contracted. If an unmarried son died, his parents instructed go-betweens to find a family with a deceased daughter who was about the age of their son. The betrothal contract and marriage ceremony were carried on as though the parties were still alive—except that tablets inscribed with the names of the bride and groom served as substitutes for them. After the ceremony, the bride's coffin was moved next to that of the groom and the bride was regarded as a deceased daughter-in-law.[4]

Among the very poor of China there are some unmarried children of marriageable age, but they are usually not single of their own volition.[5] The mortality of infant girls is high, and causes an imbalance of the sex ratio. It is the daughters of the poor, moreover, who tend to become concubines, a circumstance which creates a further imbalance in the sex ratio among the poor.[6] Even when there are potential wives available, some families simply cannot afford the expense of a wedding and the support of additional members. In many instances, however, marriage is simply delayed.

Jewish tradition advocates early marriage, and resembles Oriental culture in that the Jews are expected to marry and establish a family.[7] In the four thousand years of Israel's history, Judaism has never counseled or encouraged the celibate life. On the contrary, throughout the centuries marriage has been extolled as a divine command.[8] The family is viewed as the "bond of cohesion which

[4] Mao, "Ceremonies and Rites of Chinese Marriage Before the Republic," *op. cit.*, Chapter VI.

[5] Lee, "Research on the Chinese Family," *op. cit.*, p. 500. There has been no research on the numerical importance of this group.

[6] Lang, *Chinese Family and Society, op. cit.*, p. 126.

[7] Weiss-Rosmarin, *Jewish Survival, op. cit.*, p. 351.

[8] Goldstein, *The Meaning of Marriage, op. cit.* p. 25.

has safeguarded the purity of the race and the continuity of religious tradition"; it is "the stronghold of Jewish sentiment, in which Jewish life unfolds itself in its most typical forms and intimate phases"; its establishment "is regarded not merely as a social ideal but as religious duty." The Talmud says that an "unmarried person lives without joy, without blessing, and without good."[9]

A Jewish child who met an elderly unmarried woman for the first time recorded her impressions in these words:

. . . In the two or three visits which I paid [the neighbors] . . . I learned that their name was Graham, that the lame old man had been a soldier . . . and that the old lady was "Miss Graham." Here was an old woman who, though not even a school-teacher, seemed actually contented, and was nevertheless—unmarried. It was most amazing to me. When in describing my visit I told mother that the lady was a "Miss," she shook her head pityingly and said "Poor, poor woman!" repeating it even when I declared, "But she doesn't look unhappy, mother!"[10]

The Jews who have become thoroughly assimilated into American life sometimes remain single through choice, but this is the exception rather than the rule. An unmarried man over thirty years of age was a source of worry to his mother who feared that he would have no one to care for him when he became ill and no companionship in later life.

The Mexican family is a strong one and marriage, even of the common-law variety, is a goal. Although there are relatively few unmarried Mexicans, there is a respectable place for the single person in this culture. The Mexican people are traditionally Catholics; since this religion extols virginity, the unmarried who choose to remain single do enjoy status, especially if they enter a life of religion. On the whole, though, their number is not appreciable. Mexican society also sanctions the single state for the youngest daughter, if the mother is a widow. Should the mother be an

[9] As quoted in Tennenbaum, "Jewish Parents in a Child Guidance Clinic," *Smith College Studies in Social Work, op. cit.,* 10:54-55.
[10] Stern, *My Mother and I, op. cit.,* p. 60.

invalid, it is "unthinkable" for the last daughter to marry and leave home. These women are known as "the Mexican aunties, the unmarried women, a sort of special sisterhood, bound together in tradition and rules of self-immolation as strong as the vows which bind the nuns to their vocation." After the death of the mother, they devote themselves to nursing distant members of the family. Of one such woman it was said that she "had no home of her own but she did not need one. She was always in demand. She was wanted everywhere."[11]

Most European patterns do not differ greatly from those of Americans. Catholic cultures do, however, give status to those who are celibate, especially the clergy. Girls in Southern Italy are supposed to marry in turn according to age,[12] after the Chinese pattern. Among the Russian Molokan group one's social status is redefined at marriage, and unmarried adults are seldom tolerated. Even the parents of the single persons are stigmatized.[13]

Marriage is apparently of less importance to the rural lower-class Negro, as is evidenced by the frequency of common-law relationships and the number of illegitimate births. Undoubtedly the history of the Negro family has left its impact on attitudes toward marriage. Sometimes the importance of a legal union becomes apparent, and then an effort may be made to legalize a common-law union.

A middle-aged Negro woman had been living with a man for seven years and he was the father of her three children. Since it was time for the oldest child to start school, the mother decided that it was also time to conventionalize matters. The school authorities would question the child's last name and might ask to see the birth certificate. The children's father, however, was an elderly man and he refused to marry her because he didn't want her to have property rights. He had never acknowledged

---

[11] De Treviño, *My Heart Lies South, op. cit.,* pp. 116-119.

[12] Williams, *South Italian Folkways in Europe and America, op. cit.,* p. 83.

[13] Pauline V. Young, *The Pilgrims of Russian-Town,* Chicago, University of Chicago Press, 1932, pp. 107-108. The Molokans are a religious sectarian group.

the relationship, but had always introduced her as a "Mrs. H." He also admitted that he had another girl friend in whom he was more interested.

The children's mother thought of leaving him and establishing another home, if the agency would take care of her children until she got settled. She much preferred, however, to legalize the relationship with the children's father, "even if he divorced her the next day."

In the last few decades marriage appears to have become increasingly important. The system of allotments and allowances for wives of servicemen gave legal marriage a new significance. Many servicemen, moreover, who took out insurance papers realized the value of legal marriage.

SELECTING A MATE

The American Pattern

In America falling in love is a necessary prelude to free choice of spouses. The courtship process usually begins with dating, a social commitment between two young people intended to be pleasurable and to allow for better acquaintance with each other. Dating may be casual or occasional. A young person is said to be "playing the field" or "window-shopping" until he begins to date with the same person with some frequency. "Going steady" may begin as a matter of convenience because an amiable person of the other sex is readily available. It is generally believed that it is not wise to "go steady" at an early age, however, lest it prevent "shopping around." Informal engagement, or an understanding that at the suitable time marriage will take place, usually precedes the formal announcement of the coming marriage.

During the period of courtship, American parents do not, as a rule, impose adult duties or place much responsibility on the young people. A parent is often heard to explain this attitude by such expressions as: "They are young only once," or "She'll be doing dishes and housework for the rest of her life; I want her to enjoy her youth." Hence, American culture is known as a "youth culture," and the young girl ready for marriage is the "cynosure of American society."[14]

Today parental supervision during courtship is comparatively minimal. Earlier in the century a man was supposed to request permission to court a girl, and much of the courtship took place in the parlor or elsewhere at the girl's home. Under such circumstances, with the other family members close at hand, there was a kind of chaperonage. With the advent of the automobile, however, courtship began to occur almost anywhere else.

Some approach to sex may be a part of the dating process, depending upon the occasion and the existing rapport. Although this may stop at fondling and endearments, it appears that many American youth have apparently had premarital intercourse, often within their own class.[15] Research has "reasonably established the fact that former taboos against physical intimacies in courtship are materially weakened and to many persons practically nonexistent."[16]

Traditionally the girl is supposed to assume a passive role and let the male take the initiative in planning the dates, paying for them, and eventually proposing marriage. The present generation is, however, modifying this pattern. Since the girl may share the cost of an outing or use the family automobile, she often takes the initiative in proposing dates. If the expenses for the occasion are paid by the boy, when he takes the girl home he may stay for refreshments or the two young people may "raid the icebox." A boy is often heard to complain that his girl wants to get married while he is still economically unprepared or, perhaps, not sufficiently interested in the girl. While middle-class boys who wish to be adequately trained for good jobs require extended schooling, their

[14] Clyde Kluckhohn, *Mirror for Man, op. cit.*, p. 238.
[15] Sirjamaki, *The American Family in the Twentieth Century, op. cit.*, p. 63.
[16] John F. Cuber, "Changing Courtship and Marriage Customs," *Annals of the American Academy of Political and Social Science* (September, 1943), 229:33.

girl friends may be out of school and ready to establish a home. Hence the girl may exert pressure rather than assume a passive role.

When the young people decide to become engaged, they generally seek the approval of their respective families. If such approval is not given, however, cultural sentiments approve of love marriages in defiance of the will of the families. Moreover, the law sanctions and protects such marriages if the young people have attained the required minimum age. Sometimes the young couple elope to avoid unpleasantness. All their families can do is to sever social contacts or disinherit these children, but such measures are seldom employed. Eventually, the families tend to become reconciled to the situation.[17]

Oriental Method of Mate Selection

In family systems where family unity and welfare take precedence, courtship before marriage may be dispensed with or reduced to a brief, closely supervised affair. Among the Chinese, marriage traditionally constituted a family alliance, and the future couple might meet for the first time at the marriage ceremony. Relatives or go-betweens determined the compatibility of the young people and made the financial arrangements. Although this pattern has been altered in the last few decades,[18] family approbation continues to be a dominant consideration in the choice of a marital partner.

John C. H. Wu, who had not seen his wife before the marriage ceremony, expressed his sentiments with the following response: "[My American friend,] did you choose your parents, your brothers and your sisters? And yet you love them all the same." He adds that

[17] Joseph Kirk Folsom, The Family and Democratic Society, New York, John Wiley & Sons, Inc., 1943, p. 10.

[18] Some authorities are of the opinion that the services of go-between are decreasing and that young people in China today are meeting their spouses through friends, schoolmates, or associates. Impediments to arranged marriages are the tendencies to leave the paternal roof, to resort to protests and quarrels, or to take concubines. Lee, "Research on the Chinese Family," op. cit., 54:500. In a recent investigation of 360 marriages in a North China village, however, all the marriages except one were arranged without the consent of the couples. Lang, op. cit., p. 123.

such a betrothal had a greater dignity than the civil engagement by the free choice of the parties; because it was, as it were, registered in Heaven. If one has chosen one's own fiancée, one is liable to wonder at times if one has made the right choice. If, on the other hand, one believes, as we did, that every marriage is made in Heaven, there could be no room for regret, any more than Adam could have regretted that only Eve and none other was given to him.[19]

The Japanese pattern closely approximates that of the Chinese. A meeting of the young people may be arranged, after the families have agreed upon the suitability of the match. As a rule the go-betweens are hosts or hostesses on the occasion, which may be a chrysanthemum show or a cherry-blossom viewing at a well-known park. The young people are accompanied by their parents and if either of them voices disapproval after the "casual" meeting, the matter is dropped.[20] If the meeting is satisfactory, however, a go-between or relative begins negotiations and keeps the young couple on formal terms until the wedding takes place. It is improper for a young man and woman to be seen alone together until after marriage.

Adultery is severely censured. In China the male suffers permanent loss of social and family position if he has premarital sexual relations within his own clan and family. The woman, if unmarried, loses her chance of being properly married and may resort to suicide. Censure of the male is not as severe if he has an affair with a girl from another clan or family, but the girl always suffers.[21]

American-born Oriental children who go to coeducational schools and come into contact with American courtship patterns usually experience a cultural conflict. Parents fear that the girl's reputation will be ruined if she associates with young men, for the parental viewpoint is that males seek women only to satisfy sexual needs.[22]

[19] Wu, *Beyond East and West*, op. cit., pp. 58, 61.
[20] Benedict, *The Chrysanthemum and the Sword*, op. cit., p. 157.
[21] Yang, *A Chinese Village*, op. cit., p. 119.
[22] LaViolette, *Americans of Japanese Ancestry*, op. cit., p. 50.

A young American-born Chinese girl relates her courtship experience as follows:

After I reached my late teens, my father would often remark, "It's time now!" and I knew that he referred to the fact that I was old enough for marriage. I was kept too busy mothering my younger brothers and sisters, attending college, and working in the family grocery to put much effort into courtship, nor would the family have approved of American courtship patterns. According to the old custom, my parents felt that they had a responsibility to arrange a suitable marriage for me. There were times, then, when eligible suitors from distant states "happened" to be passing through town or when sons of family friends "happened" to visit the family. Such pre-arranged actions made me resentful, and I must admit that I refused to let myself consider some of the eligible ones simply because the family had taken the initiative. Whenever possible on such occasions I found some excuse for not entertaining the visitors.

One summer my father consented to let me attend a convention as a delegate of the college. Imagine my chagrin when I visited some family friends in the Chinese colony and found that my parents had notified these friends that I was on the matrimonial market! One woman who lived in a distant part of the state sat up with her son for a whole night on the train and when the introduction was made the following morning it was evident that the purpose of the trip was to appraise my qualifications as a prospective daughter-in-law.

Although I was raised to think of motherhood as my career, with my American background I wouldn't accept an arranged marriage. Eventually the conflict was settled when my parents agreed to let me go to school away from home. I chose a location with a large, respectable Chinese colony, and there was a tacit agreement that if I had the educational opportunity I would also utilize the opportunity to choose a husband—which I did!

European Patterns

Families with traditions of matchmaking[23] and chaperonage en-

---

[23] See discussion of European patterns and their persistence in America in Marybeth Weinstein, "Marriage by Go-Between," *The New York Times Magazine,* April 3, 1955, p. 47.

counter many problems when transplanted to American soil, especially if they settle in urban communities—which most of them do. It is impossible for the parents to know all the acquaintances of their children or to arrange marriages for them. Strict chaperonage is virtually impossible, but in an effort to maintain control over courtship, parents make themselves conspicuous or resort to undue harshness. As a consequence, the adolescent rebels against parental control and at the same time may feel insecure and inadequate when left to cope with the situation unaided.

Most Italian mothers, for instance, are very careful to keep their daughters under surveillance so that the neighbors have the correct impression. After the age of six or seven the little girl in Southern Italy is kept busy in the home or attending "school" at a neighbor's home where she learns needlework or some skills.[24] Sometimes the oldest boy acts as chaperon to his unmarried sisters. Although the Italian boys in America seldom act in this capacity, they still feel responsible for their sisters' virtue.

The sentiments of a European immigrant are revealed in the soliloquy of Julia, a Hungarian mother, whose "perceptive eyes noticed . . . that Rosy had something on her mind." After some coaxing, Rosy unburdened her hopes and fears by telling her mother that there was a dance at school and Stevey was to call for her. As the mother pondered the question, the following thoughts ran through her mind:

Was it possible that their daughter should go out with a man? Of course, Stevey was just a boy, a nice boy, so what was wrong with it. John and Julia had been living in America for a long time now, much longer than they had lived in Baranya County. Yet even the lessons of a quarter of a century could not root out certain habits.

Stevey called for Rosy and took her to the dance, but Rosy's parents were uneasy. It was eleven o'clock when the youngsters

[24] Williams, *South Italian Folkways in Europe and America, op. cit.,* p. 81.

came home and the parents "heard them raiding the icebox and then sitting down to what was probably a hearty meal. Then there was silence."

After a few minutes of unbroken silence, the panic-stricken mother whispered to her husband, "You must do something about it!"

What was he to do? The boy might be kissing Rosy at that moment. In the County of Baranya people kissed only after the marriage ceremony. Were they to force Stevey to marry Rosy? His heart was broken.

It was several days before the parents recovered from the shock. This incident was the hardest stress of their process of Americanization. Through this experience, though, they learned that their daughter "could take care of herself."[25]

The young girl whose parents will not tolerate company keeping after the American fashion may insist upon following such patterns anyhow. Should an illegitimate birth result, the repercussions in most European families would be out of all proportion to the reaction that might be expected in an American family. The chances of a good marriage for the unmarried mother would be slight, and the male members of the family might consider it a duty to avenge family honor by forcing a marriage upon the parents of the illegitimate child. A daughter whose indiscretions were publicly known among the ethnic group would bring censure upon herself and the family, even if there were no illegitimate child. Virginity is expected, and lack of it at marriage may furnish grounds for separation. To the Italians, there were two kinds of women, the "good and the bad, the virgin and the prostitute." You married the first. As for the second type, the fault lay with the girl's father who had not protected her.[26]

[25] Lengyel, Americans from Hungary, op. cit., p. 153.
[26] Campisi, "Ethnic Family Patterns," American Journal of Sociology, op. cit., 53:446. Ware, Greenwich Village, op. cit., p. 111.

Latin Courtship Procedure

The Mexican pattern of mate selection bears the imprint of Spanish culture and resembles, in varying degrees, the Southern European pattern. Like the Oriental, the young person's freedom in the choice of mate is restricted, but not to the same extent. In most Latin American countries there are opportunities to meet eligible marital partners on Sundays or festive occasions. After Sunday services the young people may mix publicly in the city plaza—a little park surrounded by a broad sidewalk—under the watchful eyes of their elders. While the band plays in the square, the boys and men march in one direction around the plaza and the women and girls in another.[27] When respectable young ladies go to public places they are always chaperoned. Family status demands premarital virginity of the daughters, and assiduous chaperonage is the culturally defined manner of safeguarding the family honor.

Young Latin girls who are sent to this country for an education often take delight in their new-found freedom. Returning to school after a summer at home where she was under constant chaperonage, a young Puerto Rican girl breathed a sigh of relief. She confided to her teachers and classmates that she had had some arguments with her parents over the matter of chaperonage. One of the listeners asked, "When you return home and raise a family, will you allow your daughters to have the privileges you enjoy here?" Without reflection, the Puerto Rican replied, "Oh, no! Not in Puerto Rico!"

The typical Latin procedure of courting a girl is the serenade beneath her balcony or window. A young Texas Mexican, whose family has been in the state since the Spanish settled it centuries ago, relates her own courtship experience in these words:

[27] Cf. Hayner, "Notes on the Changing Mexican Family," *American Sociological Review, op. cit.,* 7:491.

Just like any other girl I knew, I hoped to find a real nice boy and marry him some day when I grew up. By the time I was twenty, however, I still had not met him. I was losing hopes and therefore I blamed it on my mother's "foolish ideas"—chaperoning me to all the dances and festivities. I had noticed my girl friends having dates to go to dances or the show without a chaperon. Mother did not believe it right for a girl to go out with so many different boys before she married. I thought this old-fashioned. She would let me go out alone with girls, on a limited basis. When I went to dances, however, I was always chaperoned. I never could get well enough acquainted with any boy, I argued. Several times, after dances, boys would come to give a serenade, but mother always got the best viewing spot. Of course, she would never let me invite them in for coffee or at least thank them. The house would remain dark, and the boys left thinking I had slept through it all!

Surprising as it may seem, I finally met the man of my life at one of the family parties where a couple was celebrating a wedding anniversary. My mother liked Johnny from the start. All my brothers and sisters gave their wholehearted approval, too, as they got to know him. Mother continued to escort me for some time, however, until Johnny asked for permission to give me a ring. Then he sent two of his uncles to ask my eldest brother (my father was dead) and my mother for their consent to the marriage.

Although the older generation generally frowns upon intercultural mating, if the suitor is willing to accept Latin customs, the courtship may be sanctioned. Such was the case of Luz, a young third-generation Mexican.

Even though my family has been in Texas for three generations, we still adhere strictly to the old courtship customs. My high school sweetheart, Jose, was not my mother's idea of a suitable husband, but I had always liked him. When he visited me at home, my mother always sat in the parlor with us. If we went out to a dance or a party, mother or an elderly person chaperoned. Just when we decided to become engaged, mother made things so unpleasant that Jose couldn't swallow the insults and keep his self-respect. I was heartbroken when he left the house in anger, for what I thought was the last time.

After a few months another schoolmate began to ask me for dates. Of course, he had to come to the house for me and we were both properly chaperoned. Mother approved of Jim from the start, in spite of the fact that he didn't belong to our cultural group. Many of the social affairs to which I was invited were sponsored by Mexican groups and very little English was spoken. Jim did not speak Spanish and he must have felt out of place in those gatherings, particularly when he was stalled with mother who speaks very little English. At one ball I was chosen princess by acclamation and spent the whole evening dancing with the judges. Jim sat on the sidelines with mother, who was chattering away in Spanish.

I really didn't love Jim, even though he was willing to accept my relatives, my religion, and all aspects of my culture. When pressure for an engagement was being applied by both Jim and mother, Jose came charging back and, after many heartaches, we eventually obtained my parents' consent to marry.

Very often the young people are not as docile as this Mexican girl, and attempts to chaperon fail. Like many Southern Europeans, the Mexicans expect premarital virginity in their women, although the men are allowed to "sow their wild oats." Most Latin cultures do not permit premarital kissing and petting, and the insecure girl whose culture sanctions chaperonage but who insists upon following the American pattern may not know how much resistance to offer the amorous male. Reactions to illegitimacy are similar to those of the Europeans.

The following excerpt from a case record indicates the attitude of an aged Mexican father toward his daughter, a divorcee, who had had an illegitimate child.

Mr. C. explained that he would not accept his daughter in his home. He told me this in a manner which I thought showed he was very much ashamed about what the daughter had done, that it had hurt him to take the measures which he believed were called for—forcing her to leave his house—but that he would abide by his decision in order to protect "family honor." He went on and told me how this daughter had been married and had a child by her first husband. They separated and the daughter came back with him (her father) and Mrs. C. (his cousin), and he cared for this child while the daughter worked. He said she had turned up pregnant again and he did not know who the father of the baby was. She had left the house and returned after the baby was born and had said she would stay with them and support them all.

Mr. C. said he had refused this support because he felt that she might just want them to care for her children and she might continue to go out and get pregnant. He said he thought that regardless of how poor people might be, they should continue to maintain their standards of decency and morality.

Another custom which still prevails even in America is that of the groom's furnishing a sum of money to cover the purchase of the bride's wedding clothes and trousseau. The custom dates from an old tradition that the gentleman brings his bride a coffer in which are her wedding garments.[28] One third-generation Texas-Mexican girl strongly resented her mother's insistence that the groom abide by this custom, but the mother triumphed.

Jewish Courtship

Jewish courtship patterns follow those of the dominant American group in most respects. Traditionally, though, the *shadchan* or marriage broker served in much the same capacity as the Oriental go-between. The custom developed because the Jews of Europe and Asia were scattered over both continents, and within their small communities contacts were necessarily limited. The *shadchan* traveled from place to place and learned of eligible young men and women whom he could introduce by proxy to Jews in other communities.[29] He generally received a small percentage of the dowry when the match was arranged. The practice persisted in America, especially in earlier times.

Even in this country the practice has prevailed in varying degrees, especially on the eastern seaboard where Jews are concentrated. The marriage broker is usually male, but women may become

---

[28] De Treviño, *op. cit.*, p. 60. For an interesting account of Mexican courtship procedures, see Chapter VII of this source.

[29] Goldstein, *op. cit.*, pp. 59-60.

recognized for their ability to make matches. One woman became so adept at matchmaking that she was a challenge to a local marriage broker. When both were widowed, the broker proposed. To his surprise, he received the response: "I could not marry a marriage broker." The suitor thereupon pointed out that it was a business in which the lady herself was engaged, even though as an amateur. To this rejoinder, the lady answered, "It's all right for a woman, but it's no business for a man."[30]

Today most young Jewish people choose their own mates after the American pattern, with the exception of the World War II influx of Jewish immigrants. Some observers in the Jewish community have noted the revival of the *shadchan* among these Jewish newcomers.

Negro Attitudes

The Negro family system in the rural South is an outgrowth of history and environment, as has been noted. As a consequence, the Negro family lacks the kind of institutional character found among other groups, and family tradition permits the sexual freedom which other family systems traditionally prohibit.[31] The Negro family originated in the mating of young people "who regarded sex relations outside of marriage as normal behavior,"[32] and when children were born they became a part of the mother's family group. After emancipation, these attitudes persisted and even today they are still common among lower-class Negroes. Marriage may or may not take place, following the birth of a child. Sometimes the girl is regarded as too young, as was the case in the following family:

An adolescent Negro girl, Jane, was referred to the agency because of habitual incorrigibility. Her mother was married to a Mr. D. in 1933.

---

[30] Behrman, *The Worcester Account, op. cit.,* p. 135. Chapter VI is devoted to the activities of the woman broker.

[31] E. Franklin Frazier, "The Negro Family," *The Family: Its Function and Destiny,* ed. by Ruth N. Anshen, New York, Harper & Brothers, 1949, p. 149.

[32] Frazier, "The Negro Family," *op. cit.,* p. 150.

She was not divorced, but had not lived with her husband since 1940. Four children were born prior to their separation and five were born since then, all of different fathers. The mother was not sure of the name of the client's father.

The relationship between the mother and daughter became strained when the girl entered puberty. Fear of the girl's becoming pregnant caused the mother to become unreasonable and rigid. The daughter now reminds the mother of her own illicit relationships and the fear of her daughter's following her example makes the pressure more acute. The situation seems to be one in which the mother teaches, "Do as I say, not as I do." What the girl does is not seen as something wrong, but it is forbidden simply because the girl is too young to do it.

In one study it was found that over three-quarters of the total group of Negro illegitimate mothers had more or less accepted illegitimacy so far as its moral implications were concerned, while less than a quarter felt that they had violated a rigid moral prohibition.[33] Negroes who value traditional religion would fall into the latter category.

Sometimes Negro parents will attempt to instill conventional attitudes in their children in spite of the odds against them, as is seen in the following case record:

A thirteen-year-old Negro girl was brought to the agency for running away from home. The girl reports having sexual relations three different times, but medical reports do not substantiate her statements. She seems to feel that having her group as well as her parents feel that she has had such experiences will prove helpful to her. In talking about the other girls at her school she mentioned that all of them in her grade are pregnant except herself and one other girl.

The family apparently has more to offer in the way of stability, physical comfort, and emotional satisfaction than most families with children that get into difficulty. Despite this fact, the client seems to have a very strong motivation to appear to be the very thing that she has been taught is not nice. She seems to have a desire to punish her parents. Such a desire could stem from the parents' inconsistent handling of the prob-

[33] Knapp and Cambria, "The Attitudes of Negro Unmarried Mothers Toward Illegitimacy," *Smith College Studies in Social Work, op. cit.,* 17:202.

lem of sex. The girl detects her parents' rigidity in this area. As an only girl she was allowed more freedom than the boys. Now that she has reached adolescence her parents are more exacting and particularly concerned about her relations with boys. This may possibly be due to the parents' own experiences in what was apparently a forced marriage. There has already been a repetition of this type of marriage in the family as one of the boys was married at seventeen to his girl friend who was pregnant.

Reliable sources seem to indicate that the rates of illegitimacy in rural communities range from 10 to 20 percent of Negro children born.[34] In the relatively isolated and stable Negro population on St. Helena Island as many as 30 percent of births were believed to be illegitimate.[35]

Percentages of illegitimacy in certain urban communities in 1947 were more than 22 percent for Philadelphia, 20 percent for Washington, D. C., and nearly 19 percent for Cincinnati. Kansas City, Pittsburgh, and St. Louis had more than 16 percent.[36]

When children are born out of wedlock, the mother is expected to assume obligations toward them. The unmarried mother is usually "as sensitive as the legally married mother to what is expected of the woman who is a mother."[37] In some instances, however, a very young mother may depend upon her own mother to care for the children. Such was the situation revealed in the following record:

A Negro woman with three daughters was referred to an agency because of limited income. All three daughters had illegitimate children. The eldest daughter assumed the responsibility for her child; the second daughter provided financially for her child but did not assume the mother role; and the youngest girl, aged seventeen, had an eleven-month-old baby who was cared for by its grandmother. Since the youngest girl had to be forced to mother the baby, the social worker asked the grandmother if she had thought of placing the grandchildren

[34] Frazier, *The Negro Family in the United States, op. cit.*, p. 90.
[35] *Ibid.*
[36] Elliott and Merrill, *op. cit.*, p. 150.
[37] Frazier, *The Negro Family in the United States, op. cit.*, p. 94.

for adoption. She replied, a bit indignantly, that they had never discussed such a possibility. To give children away was out of the question;
it would be treating them "just like cats."

The father of the child is generally not regarded as "guilty in
the eyes either of [the girl's] family or of the community of any
offense against the integrity of her family."[38] His responsibilities
tend to be minimal. He may bring gifts or clothes for the child,
or he may leave the responsibility to the mother and her family.

FACTORS INFLUENCING CHOICE OF MATE

People in America marry because of such factors as social pressures from parents and relatives, and possibly from the fear of being
considered unsuccessful in competing for a marital partner. In
addition to these pressures, there are other factors involved such as
the desire for companionship, the wish to have a home of one's
own, a love of children accompanied by a strong paternal urge,
and the need for response and romantic love.[39]

Although studies have shown that romantic love tends to rank
lower than the other factors mentioned, it would appear to be a
strong motive judging from such evidence as themes in literature,
movies, and radio or television scripts. The movies, in particular,
stress love as a major value, often making it "the end and be-all of
existence. Making money, work, friendships, one's place in the
world, are all secondary," according to the findings of one analyst.[40]

.The reasons why persons from such ethnic groups as the Chinese,
Mexicans, and some Europeans marry include many of these factors, with more emphasis on family pressure, but little or no competitiveness. Romantic love is seldom a consideration, except among

---

[38] *Ibid.,* p. 95.
[39] Kane, *op. cit.,* p. 100.
[40] Hortense Powdermaker, "An Anthropologist Looks at the Movies," *Annals of
the American Academy of Political and Social Science* (November, 1947), 254:83.

the ethnics who are almost completely assimilated into American culture. In fact, the desire for public emotional response is taboo even among Chinese married couples. Signs of affection are seldom shown openly, even within the family circle. Most Italians, too, are reticent about making a display of affection.[41] A young Mexican wife remarked that outward signs of affection were considered undignified in her own family, but that her husband's relatives—also Mexican—believed in kissing as a form of greeting or farewell.

Once the search has begun for a marital partner, there are various factors involved in the preferences of Americans. During the exploration stage, appeal may be based on physical attractiveness, similarity of interests, and age. Personality and emotional qualities usually rate high. Ray E. Baber found in an investigation of students' preferences in New York over a period of years that the young people were adamant in considering the matters of disposition and personality the basic elements of a happy marriage.[42] Other studies of student groups substantiate these findings.[43] This is significant inasmuch as it indicates a trend away from the traditional family roles toward the family as a group knit together by the strength of personal interrelationships.[44]

Personality and emotional needs include a pleasing disposition, maturity, dependability, affection and attention, acceptance and approval, trust and sympathy, as well as security. Sometimes a person looks for a mate who has the same needs and whose personality matches his own. Another person may prefer a mate who has complementary traits. Thus, the virile, dominating male may look for a passive, dependent wife.[45]

[41] For a witty account of attitudes toward flirtation around the world, see Robert Payne, "Flirtation Is a Serious Business," *The New York Times Magazine*, March 21, 1954, p. 14.
[42] Baber, *Marriage and the Family*, op. cit., p. 120.
[43] Cavan, *The American Family*, op. cit., p. 349.
[44] *Ibid.*
[45] *Ibid.*, pp. 350-351.

Families at the other extreme of the conceptual pole, especially the Chinese, place less emphasis on personality. Stress is placed upon a young woman's sound mental and physical health (the latter being an assurance of fecundity), efficiency in domestic work, and good reputation. Chastity and obedience to parental authority are implicit in a good reputation. Unusual beauty is not desirable.[46] Economic considerations are primary in the choice of a son-in-law, and the amount of property possessed by his family and the number of sons among whom it will be divided are of great importance. If the economic situation is satisfactory, personal qualifications are considered. Again, a strong rather than a handsome body is what matters.[47]

The Italians, too, traditionally value chastity, especially in the girl, and take into consideration the reputation of her family, her skill at housework, and her potential fecundity and health. Second- or third-generation Italians, however, may choose a wife for sentimental reasons. In men such virtues as industry and the possibility of having steady work as well as health, sobriety, and religious devotion are traditionally important.[48]

Among the Jews, scholarship is highly valued in a spouse. "A poor scholar," it is said, "would be preferred in the marriage market to a rich ignoramus," and "a boy stuffed with learning was worth more than a girl stuffed with bank notes."[49] Although girls are not generally as well educated as boys, an educated girl tells that the matchmakers asked her parents if "they had not best be looking for some young doctor or lawyer" for her. The mother was "filled with immeasurable pride," for she saw her daughter "the wife of the haughtiest doctor in the ghetto."[50]

[46] Yang, op. cit., p. 107.
[47] Ibid.
[48] Ware, op. cit., p. 174; Williams, South Italian Folkways in Europe and America, op. cit., p. 83.
[49] Mary Antin, The Promised Land, Boston, Houghton Mifflin Co., 1912, p. 37.
[50] Stern, op. cit., p. 106.

Among Negroes psychological factors may be related to color. A light-colored wife may represent status, or the mother-figure and may be a strong motive in influencing choice. Sometimes men choose to marry a dark woman because they are able to love only those persons who closely resemble themselves.[51]

Intelligence and education are cultural factors which play relatively important roles in mate selection in all ethnic groups. Since males are generally expected to be breadwinners, the higher their education, the more security they tend to offer and the more status their families would seem to enjoy. Research data have not, however, given support to the belief that disparity in education is undesirable between spouses.[52]

Propinquity or physical proximity is important, especially among Americans where young people exercise freedom of choice. Many an ardent swain has been deterred by the distance he has had to travel to see his lady love. Young men in uniform who have been stationed far from their girl friends often find that the Romeo near at hand has the advantage. Among groups which tend to use go-betweens or *shadchans*,[53] propinquity is not so important. It may be a considerable factor, though, in small ethnic colonies that stress group intramarriage and that offer little selection to the young people of marriageable age. Pressure toward marriage may outweigh the social disapproval of intercultural or interclass mating.

There are, of course, other factors involved in mate selection such as parental influence, social class, occupation, and the varied legal requirements including that of minimum age. A very forceful motive in mate selection is the tendency to marry within one's own ethnic group, for marriages that cross homogamous barriers generally result in social disapproval.

[51] John Caswell Smith, "Understanding the Negro Client," *The Family, op. cit.,* 27:90-91.
[52] Landis and Landis, *op. cit.,* p. 157.
[53] See p. 204.

CROSS-CULTURAL MATING

American culture, it has been noted, stresses individuality and freedom to choose a mate regardless of cultural differences. When young people choose to marry someone of another racial or cultural group, however, it is considered "news," especially if one of the young persons comes from a well-known family. For example, when Anne Mather, heiress to an iron-ore fortune, married Frank Montero, a Negro social worker, this event was considered newsworthy.[54]

There are a number of factors to account for cross-cultural mating. Among other things, these include: the freedom to move about and choose one's own friends; the concentration of diverse peoples in urban centers where one comes to know many different kinds of individuals; the tendency to recreate outside the home; the increased number of women working and earning who are less passive in the mate selection process than were their older sisters; and the lessening of discrimination and segregation in housing, education, and employment, making it possible for young people of varied cultural backgrounds to become better acquainted than formerly.[55]

On the other hand, however, there are laws prohibiting cross-cultural marriages in some thirty states. Most of the Southern states, for instance, will not permit Negro-white intermarriages. Similarly, on the West Coast where Orientals are numerically strong, there are laws restricting choice of mate. Other states outlaw the marriages of Indians with native white persons.[56]

Many studies have indicated the strength of cultural motives in

[54] "Split Decision," *Time* (July 24, 1950), 56:62.
[55] Cf. Algernon D. Black, *If I Marry Outside My Religion,* New York, Public Affairs Committee, 1954, pp. 4-5.
[56] Cf. Kane, *op. cit.,* pp. 109-110.

making a choice of mate. In New Haven about two thirds of all marriages are within the ethnic group, but among Jews and Italians the percentages are 90.1 and 85.5 respectively. Two thirds of the marriages in rural Minnesota were also found to be endogamous. In Los Angeles County the rate for intramarriage among Chinese, Japanese, Mexicans, and Negroes was 97.3 percent.[57] Thus it would seem that despite the insistence upon freedom of choice of mate and the factors contributing toward intercultural fusion, the tendency is toward endogamy.

There are problems which frequently arise out of cross-cultural mating when it does occur. Sometimes religious differences are at the basis of the difficulty. Jews and Catholics to whom religion is a value prefer not to make compromises in this area.

The Central Conference of American Rabbis has declared that mixed marriages are contrary to the Jewish religion. Because the Jewish people constitute a minority, it is deemed inadvisable to weaken the group by intermarriage. Even when the outsider embraces Judaism, an alien element is introduced.[58] Psychological factors are also regarded as a hindrance to successful marriages between Jews and non-Jews.[59]

Despite these warnings, however, there appears to be an increase of intermarriage in some communities, such as Minneapolis. In this city it is usually the Jewish boy who marries a non-Jew and, as a rule, he is financially better off than the girl.[60] As a preventive measure, some parents and relatives have stipulated in their wills that heirs who marry outside the group cannot claim their heritage. Such was the case with Jean Tanburn, a Jewish girl who contested the will.

[57] Samuel Koenig, "Second- and Third-Generation Americans," *One America*, eds. Francis J. Brown and Joseph S. Roucek, New York, Prentice-Hall, Inc., 1945, pp. 481-482.
[58] Goldstein, *op. cit.*, pp. 160-162.
[59] *Ibid.*, pp. 163-165.
[60] Gordon, *Jews in Transition, op. cit.*, pp. 206-207.

Jean Tanburn's great-grandfather, a silk importer who died in 1938, stipulated in his will that "no descendant of the testator who marries a person not of Jewish faith or not of Jewish blood can take any legacy." His million-dollar estate was handed down to Jean Tanburn's father who died in 1952, willing her $10,000 plus an income of $6,500 a year. She was to come into her legacy in May, 1953, when she reached the age of twenty-one. She went to court in advance to determine if her pending marriage with Donelson Morrison Kelley, Jr., a non-Jew, would prevent her from gaining the inheritance. On February 16, 1954, the New York State Supreme Court reversed a lower court ruling that she must give up either the legacy or the fiancé.[61]

Not too long ago a Jewish father tended to say Kaddish—a prayer for the dead—over the child who had married outside the fold.[62] Intermarriage, then, was tantamount to death as far as the family was concerned. The Jewish attitude is expressed in this statement: "It is certain that, if nothing is done to prevent the tendency to intermarriage, Judaism can barely survive another century, and, even if it does survive, it will have become hopelessly devitalized."[63]

The Catholic Church, too, is opposed to interfaith marriages. From the Catholic standpoint, there is no such thing as equality of religion. Consequently, "to have offspring reared in another faith is a catastrophe, since it denies to the persons for whom one has the greatest love the Grace of the sacraments and the solaces of Roman Catholicism in life and death."[64] In an effort to discourage mixed marriages, the Catholic Church requires the Catholic party to obtain a dispensation from the bishop and to give reasons for requesting such a dispensation. The non-Catholic party must promise that the Catholic party will be permitted to exercise his

---

[61] See "Pretty Jewish Girl Wins Legacy Fight," *San Antonio Express,* February 17, 1954, p. 1.

[62] J. O. Hertzler, "The Sociology of Anti-Semitism Through History," *Jews in a Gentile World: The Problem of Anti-Semitism,* eds. Isacque Graeber and Steuart H. Britt, New York, The Macmillan Co., 1942, p. 79.

[63] Mordecai M. Kaplan, *Judaism as a Civilization,* New York, The Macmillan Co., 1934, p. 417.

[64] Kane, *op. cit.,* p. 152.

religion freely, that children will be raised in the faith, that there will be no other form of marriage ceremony, and that Church laws regarding birth control, sterilization, and divorce will be obeyed. The marriage ceremony cannot be performed solemnly in the Church at a nuptial Mass where special prayers are said for the couple. All these measures are intended to serve as impediments to interfaith marriages in order to preserve intact the cultural element of religion.

Several Protestant denominations have adopted resolutions warning their members against intermarriage, especially with Roman Catholics. Such church policies were adopted by the Protestant Episcopal Church in 1948, by the United Lutheran Church in America and by the Southern Baptist Convention in 1950, and by the Disciples of Christ in 1951. Despite these declarations, Protestant churches generally have no regulations or rules, such as those of Jews and Catholics, binding their members and clergy.[65]

Since culture is a plan for living, or a way of life, cross-cultural mating creates problems in addition to those which married persons ordinarily experience. Insight into certain cultural differences are revealed in excerpts from the following record of an American man who had a legal wife from his own cultural group and a common-law wife from the Mexican group.

Mr. D. has a legal wife and eight children as well as a common-law wife, Luz, and six children. Luz says that after every pregnancy, Mr. D. "goes off and hides" and she takes the children to her mother's house. Her mother is now ill and no longer able to care for Luz, and with another baby coming soon, Luz applied for assistance.

When contacted, Mr. D. said Luz and the six children had no legal demands on him. He remarked that he didn't know if anybody would ever be able to keep him away from Luz—that he never had been able to stay away from her.

Luz eventually took matters into her own hands. Mr. D. came into the office and said that she had been to his office and taken some of his

[65] Black, *op. cit.*, p. 15.

books and things in order to force him to come to see her. He states that Luz had written Luz D. and the names of her children all over his office walls, and she had used a bobby pin to scratch her name on the enamel of his car. He did not dare take the car to the home of his wife.

Mr. D. states that when his wife gets angry she does not take it out on the children. She cooks for them, keeps them clean, and sends them to school. She does not call him names or fight with him. He lives at his office; he has a bedroom there and keeps his clothes there. He goes to his wife's home every morning and gets the four older children and takes them to school. He also goes to the store and buys groceries and takes them to her house. She never makes scenes. Mr. D. says he considered a divorce in order to marry Luz, but her house was filthy and the children were neglected. She hands them a "pan dulce" or doughnut rather than cook for them.

Further insight into Mexican patterns are evident in a Jewish-Mexican union, a second marriage for the Mexican wife, a woman of middle-class status.

Mrs. S. was first married to a man who was about twelve years her senior—a wealthy Mexican Government official. This marriage lasted only a short period of time, although the marriage was not dissolved legally for about five years. Mrs. S. apparently got a great deal of satisfaction out of her first marriage. She was wealthy and could have everything money could buy. She feels that she was ill prepared to meet the social obligations which were made for her. She was too young, and the marriage ended in divorce.

Mrs. S. describes "episodes of amnesia" to which she has been subject, and it was during one of these episodes that she married Mr. S. She says that she remembers nothing of the wedding and expressed a great deal of feeling because she married someone of other than Mexican descent. Mrs. S. told her husband that she did not want any more children because she felt that the marriage was not going to last. She asked that he be sterilized or that she be permitted to be sterilized, but Mr. S. would not agree to this. As a result, two children were born to the marriage, and Mrs. S. cannot accept them. She describes her husband as "a good man with good intentions, but something of a clod." She feels that they have no common meeting ground, and she has made up her mind to get a divorce. She would like to go back to Mexico to live, because the men there are "more alive; you know what I mean."

Mr. S. feels that he is very much in love with his wife, but he thinks there are too many obstacles to overcome to have the marriage work out. He is willing, however, to try to work through the difficulties. He has felt somewhat threatened by his stepson because he feels that the latter rules his wife. As a result, he has been overly strict as a disciplinarian and has been very severe with the boy. He states that his wife has never cooked a meal since they have been married and that he has to do all the housework, all the shopping, and that as a result he has felt financial pressure. He describes rather compulsive behavior on the part of the wife in that when she does occasionally clean, she will spend a whole day on just one room. He states that it will be immaculately clean, but that she is not able to do more than one task. He feels that she "lives in a dream world."

Like Mrs. S., many Mexicans have strong feeling about marrying outside the cultural group. Proximity to the mother country and steady immigration from the cultural source have both served to strengthen cultural ties.

Orientals may have even stronger reactions toward cross-cultural marriages, which are generally unacceptable socially and infrequent even in America. Since Chinese immigration was predominantly male, there was some intermarriage among the first generation immigrants, but the rate of intermarriage decreased as the sex ratio became less imbalanced. In a study of the ethnic group in New York City, there were no cases of Chinese females marrying non-Chinese males.[66] One young man, educated at Harvard, remarked that "charming as these American ladies are, they are not for me. I must marry one of my own kind with whom I can feel at home even in 'Inferno.' "[67] Parental consent for marriage is mandatory,[68] and consent to marry outside the group is exceptional. Parents may disinherit children who fail in this respect. So strong is the

[66] Shepard Schwartz, "Mate-Selection Among New York City's Chinese Males, 1931-38," *American Journal of Sociology* (May, 1951), 56:564.

[67] No-Yong Park, *Chinaman's Chance, op. cit.,* pp. 122-123.

[68] Matsumiya, "Family Organization in Present-Day Japan," *American Journal of Sociology, op. cit.,* 53:109.

tradition that a Chinese grandfather who had lived most of his life in America refused to acknowledge his only grandson, the child of a mixed union which he had not sanctioned.

With the Oriental such a union involves not merely a cultural mixture of language, religion, family patterns, and the like, but it also involves a racial mixture. Marked physical differences are, for some persons, harder to accept than are other differences. This was the experience of an American who had married an Oriental wife. He divorced this wife, and brought the daughter to his family in America. She was, however, unacceptable to his American relatives. According to the case record:

Natalie's stepmother rejected the child and expressed a feeling that Natalie is a very disturbing factor in the family and also throughout the neighborhood. The stepmother stated that the child looks much like "a Negro or Mexican." This has caused ostracism not only of the child but of the entire family. The stepmother further stated that the problem is acute since the whole family is blond haired and light complexioned, whereas Natalie is dark skinned, black haired and Oriental in appearance. The stepmother's maternal grandfather is also rejecting the child because of her color.

Negroes, too, have problems revolving around color. The native whites are not the only ones who oppose mixed marriages. According to a Negro journalist:

The truth is that a Negro incurs the wrath of other Negroes when he crosses the color line in marriage, often to a greater degree than a white is scorned by other whites. It is a matter of pride with a lot of Negroes, especially women, and for this reason Negroes often heap as much misery upon interracial couples as do whites.[69]

Negroes are not, of course, wholly of African descent. It is estimated that less than 20 percent of American Negroes have no racial intermixture. In the words of John Gunther: "A lot of people have been intimate with a lot of people."[70]

[69] Rowan, *South of Freedom, op. cit.,* p. 223.
[70] *Ibid.*

Apart from the difficulties already mentioned, a host of others plague the couple who have diverse cultural backgrounds. Although they may have made seemingly effective compromises at the time of marriage, conflicts will tend to arise as to which culture shall prevail in rearing the children. Many arguments have their roots in such cultural differences.

Even the matter of food preferences may cause lack of harmony. Food is related to religious beliefs, to social prestige, to the time of day, to the season, to where one lives, and to how much money one has.[71] The American Indian may regard grasshoppers as a delicacy, while others think of them merely as pests. Mexicans enjoy *gusanitos del maguey,* but Americans are shocked when they learn that these tidbits are fried, salted caterpillar grubs. Chinese consider rice a staple, but if it is prepared "soft and slippery," it is a symbol of sickness.[72] If a husband's reference to "mother's cooking" may be a source of irritation to a wife from the same cultural group, with how much more reason might a wife from another ethnic group resent such references.

One of the chief reasons given by Italian men in New Haven for marrying within the ethnic group was the fact that Italian girls knew how to prepare Italian meals.[73] Italians season food to give it a special flavor, and the same holds true for the Chinese, Japanese, Mexicans, and others. They may be forced to substitute American condiments, however, if the preferred seasonings are difficult to procure or if they are too expensive.

As a rule, there is greater harmony when both parties to a marriage share interests in such areas as food, budgeting the family income, recreation, language, religion, and attitudes toward cleanliness and child rearing.

[71] Alfred J. Marrow, *Living Without Hate,* New York, Harper & Brothers, 1951, p. 37.
[72] "Global Food for Thought," *Newsweek* (November 29, 1954), 44:103.
[73] Child, *Italian or American? op. cit.,* p. 138.

LEGAL MARRIAGE AND COMMON-LAW MARRIAGE

After complying with legal prerequisites, four out of five American couples marry in church with as much ceremony as they desire or can afford.[74] Civil marriages are contracted by others for various reasons. Perhaps religion is of little value to them, or they feel they cannot afford a church wedding, or they are entering religiously mixed marriages. Others use a civil ceremony when they are remarrying or marrying in haste. Common-law marriages are not unknown, but they are infrequent among the middle and upper classes.

The marriage ceremony, especially in rural China, is an elaborate family celebration which may cost about four months net family income.[75] There are three elements which are essential to the traditional marriage ceremony—the bridal chair which brings the bride to her husband's family; the parade from the bride's home which shows publicly that the marriage is being properly performed, and allows the people to see the dowry; and the ritual homage to the gods of Heaven and Earth and to the ancestors of the husband's family. The latter ceremony is a way of informing the ancestors that hereafter the bride is one of them.[76]

The Chinese in America continue to emphasize the marriage ceremony, but with obvious modifications. For one thing, many Chinese have become Christianized and the ceremony is performed in church. This public ceremony—rather than the parade of the bridal chair and dowry—testifies to the authenticity of the marriage. Elaborate weddings, however, are generally preferred to simple ceremonies attended only by the immediate family. If the family is

[74] Sirjamaki, *The American Family in the Twentieth Century, op. cit.,* p. 70.
[75] Hsu, *Americans and Chinese, op. cit.,* p. 305.
[76] Yang, *op. cit.,* p. 113.

prominent, the entire Chinese colony may be invited to the wedding, provided that accommodations can be made for large numbers.

Latin-American custom decrees that a wedding be a festive occasion, and status requires that the invited guests be numerous. The larger the attendance, the greater the family's prestige. In American urban communities where it is difficult to cease business transactions on a week day, most large weddings are on Saturday afternoons or on Sundays. A large reception is usually held in a hotel or club, if the family can afford it. Families of moderate means tend to invest large sums in elaborate weddings, even though they deprive themselves of necessities or go into debt to meet the wedding expenses.

There are, however, many common-law marriages among the Mexicans. Sometimes a couple feel that they cannot afford a big wedding and hence they enter into a common-law relationship. For others, the common-law arrangement is a prelude to a legal or church ceremony. One woman who had three children by a common-law husband was undetermined about the feasibility of legalizing the relationship since she wasn't sure that she cared to be married to her husband "for life."

The following excerpt from the case of a thirty-year-old Mexican of mixed Spanish and Indian ancestry illustrates this tendency.

The client has been married legally to the present wife for about a year. Prior to that time a common-law relationship had existed for five years. She is Indian, and he met her when he went to Wisconsin and Michigan where his brothers had settled. She had a small child from a previous marriage; this boy was nearly seven. The client supported this child from infancy, and has repeatedly made efforts to adopt him legally. His affection and feelings of responsibility toward the child seem quite genuine. Recently the patient and his wife took another infant to raise —the child of his wife's sister who was "in trouble."

Although many European groups prefer a church ceremony, they are not always as insistent upon the same degree of ostentation as are the Chinese and the Mexicans. Among the South Italians, if both families approve a match and have sufficient money they will generally provide an elaborate wedding. A legal ceremony—which might be a simple affair—is not considered valid by Italians or others who are practicing Catholics.[77] Custom decrees that the church ceremony be more elaborate than that of a middle-class American marriage tends to be. In Detroit, for example, a Polish wedding began with the old-country custom of marching to church with music. After the church ceremony, five hundred friends joined the bride and groom in a sixteen-hour wedding party consisting of eating, drinking, and dancing. At midnight the festivities ended with the "lifting of the veil" from the bride. According to custom, the wedding gifts paid the cost of the festivities, and the young people had some money left to help set up housekeeping.[78]

The Jews who have long resided in America have generally adopted the prevailing attitudes. Orthodox Jews, however, as well as first-generation Jews, may adhere to traditional patterns. Ideally, the marriage ceremony is to be "treated as an event of significance to the Jewish community as a whole, . . . solemnized by a representative of Jewish communal life, and recorded in a Jewish communal register."[79] The *chuppah* may be employed in the service. It is an ornate canopy generally made of velvet, richly ornamented, and embroidered with gold. The bridal couple stand under it while the marriage ceremony is being performed. The *chuppah* need not be elaborate, but may be a bower of ferns or flowers.[80] Unless the union is properly sanctioned by the Jewish representative, the Jewish couple "should be regarded as reading themselves out of the Jewish community."[81]

---

[77] Williams, *South Italian Folkways in Europe and America, op. cit.,* p. 101.
[78] "A Lively World's Last Days," *Life* (April 25, 1955), 38:140-141.
[79] Kaplan, *op. cit.,* p. 422. In italics.
[80] Goldstein, *op. cit.,* p. 56.
[81] Kaplan, *op. cit.,* p. 422. See illustrations in "Judaism," *Life, op. cit.,* 38:93.

Ceremonial marriage is still a mark of prestige for the American Negro. Common-law marriage, which is frequent, tends to be acceptable, but promiscuity is censured. One widow who was "slipping up on the hill" to see the father of her unborn child boasted that she never bothered other women's husbands, and made it clear that she wanted no marriage ceremony. She was glad that her first husband was dead and did not want to be bothered with another one.[82] The possibility of mistreatment is, at times, a factor which restrains Negro women from forming legal unions.[83] Many women prefer economic independence to the probable responsibility of supporting a husband as well as their children.[84] Parents may not approve of a daughter's marriage on the grounds that she is too young, even though she has mothered an illegitimate child.[85]

Sometimes the common-law Negro father feels the same as the mother about the responsibilities involved in a legal marriage. Such was the case of a tubercular Negro client, a thirty-nine-year-old man who was himself the child of a common-law union.

The client's marital status is confusing in so far as records are concerned. He interchanged the terms "girl friend" and "wife" with no intent of misrepresentation. He lived with the mother of his two little girls for some time but they were not legally married. He gives her money and supports the children. The latter mean a great deal to him and he speaks of the children lovingly, individualizes them, and plans for them. Since he feels his illness incapacitates him as a "husband," and there are no legal ties, this "wife" is now apparently being a "girl friend" again.

These attitudes on the part of the Negro are an outgrowth of their tradition. During slavery certain cultural patterns developed that have been retained to the present time. For example, marriages

---

[82] Frazier, *The Negro Family in the United States, op. cit.*, p. 93.
[83] Burgess and Locke, *The Family, op. cit.*, p. 169.
[84] *Ibid.*
[85] Frazier, *The Negro Family in the United States, op. cit.*, p. 95.

sometimes occurred by simple public declaration or with a ceremony conducted by a minister but without a marriage license. It was also popularly believed that divorce could occur by public declaration or simply by crossing state or county lines.[86] Judgments about the unconventional actions of Negroes, then, should be made in the light of Negro history and tradition.

[86] Myrdal, *An American Dilemma, op. cit.,* p. 931.

11

Paternal Role

THE AMERICAN FATHER

THE paternal role in American society has been variously defined. It is, of course, interrelated with that of the wife and mother, and will depend largely upon the role of the latter. Family members bear the surname of the father who is generally recognized as family head and representative. He is traditionally expected to be protector and provider for the family, and to set a good example. Traditionally, too, his wife and children expect him to act as disciplinarian.

Two generations ago the American father was more closely associated with the home and exercised more authority over family members. His role as economic provider now takes him out of the home for most of the day. The consequences of these long absences have been variously interpreted. Some analysts believe that the stress placed upon economic success outweighs that placed upon success as a parent and that the psychological impact of economic failure is harder to endure than a child's defection. The mother, after all, bears the major responsibility in child rearing.[1] Other commentators say that the father who disappears so mysteriously after breakfast and is not seen again until the twilight hours, assumes a light cloak of romance. Quality is better than quantity

[1] Cavan, *The American Family, op. cit.,* p. 585.

225

in evaluating a good father, and children prefer "an Old Man that they can count on much more than they want him hanging around the house all day."[2]

The father's attitude toward his children has been described as "autumnal," since he tends to regard himself as their custodian for "a brief and passing season."[3] Such remarks as: "In another year, boy, you'll be out of school and on your own!" are indicative of this attitude. Not that the father necessarily relinquishes all solicitude once a child is educated, but parental responsibility is lessened after a boy begins full-time work and a daughter is married or employed.

A typical American boy does not ordinarily follow in his father's occupational footsteps. He is expected to aim for a higher social and economic level. Hence, the father does not enjoy the status which would be his if he were imparting his own occupational knowledge and skill to his offspring. Sometimes, of course, the boy whose father is in a profession, such as medicine, may decide to become a doctor also. In that event, the father, by virtue of his occupation, would have prestige in his son's eyes. Not all professional fathers, though, can expect their sons to choose the same profession. A young man who was before the examining board prior to admission to medical school was asked the area in which he felt least prepared academically. He replied, "Mathematics." One of the examiners then remarked, "That's the son of a certified public accountant talking."

The developmental father, when asked something he does not know, will tend to tell the child outright that he does not know the answer. The traditional father, however, is more inclined to ignore the question, answer vaguely, or send the child to his mother.[4]

---

[2] Edward Streeter, "Have Fathers Changed?" *The New York Times Magazine*, May 9, 1954, p. 14.
[3] Mead, *And Keep Your Powder Dry, op. cit.*, p. 45.
[4] Elder, "Traditional and Developmental Conceptions of Fatherhood," *Marriage and Family Living, op. cit.*, 11:99. See variations between the traditional and developmental roles in Table 1.

Developmental fathers place more emphasis on mutual activities such as picnicking, riding, hunting, fishing, and visiting, while the traditional fathers tend to emphasize commercial or spectator activities. Developmental fathers usually think that they should help regularly with certain household tasks, but traditional fathers regard domestic tasks as "women's work."[5] In one study it was found that the skilled tradesmen were oriented toward the developmental school while the semiskilled workers were of the traditional school.[6]

An English observer notes that the father role as portrayed by Dagwood in the comic strip *Blondie* seems to be representative of the attitude toward the American man as husband and father. He is, like Dagwood, "kind, dutiful, diligent, well-meaning within his limits; but he has so completely given up any claim to authority that the family would constantly risk disintegration and disaster, if it were not for Blondie."[7]

Certainly, the paternal role as it has developed bears some resemblance to this description. Exercising authority is not as important to the developmental role as are the father's kind and loving relationships with his wife and children. The father sees himself as a "pal" to his children and the latter wish their father to be seriously interested in their problems. Both father and children envision helping around the house as a part of the developmental paternal role. (See Table I, p. 228)

The mid-century has witnessed a revival of parental interest in domestic activities.[8] After work hours and on week ends the father has become "an amateur painter, paperhanger, and builder" and even engages in such domestic pursuits as "baby tender, dishwasher, cook, repairman" and yard man.[9] Such activities within

[5] *Ibid.*, p. 100.
[6] *Ibid.*, p. 98.
[7] Gorer, *The American People, op. cit.*, p. 49. See also John J. Kane, "Momma, What's Happened to Daddy?" *Jubilee* (July, 1954), 2:24.
[8] Cf. Lester David, "Should Husbands Do Housework?" *This Week Magazine.* July 4, 1954, p. 5.
[9] "The New American Domesticated Male," *Life* (January 4, 1954), 36:43.

TABLE 1.   Typical Responses of Respondents Revealing Traditional and Developmental Conceptions of a Good Father[a]

Respondent	Traditional Role Conceptions	Developmental Role Conceptions
Father	1. Provides adequate financial support	1. Helps provide a harmonious home atmosphere
	2. Teaches the child right from wrong	2. Cultivates the child as a pal
	3. Is active in church and makes children active in church	3. Spends as much time as possible with the children when home
	4. Furnishes good advice	4. Keeps in touch with school and community as they relate to child growth
	5. Sets an example; is the man in the family	5. Helps with the household duties
Mother	1. Is a good provider	1. Builds up wholesome family relationships
	2. Corrects the children when they are at fault	2. Tries to follow interests displayed by the child
	3. Provides a religious background	3. Includes the child in social activities in which the parents participate
	4. Provides for the child's education	4. Is loving and kind and interested in the children's personal problems
	5. Sets a good moral example	5. Strives to understand the child's point of view
Adolescent	1. Provides enough money for the family to live comfortably	1. Shares in the development of the child
	2. Is responsible for the discipline of the children	2. Gains a close relationship with children and mother
	3. Provides material security	3. Considers the child's problems as seriously as he does his own
	4. Gives wise advice	4. Does not teach by threatening, fear, or distrust
	5. Sets a good example	5. Does his share of the household tasks

[a] Table derived from study by Ruth Connor, Theodore B. Johannis, Jr., and James Walters, "Parent-Adolescent Relationships," *Journal of Home Economics* (March, 1954), 46:189.

the family bring him into closer association with the children and should, if persisted in over a period of years, give tonicity to inter-familial relationships.

"Why don't you assert yourself? In our house, I just change mine, feed him and walk the floor with him." (Courtesy of Jeffrey J. Monahan and *The Ladies' Home Journal.*)

ORIENTAL PATERNAL ROLE

Among both the Chinese and the Japanese the father is traditionally the undisputed head of the household. He is master of his wife and concubines and practically a "demigod" to his children. By law and custom he has full power over them.[10] He is "first in all things, in the bath, in being served at meals, and in all preferential activities."[11] Traditional Chinese fathers may consider it their duty to demand unquestioning obedience.[12] Japanese fathers, too, may take obedience and subservience for granted.[13] In theory, however, submissiveness to the paternal figure is demanded in the name of a supreme value in which all family members have a stake; family loyalty and honor are involved.[14] The Japanese father is supposed to call a family council when matters of real importance arise, and later enforce the decision of the council.[15]

The term "Old Man" in American society may connote familiarity or even disrespect, but among the Chinese it is often a term of reverence given to the patriarch who manages and presides over family affairs.[16] Filial piety is the keynote of both the Chinese and the Japanese family.[17] The male head of the house is the "living symbol of the past and the functioning representative of the dead"[18] to whom is due all honor.

All family members are entrusted to the care of the paternal figure. He is responsible not only for their material well-being but also for their good conduct. In the capacity of trustee of family honor, the father is charged with protecting the virtue of the womenfolk and arranging suitable marriages for them. Even sons who are themselves fathers of young adults will dutifully respect

[10] Kiang Kang-Hu, "The Chinese Family System," *Annals of the American Academy of Political and Social Science* (November, 1930), 152:41.

[11] Queen and Adams, *The Family in Various Cultures, op. cit.,* p. 90.

[12] Osborne, "Problems of the Chinese Family," *Marriage and Family Living, op. cit.,* 10:8.

[13] Smith, *Americans from Japan, op. cit.,* p. 52.

[14] Benedict, *The Chrysanthemum and the Sword, op. cit.,* p. 55.

[15] *Ibid.*

[16] Burgess and Locke, *The Family, op. cit.,* p. 44.

[17] Cf. Queen and Adams, *op. cit.,* p. 90.

[18] LaViolette, *Americans of Japanese Ancestry, op. cit.,* p. 17.

paternal authority and consult the family head on all important matters.[19] Paternal authority is not lessened when a son comes of age, but is continued as long as the father is alive.[20]

This respect for paternal authority persists, in varying degrees, in the Chinese family in America. According to the following case record, a second-generation Chinese man valued paternal authority so highly that he would not exercise initiative.

A twenty-five-year-old Chinese patient refused to make any commitment in the hospital about vacation plans without first consulting his father and cousin to learn what they "expect of him." He explained his hesitancy by saying that he had entered into business with his cousin, and that his father had financed his share of the enterprise. Although it was a gift, the patient feels that he has an obligation to follow his father's wishes regarding leave from the hospital.

Family members are not expected, then, to act with any degree of independence; they are supposed to seek advice in matters that would be regarded as trivial in American culture.

The Chinese woman, too, will tend to be noncommittal when the professional worker attempts to help her formulate plans for the children or for a household budget. Until the family head has indicated his wishes, the mother generally does not consider it within her province to make any commitments.[21]

The role of the father as a good provider has persisted among America's Chinese[22] and Japanese. As family financier, the father makes decisions in business matters, is custodian of the funds, and dispenses them as they are needed. Because of limited opportunities, the Chinese and Japanese who are not concentrated in urban

---

[19] Benedict, *The Chrysanthemum and the Sword, op. cit.,* p. 52.

[20] Hsu, *Under the Ancestor's Shadow, op. cit.,* p. 258.

[21] See Blackey, "Some Cultural Aspects of Social Casework in Hawaii," *op. cit.,* p. 47.

[22] Norman S. Hayner and Charles N. Reynolds, "Chinese Family Life in America," *American Sociological Review* (October, 1937), 2:633.

colonies have engaged in the service industries such as laundries and restaurants, or in the grocery business.[23] All family members, including the smaller children, tend to make some contribution to the business enterprise. In one family the younger children unload cartons of groceries, carry packages to customers' cars, and perform other odd jobs around the grocery store. The older children serve as clerks and as cashiers. No cash payment is made for these services; everything goes into the family purse to be distributed at the discretion of the father.

The paternal role in a transplanted extended family presents several psychological problems. If the father follows the old pattern, he seems harsh and dictatorial, but the American pattern appears, in contrast, pusillanimous. His American-born children see him as overrestrictive—enforcing chaperonage, administering corporal punishment,[24] and quelling initiative by making decisions for the children. If the children insist too strongly on following American patterns, there is danger of a rift between generations. Older sons may leave the paternal home rather than accept traditional filial roles of reverence and submission. Of all family roles that of the Chinese father is perhaps the most difficult to adapt to the American pattern, since it contrasts so sharply with the American developmental role.

The Mexican Father

In many respects the Mexican father's role resembles that of the Oriental. He is traditionally an authoritarian, patriarchal figure who is lord of his household. His prerogatives are to receive the obedience and respect of his wife and children, as well as their

---

[23] In large centers on the West Coast and in New York City the colonies are large enough to provide many other business opportunities serving the ethnic group.

[24] In China spanking is often endured by young people until they marry. Cf. Lang, *Chinese Family and Society, op. cit.,* p. 240.

services.[25] According to tradition, he keeps aloof from the petty details of the household and does not wish to be bothered with complaints or requests. When he returns home in the evening he does not customarily inquire about the children or what happened in his absence. Maintaining the proper social distance and avoiding intimacies are believed to enhance the respect which is due him.[26]

A young third-generation middle-class Mexican girl describes such a paternal figure in an account of her own family.

I belong to a family of ten children. As small children, we lived in constant dread of our father. We dared not disobey him. As long as I can remember, my mother inculcated in us a deep respect for our father. She pictured him as the best man in the world to whom all respect was due.

Father was quiet and appeared to be stern. He seldom punished us, nor did he show any interest in the everyday happenings of our childhood. In fact, he spent little time with us. Hence, we children gave all our love to our mother who was kind and gentle.

Father always had his way. He insisted that mother cook his meals. He was very methodical, rising early in the morning and having his breakfast always at the same time each day. The servants took care of us and cooked our meals. But nobody except mother could take care of father.

The husband is traditionally the breadwinner and he generally turns over his earnings to his wife, since she does most of the spending. She is not supposed to refuse her husband's request for money, although she often does so if she suspects that it is to be used on another woman or for drinking.[27] Men who keep their earnings and dole out small sums daily are considered miserly.[28]

In the rural economy from which many Mexicans came, the father had little difficulty in maintaining his position as economic

---

[25] Oscar Lewis, "Husband and Wives in a Mexican Village: A Study of Role Conflict," *American Anthropologist* (October-December, 1949), 51:602.

[26] *Ibid.*, p. 605.

[27] *Ibid.*, p. 604.

[28] *Ibid.*

provider. The frugal, industrious wife, of course, contributed her services and often managed to save some money. Very often in the transplanted family the husband's economic role is challenged. During long periods of unemployment, his wife and children manage to earn enough to supply the family's pressing needs, while the husband loses status. The oldest son, especially, tends to supersede the father as protector of the younger children inasmuch as he is better acquainted with American culture.[29]

The unemployed Mexican father rarely performs any household task, except for making occasional repairs. He is averse to doing "women's work." Even though his wife has to act in the capacity of economic provider, she is still responsible for household duties. Unskilled Mexican laborers working at a large institution in Texas berated their fellow man who had to manage heavy machinery in the laundry. To the yardmen, washing clothes was women's work and any man who worked in a laundry—regardless of the nature of his work—was unfortunate. In order to placate the laundry worker, provision had to be made to allow him to spend time working in the yard periodically.

A sickly, unemployed Mexican father indicated his conception of his own importance by the following statement to a social worker who made inquiries about the health of the rest of the family.

"Oh, yes, they are fine. My wife is young, you know. She was only eighteen when we married and she just had one right after another which was a little tough luck for me, but she was just young and never missed a one. My boys are in good shape, too."

To show me the condition of his boys, he called one of the larger ones over and took off his shirt, showing me how well built he was. I commented that the boy looked strong.

"Yes, he is, and they all are," replied Mr. D. "You know, they get some of that from me, too; it's not all from their mother. She is big and fat, but I am strong. I must be or I would be dead from this ulcer after

[29] Burma, *Spanish-Speaking Groups in the United States, op. cit.*, p. 86.

so many years. They have good bones and they get them from me. Their mother has weak bones."

Throughout the discussion, Mrs. D. was present and listening, but she made no comment whatever.

Another man might think bearing ten children would be a "little tough" on the mother, but not this father who was a poor provider. That the wife made no rejoinder is typical. In front of outsiders the father is not to be contradicted or questioned.

In order to maintain status, the traditional father may resort to wife-beating. This occurs most frequently when he is drunk. Sometimes, however, a man gets violent over his wife's neglect of such responsibilities as preparing a hot meal or having clean clothes ready for him. Suspicion of adultery is a major cause of wife-beating.[30] The wife is not supposed to fight back or report the incident to civil authorities.[31]

The following account of a Mexican woman's attitude toward her husband's severity is reported by an American-born woman who extended an invitation to her Mexican friend:

"Oh, I can't," Adela told me, importantly. "I'm being punished."

"Punished? For what?"

"I had permission to use Roberto's car yesterday until six, but I didn't get home until seven. He was so jealous! So he locked me in my room, and here I am."

"Well, climb out of the window! I never heard of such a thing!" I shouted, thoroughly outraged.

"Oh no," cried Adela. "I have to stay in my room three days. . . ." But she sounded very proud and happy, as indeed she was.

When after due chastisement, Roberto let her out . . . and she asked and was granted permission to come to see me, I asked what in the world she meant by this childish business of staying locked in her room.

Adela was eager to explain.

"Why I've been trying to make him jealous for *months*," she crowed,

[30] Lewis, *op. cit.*, p. 605.
[31] *Ibid.*

"and at last, when I came home so late and wouldn't say where I had been, he got really wild! It was wonderful."[32]

As noted previously[33] the father may traditionally engage in an extramarital affair, even though he beats his wife if he suspects her of doing in like manner. Although second- and third-generation Mexican women accept this cultural pattern, the acceptance is not as passive as it was traditionally. This change in attitude is evident in the following account:

Father had always been undisputed head of the family until he committed a serious offense against my mother. A strong family disagreement resulted. One of my brothers took my father's side, but the rest of us children stood beside mother. Mother was highly offended by father's action and terribly hurt to see one of her sons against her. As a result, she was transformed from a warm, submissive wife to a cold, authoritarian one. She told my father that she would no longer be under his yoke, and she has kept her word for the past six years. Today she has a strong voice—and sometimes the final one—in family affairs.

While the American father is traditionally expected to be active in the church, there is no parallel expectation of the Mexican father. Religion and the church are associated primarily with the role of women. The average Mexican adult male may value the proper rites of passage, but he is not renowned for his other religious observances. Contact with American patterns will hardly alter this traditional pattern, for the American male is not regarded as especially observant either.

Even though Mexican ethnics value marriage within the group, there may be some question of the advisability of a girl's marrying one of her own if she has an equally desirable American suitor. One girl in this predicament sought counsel of her father and was told that an American husband would be "better to her, less apt to associate familiarly with other women, help with the housework, and

---

[32] De Treviño, *My Heart Lies South, op. cit.,* pp. 171-172.
[33] See Chapter 10, p. 203; Chapter 12, p. 261.

share the care of the children." When the time for decision came, however, the girl chose to marry within the ethnic group.

The traditional Mexican father is generally unwilling to allow his adult children complete economic independence. If possible, he will take his sons to work with him and collect one pay check. Even married sons feel obliged to continue this practice. When a third-generation Mexican couple wished to marry, the girl's parents gave their consent only on condition that she continue to surrender her pay check. More often it is the young man's parents who make such stipulations, for it is still customary for the married sons to bring their wives to the paternal home. This custom, however, is not as persistent as it was formerly.

The paternal developmental role, then, makes some allowances for children to keep part of their earnings and to make some decisions for themselves. Alterations in the traditional patterns, though, are due in large part to the fact that many Mexican fathers find it difficult to preserve status in an environment where tradition meets with constant challenges.

EUROPEAN PATERNAL ROLES

The traditional Southern European paternal role bears resemblance to that of other paternalistic societies. Family members, especially the young, were expected to obey "him who stood at the head of the family, him whom they were to approach always in fear and with respect as the source of all authority."[34] Among South Italians it is still customary for a child to obtain the father's blessing before undertaking an enterprise.[35] Paternal authority over a child is traditionally regarded as absolute, at least until the latter's mar-

---

[34] Handlin, *The Uprooted, op. cit.*, p. 241.
[35] Williams, *South Italian Folkways in Europe and America, op. cit.*, p. 76.

riage. Even after marriage this authority may be maintained to a high degree.[36]

Culture permits aggressive domination by the father of his wife and children.[37] It seems as though the Italian father may be rather severely tyrannical without incurring the general disapproval of the group.[38] In America, too, the father may assert his right to force a child into any occupation, to select a marital partner for him, and to beat him.[39] The wife, too, is expected to be subject to the authority of her husband. If she questions his authority, her waywardness is blamed on lack of discipline in childhood.[40]

The patriarchal pattern of many European families is radically altered when the husband takes his place in the industrial economy of the American community. The father is more respected than consciously feared or imitated.[41] He often loses status as his wife and children become acquainted with American patterns and begin to adopt them.[42] Very often, the father merely makes a pretense of maintaining his former status.

Among the Poles and Russians in Yankee City, the husband retains his dominance rather completely. Greek women, however, participate more actively in the economic system than do the Polish and Russian women.[43] As a consequence, the Greek women assert themselves more than the women in the other two ethnic groups. The Greek husbands, though, make an attempt to keep their women identified with the home.[44]

[36] Child, *Italian or American?* op. cit., p. 27.

[37] *Ibid.*, p. 30.

[38] *Ibid.*, p. 27.

[39] *Ibid.*

[40] Williams, *South Italian Folkways in Europe and America*, op. cit., p. 93.

[41] Campisi, "Ethnic Family Patterns," *American Journal of Sociology*, op. cit., 53:445.

[42] *Ibid.*, p. 444.

[43] W. Lloyd Warner and Leo Srole, *The Social Systems of American Ethnic Groups*, "Yankee City Series," III, New Haven, Yale University Press, 1945, p. 109.

[44] *Ibid.*

Despite the fact that the women of all ethnic groups in Yankee City—except among the long established Irish and Jewish groups—are gainfully employed, this work does not alter perceptibly the husband's domination of his wife.[45] The husband generally controls the purse and portions out small sums for immediate needs. As a rule, he makes all important purchases, including clothing and furniture.[46]

Like their Mexican sisters, the Greek women of Yankee City are the more ardent family church members. Yet, even within the church structure the Greek women have no status except through their husbands. Only men are recognized as church members, and the women sit in a reserved section of the church during services. Woman's role is a passive one, while the men chant the responses.[47]

ROLE OF THE JEWISH FATHER

Traditionally, the Jewish father's role was similar to that found in the European family. The father's authority over his child was uncontested and almost supreme. Abraham, for example, was ready to sacrifice Isaac, his son. Sometimes children were seized in payment for debts, since children were regarded as the property of their fathers.[48]

Children were expected to honor and respect their parents as God's representatives on earth, and severe punishments were prescribed by law for those children who disobeyed or cursed their parents. A child who struck a parent, for instance, might be put to death.[49]

Among some first-generation and orthodox Jews the father has

[45] *Ibid.,* p. 110.
[46] *Ibid.,* p. 108.
[47] *Ibid.,* p. 110.
[48] "Family and Family Life," *The Jewish Encyclopedia, op. cit.,* 5:336.
[49] *Ibid.,* p. 337.

retained many of his traditional prerogatives. The daughter in such a family gives the following description of her home life.

The home life of myself and my three sisters and four brothers was one in which my father, an orthodox Jew, was the central and controlling figure. As is traditional in Jewish home life, my mother's duties and practices followed the pattern prescribed by my father. There was no question in our home of noncompliance on the part of any of us in the religious behavior set down by my father which, among other things, included Sabbath observance, the dietary laws, and daily prayers.

As this family exemplifies, the father's primary role appears to be a religious one. He is accountable before God and the community for the Jewish character of his household; hence, the "socioreligious activities are the crucial functions of the male."[50]

In Eastern European Jewish communities the father's authority rests upon "the quality of his intellect, upon his moral character and his ability to guide and inspire the child."[51] He may be physically strong or frail, assertive or gentle by nature, a good or a bad provider, and nevertheless retain his status. Under all circumstances he tends to remain titular head of the family, for his authority is not measured in terms of superior physical power or economic services.[52]

The father may also be the chief disciplinarian in the family. Such was the case in the first-generation family of Mary Antin.

The real disciplinarian in our family was my father. Present or absent, it was fear of his displeasure that kept us in the straight and narrow path. In the minds of us children he was as much represented, when away from home, by the strap hanging on the wall as by his portrait which stood on a parlor table. . . . Almost everybody's father had a strap, but our father's strap was more formidable than the ordinary.[53]

---

[50] Theodore Bienenstok, "Antiauthoritarian Attitudes in the Eastern European *Shtetel* Community," *American Journal of Sociology* (September, 1951), 57:153. The *Shtetel* is a small Jewish community in Eastern Europe.

[51] *Ibid.*, p. 152.

[52] *Ibid.*, p. 153.

[53] Antin, *The Promised Land, op. cit.*, p. 70.

More often, however, the father has very little to do with the child's early training, except that which is religious in nature. Even in Europe, the father was away from home much of the time, trying to earn a living for his family.[54] Mary Antin's grandfather, for example, was a country peddler who "was doing well if he got home for the holidays with a little white flour for a cake, and money enough to take his best coat out of pawn."[55] Her father who acted as disciplinarian of the children did not learn this role from his father.

In giving orders, the father seldom demands unquestioning obedience, nor does he tend to interpret a disregard of his wishes as a slur upon his authority.[56] Unhesitant acquiescence is generally expected only when there is a question of preserving the traditional way of life.[57] Nonrepressive methods and persuasion are generally preferred to coercion. Corporal punishment is a last resort, rather than a primary disciplinary measure.[58] According to the following statement by a Minneapolis Jew, some fathers may think they should discipline the first child, but later relinquish the practice.

My wife and I have a happy home. Externally I'm supposed to be the head of the house. But she certainly has as much influence as I. She isn't as strict a disciplinarian as I am. I used to punish my first child on occasion, but I have never given the others a licking.[59]

The Jews of Yankee City are fairly representative of those ethnics who have been in America for generations. Hence, they typify a further developmental phase than the more recent immigrants from Eastern Europe. Among the Yankee City group, wives have a marked subordination to their husbands, but it is not as strong as in the traditional Jewish family structure. The roles of husband

---

[54] Cf. Gordon, *Jews in Transition, op. cit.,* p. 193.
[55] Antin, *op. cit.,* pp. 44-45.
[56] Bienenstok, *op. cit.,* p. 154.
[57] *Ibid.*
[58] *Ibid.,* p. 155.
[59] Gordon, *op. cit.,* p. 259.

and wife are as reciprocal as those of the modern American family. Both parents share authority and control. The wives make most of the purchases for the family, except for real property and the family car. They have leisure time and have ceased to be identified with the personalities of their husbands. Only in the synagogue has the male retained traditional status.[60]

NEGRO FATHER

The subordinate position of the Negro father has its roots in history and tradition. During slavery, the father's function was biological rather than sociological or economical. The mother reared and cared for the children, and they were considered hers.[61] The father's name was seldom indicated on the records of the plantation; the children were listed as belonging to the mother.[62] In many instances children did not know who their father was; when he did live with them, he had little authority.[63] The slave owner could take the mother for his concubine, or separate the mother from the father without any interference from the latter.

With emancipation, some Negro men had become so accustomed to this pattern that they made little effort to alter it.[64] Other men, however, had assimilated the sentiments and family ideals of the dominant group and made every effort to strengthen their paternal position.[65] Even during slavery, some freedmen had purchased freedom for their wives and children.[66] Shortly after they emerged

---

[60] Warner and Srole, op. cit., pp. 115-116.
[61] Cf. King, "The Negro Maternal Family," Social Forces, op. cit., 24:101.
[62] Davie, Negroes in American Society, op. cit., p. 207.
[63] Ibid.
[64] King, op. cit., p. 101.
[65] Frazier, The Negro Family in United States, op. cit., p. 130.
[66] Ibid., p. 134.

from slavery, those Negroes who enjoyed social and economic advantages developed a "feeling of solidarity and some community of interest under the authority and discipline of the father."[67] They purchased land and attempted to set up the family on a traditional institutional basis. The man who claimed ownership of his wife and children had a substantial claim to authority.[68] Most of these families became the backbone of the Negro middle classes.

For many Negro fathers, however, it was difficult to adjust to the responsibilities of family headship. They did not attempt to assert themselves, but were content to leave the family authority in the hands of their women.[69]

Tradition and personality have not been the only factors responsible for the Negro father's position. One authority believes the "real key to the organization of the Negro family today is found in the relative economic positions of men and women."[70] The average Negro woman is capable of economic independence. Even on the farm where the father assumes greater economic responsibility for his family, the woman works in the field and contributes a "man's share" to the purse. In towns and villages she has a definite advantage over her husband. Negro men have "suffered from irregularity of employment and from actual unemployment more than any other segment of America's lower class."[71] They have never been able as a group to obtain and hold good jobs long enough "to build a solid economic base for family support."[72] Lack of economic opportunity and poor education have undoubtedly been important factors in the Negro father's status. He roams around to find work,

[67] *Ibid.*, p. 132.
[68] *Ibid.*, p. 140.
[69] King, *loc. cit.*
[70] Charles S. Johnson, *Growing Up in the Black Belt*, Washington, American Council on Education, 1941, p. 59.
[71] St. Clair Drake and Horace R. Cayton, *Black Metropolis*, New York, Harcourt, Brace & Co., 1945, p. 582.
[72] *Ibid.*

and may keep roving—deserting his family and preventing the formation of a stable family organization.[73]

The Negro mother, on the other hand, procures domestic work with relative ease.[74] Even during the dark days of the depression she "brought home the butter in the bag."[75] The white families for whom Negro women work tend to give cast-off clothing and left-overs from the table to the Negro domestics. Hence, both husband and children came to look upon the mother as the economic support when the family migrated to larger communities.

Insecure in their economic position, men may trade love for a living.[76] Negro lower-class women look to them for affectional and sexual satisfaction, and the men often take advantage of the situation. Even though a man may be able to contribute substantially toward family support, he may not do so, as in the following instance.

After living in the community for some time, Mrs. S. took up living with George T. There is no issue from the present liaison; however, it is of great advantage to Mr. T. as he has a woman to care for his home and he enjoys all the advantages of married life but does not contribute greatly to the support of the home. He provides a roof for himself, his common-law wife and her children. Mr. T. states that he sees no reason why he should contribute to the support of Mrs. S. or her children. He donates a five-dollar bill occasionally for groceries, which just about takes care of his own food. His wife works as a part-time maid at various places and spends the main portion of her earnings for the home expenses as well as for clothing. Mr. T. has this attitude despite the fact that he has a bank account and has just received $1,000 in severance pay from his government job.

The lower-class Negro man may act on the assumption that his family does not need him. A woman seldom forces a father to sup-

[73] *Ibid.*, p. 583.
[74] Johnson, *op. cit.*, p. 59.
[75] Drake and Cayton, *op. cit.*, p. 583.
[76] *Ibid.*, p. 584.

port her or the children; legal recourse is expensive and violates tradition.[77] Nor does she expect complete sexual fidelity. As long as he is sober, does not beat her nor lavish his money on other women, she may think of him as a "good old man."[78]

[77] Johnson, *op. cit.*, p. 59.
[78] Drake and Cayton, *op. cit.*, p. 586.

12

Maternal Role

AMERICAN MOTHERS

THE solidarity of the American family, as previously noted, rests to a large extent on companionship and affectional ties. Traditional feminine roles (see Table 2) have been altered, and the contemporary woman is expected to be efficient not only as a mother and housewife but also as a companion to her husband. Companionship "develops out of mutual affection and intimate association."[1] Demonstrations of affection are expected, and gifts on such occasions as anniversaries, birthdays, or after an absence from home are taken as a matter of course.[2]

While the wifely aspects of her role are never dormant, they tend to be superseded by the maternal aspects when there are small children. The average mother usually cares for the personal needs of her children without the assistance of nurses or governesses. Hence, strong emotional bonds tend to exist between mother and children.[3] In fact, the mother has assumed functions which were traditionally associated with the father, especially in respect to authority. So marked has this trend been that, in the opinion of many Europeans, American society is "dominated by petticoats." Not

[1] Burgess and Locke, *The Family, op. cit.,* p. 27.
[2] See Chapter 8, p. 161.
[3] Cavan, *op. cit.,* pp. 156-157.

TABLE 2. Typical Responses of Respondents Revealing Traditional and Developmental Conceptions of a Good Mother[a]

Respondent	Traditional Role Conceptions	Developmental Role Conceptions
Father	1. Keeps the home properly	1. Gives the child of her time in way the child wishes
	2. Teaches daughter homemaking	2. Educates the children to think for themselves
	3. Is a good cook and housekeeper	3. Leads the family into coöperative planning
	4. Teaches child religion	4. Helps the father understand the daughter
	5. Provides wholesome meals	5. Has outside interests, P.T.A., etc.
Mother	1. Tries to teach children proper manners	1. Attempts to understand the child and his needs
	2. Puts family needs and welfare ahead of her own	2. Builds up wholesome family relationships
	3. Cooks good healthy meals	3. Shares and coöperates with the child
	4. Teaches religious values	4. Strives to understand the child's point of view
	5. Sets a good example	5. Aids in civic ventures for betterment of the community
Adolescent	1. Cares for the house and cooks	1. Respects children's feelings and listens to their troubles
	2. Is a good wife and mother	2. Plays and has fun with children
	3. Keeps the house neat and clean	3. Allows children to share family pleasures and responsibilities
	4. Teaches children right from wrong	4. Provides children with plenty of love and affection
	5. Is a good example	5. Tries to keep up with current times and ideas

[a] Table derived from study by Connor, et al., "Parent-Adolescent Relationships," *Journal of Home Economics, op. cit.,* 46:189.

only the daughters but also the sons are under "almost undiluted feminine authority" in the home as well as in the school.[4]

In addition to child care, the mother in the majority of American

[4] Clyde Kluckhohn, *Mirror for Man, op. cit.,* p. 231; Gorer, *The American People, op. cit.,* pp. 58-59.

families does most of the cooking, laundering, cleaning, and shopping. Domestics may come in once or twice a week to help with the heavy work or to do a thorough job of cleaning—if the family can afford it. Labor-saving devices are rather common and lighten the work of most housewives. Some women prefer these devices to having domestic help. Attitudes toward doing domestic work vary. While such work may be looked upon as an isolating and interminable chore, most women accept it as one of the wifely functions.[5] Most American women are not overburdened with such work, but have leisure time at their disposal, especially after the children reach school age.

Leisure time activities range from listening to the radio or watching television in the home to active participation in social, civic, and educational groups. Americans tend to be "joiners" and they usually belong to several clubs, depending upon their interests. The alleged supremacy of American women is based partially on their influence in schools, churches, and in economic life. Statistics of property ownership, insurance, and education attest women's importance. There are, moreover, "a hundred magazines designed especially for their entertainment or edification." Most metropolitan papers have a page for women, and "every radio station a series of programs directed exclusively to their supposed needs."[6] Since women spend most of the money,[7] the overwhelming body of advertisements is directed to them. Women in other cultures may be the rulers in the homes, but in America they also "design it, build it, furnish it, direct its activities, and fix its standards."[8]

The middle-aged American women whose husbands are good providers and whose children are grown are said to be "favored

[5] Cf. Mirra Komarovsky, *Women in the Modern World*, Boston, Little, Brown & Co., 1953, p. 97.

[6] Commager, *The American Mind, op. cit.,* p. 424.

[7] Gorer, *op. cit.,* p. 61, notes that market researchers estimate that women make more than three fourths of the retail purchases in the United States.

[8] Commager, *op. cit.,* p. 424.

beyond any such great numbers of women in any other part of the world"[9] in that their lives are often a "round of card parties and clubs and window shopping and movies."[10] Very often, however, the middle-aged American woman who has centered her interests in her children feels a loss of function and status when the children marry and leave home. In other cultures, especially the Chinese, middle age is marked by high status inasmuch as the mother then has not only her grown sons, but also her daughters-in-law under her roof and authority. Many American homes, however, become "empty" when the children have married and settled elsewhere.

Another threat which often accompanies middle age is the fear that loss of physical appeal will lessen the husband's affection. Every average woman tends to spend considerable time and money on enhancing or preserving her physical charms. She does not, as a rule, resent the admiration of her charms by strangers or the general public.[11] Adulation is acceptable, whatever the source. The popularity of beauty contests, even on a nationwide scale, is an indication of prevalent attitudes. Not only the young unmarried girl is crowned "Miss Sweet Potato" or "Apple Blossom Queen" or "Maid of Cotton," but the married woman also vies with other housewives for the title of "Mrs. U.S.A." The mother and housewife often feels that she must retain her physical attractiveness in order to keep her husband's affection and interest.

America is noted for her beautiful women, and much value is placed on physical attractiveness. A Frenchman remarked on the wartime custom of having orchestras conducted by pretty women, even when they were ignorant of music. "The public did not come so much for the music as to eye delicious figures," he noted.[12]

[9] Benedict, "The Family: Genus Americanum," *op. cit.*, p. 167.

[10] *Ibid.*, pp. 163-164.

[11] Hsu, *Americans and Chinese, op. cit.*, p. 155, contrasts the ideas of the Chinese woman with those of the American women. The former would consider it an insult if she were admired by a total stranger.

[12] Duteil, *The Great American Parade, op. cit.*, p. 175.

In the face of all this physical appeal, the American housewife feels that she must strive to keep her husband's interest and affec-

"So you're Rexford's new secretary! I'd never have recognized you from his description!" (Courtesy of George Wolfe and *The Saturday Evening Post.*)

tion. The women he meets at work are often regarded as competitors, too. One type of American sales girl has been classified as

"The Charmer" because she focuses attention upon herself. "People do things for me, especially men," said one charmer, "when I give them that slow smile and look up through my lashes."[13]

In addition to being a homemaker, the contemporary American woman may work outside the home. The number of married women in the labor force has been gradually increasing until today nearly one third of the total labor force is comprised of women—twice as big a proportion as sixty years ago.[14] If there are small children it is deemed inadvisable to deprive them of a mother's care, unless the income is low or uncertain. However, a career-minded mother who is highly trained may wish to work outside the home despite the fact that her husband is a good provider and that her children are small.[15] Widowed, divorced, or separated women may have to support themselves and their children. Women workers tend to be concentrated in occupations closely allied to the traditional homemaking roles such as employment in teaching, nursing, domestic service, or as waitresses, beauticians, dieticians, and so forth.

When women began to work outside the home, they began to effect a change in status. Chaperons, of course, could not escort the teacher or saleslady to her job, and the convention against ladies appearing unescorted in public became a thing of the past. The new-style feminist, according to one analyst, differs from the old with respect to the emotional source of her career drive. It seems to stem from a positive interest in some field and a desire to achieve in it rather than from a revulsion against being a mere housewife.[16]

The American kinship pattern has contributed to the equality which American women have with their husbands. Other kinship systems tend to place a structural premium on the role of either

[13] Mills, *White Collar, op. cit.*, p. 175.
[14] "Women Executives," *Time* (January 11, 1954), 63:72.
[15] Sirjamaki, *The American Family in the Twentieth Century, op. cit.*, p. 91.
[16] Komarovsky, *Women in the Modern World, op. cit.*, pp. 96-97.

sex in the maintenance of the continuity of kinship relations.[17] In the American system, however, the multilineal pattern favors equally both parties to a marriage.

Isolation from other members of the consanguinal family is another factor which contributes to the equality of husband and wife. Within the confines of the small conjugal unit the emotional needs for response and security are ordinarily satisfied. Since these needs tend to be best met on the basis of congeniality and companionship, the situation usually fosters equality between the spouses.

Companionship of husband and wife also implies equality. In middle-class urban American society it is customary to invite both husband and wife to any mixed social gathering, whether it be a card party, a dance, a dinner, or any similar occasion. American culture also tends to consider as ideal the marriage relationship in which joint decisions are reached—a possible reflection of democratic values.

Government machinery has gradually equalized the civil rights of husbands and wives. In present-day America a married woman may make contracts and wills, sue and be sued, and own property in her own name. Other legal provisions, however, are of a protective nature and do not imply strict legal equality. Such, for example, are the provisions for economic support and alimony, both of which are the obligation of the husband.

Finally, there is in America a tradition of chivalry and romantic love, both of which are incompatible with the view that woman is "inferior." With the equality that American women have gained socially, politically, and economically, the tradition of chivalry might be expected to be extinct, but the elements of chivalry still govern

[17] Parsons, "Kinship Systems of the Contemporary United States," *American Anthropologist, op. cit.,* 28:33. For an analysis of Oriental impressions of American women's rights, see Herbert Passin and John W. Bennett, "The America-educated Japanese, I," *Annals of the American Academy of Political and Social Science* (September, 1954), 295:88.

to a certain extent the patterns of behavior between the sexes—to the woman's advantage.

ROLE OF ORIENTAL WOMEN

The role of the wife and mother among Orientals is a secondary one, for authority and prestige are vested primarily in the male. Since the wife is not considered her husband's equal, companionship is a negligible factor in family unity. Expressions of affection are almost never given publicly and seldom openly within the family circle. Husband and wife are supposed to "take each other for granted,"[18] and the latter must not let her love interfere with her husband's career, or with the duty he has toward his parents.[19]

Chinese written characters are indicative of the roles which are expected of family members. The symbol for "husband" means "the supporter," that for "married woman" is a combination of the symbols for "girl" and for "broom," and that for "father" indicates "handling a staff."[20]

Among the rural Chinese, most women tend to have a life of toil. The little girl is trained to gather fuel and herd cattle, while her mother not only cares for the house and the children, but also helps in the field.[21] Traditionally, the low status of women was attested to by such practices as abandoning or killing female babies; selling of women of all ages, even after the practice was made illegal; prohibiting women from having property rights; binding of women's feet; and forbidding the remarriage of widows.[22]

[18] Hsu, *Americans and Chinese, op. cit.,* p. 46.
[19] Yang, *A Chinese Village, op. cit.,* p. 54.
[20] Kang-Hu, "The Chinese Family System," *Annals of the American Academy of Political and Social Science, op. cit.,* 152:41.
[21] Kenneth S. Latourette, *The Chinese: Their History and Culture,* 3d ed., rev., New York, The Macmillan Co., 1946, p. 680.
[22] Lang, *Chinese Family and Society, op. cit.,* p. 332.

The Japanese woman seems to have greater freedom than other Asiatic women, but her position is nonetheless one of subordination. Female foot-binding has never been practiced and she can shop quite freely, carrying the family purse.[23] She seldom walks side by side with her husband, however, but follows a few paces behind him. She has never been as well educated as her brothers, for emphasis in her training is on etiquette and graceful movements.[24] A woman always bows lower than a man of the same social class, as an indication of her inferior position.[25]

The Oriental woman's role is viewed as one of childbearing and housekeeping, although she may also be expected to make a direct contribution toward family economic enterprises. Her status is enhanced when she bears a male child who will carry on the family name. Within the home she usually has the respect and affection of her children, even though the children are trained not to be demonstrative.

The Chinese woman may have to share her husband's affection with concubines, a situation which is traditionally accepted with equanimity. If the wife has borne no sons, a concubine may be taken at the insistence of the wife or of her husband's family. There is no sense of guilt,[26] but there may be a feeling of responsibility toward the family to insure male progeny. Of course, the family has to be economically able to purchase and support another woman, a fact which places a limitation on the practice. Concubinage is most frequent among army men, officials, and businessmen, and is viewed as less of a problem than divorce.[27] One authority predicts

[23] Benedict, *The Chrysanthemum and the Sword, op. cit.,* pp. 53-54.
[24] *Ibid.*
[25] Yoko Matsuoka, *Daughter of the Pacific,* New York, Harper & Brothers, 1952, p. 139.
[26] Hsu attributes this lack of a sense of guilt to the fact that Chinese culture is neither Christian nor Puritan. "The Family in China," *The Family: Its Function and Destiny,* ed. by Ruth N. Anshen, New York, Harper & Brothers, 1949, pp. 89-90.
[27] Lang, *op. cit.,* p. 221.

that the practice will probably "show a cultural lag in China for generations to come, even after technology, government, and other aspects of the culture have all undergone considerable modernization."[28]

Although the Chinese family is one of the strongest and most secure of all families, there are nonetheless some circumstances which are especially unfavorable to women. The young married woman who becomes a widow before she has borne a son may find herself a "surplus commodity" in her husband's family. She is likely to be disposed of at the first opportunity. The concubine, too, may be quite insecure in a household where she is unacceptable to the wife. If she bears no male children, her position may become untenable.[29]

As the Chinese family has developed, however, there have been many modifications of the traditional pattern. The older woman tends to acquire increased status when her sons bring their wives into her household. She becomes, in fact, a sort of dowager reigning over a large establishment.[30] The widowed woman is not always at the mercy of her husband's family, for although remarriage is still frowned upon, it does occur, nonetheless.[31] Urbanization and increasing contact with Western culture are making an impact on the status of women. Village girls are going to cities in order to find work and are experiencing more freedom in an urban environment.[32] City girls are receiving more education than formerly, and men of the younger generation have been making voluntary concessions to them.[33] In urban areas husbands and wives sometimes approach Western norms in that husbands consult their wives and even share activities outside the home with them.

[28] Hsu, "The Family in China," *op. cit.*, p. 90.
[29] *Ibid.*, pp. 80-81.
[30] *Ibid.*, p. 79.
[31] *Ibid.*
[32] *Ibid.*, p. 91. Hsu discusses the detrimental effects of Hollywood movies and of lack of family controls in the cities on the morals of the Chinese people.
[33] *Ibid.*, pp. 90-91.

The Japanese, however, have gone further than the Chinese in adapting to Western culture—a probable effect of World War II and the occupation of Japan. At a meeting in Tokyo in 1954, a group of Japanese women enumerated the following indications of progress: "divorce, women's suffrage, the acceptance of women in an ever expanding range of jobs (as legislators, police officers, taxi drivers, even judges), increased coeducation, the spread of women's clubs, and a general increased freedom for women to speak their minds."[34] Of course, tradition does not die without a struggle. Japanese feminists point out such problem areas as the continued sale of girls, male preference for geisha girls, unequal pay for women, and arranged marriages.[35]

The Oriental woman in America has retained many traditional aspects of the feminine role. It is as a mother that she gains status, and male progeny is a prerequisite for the fulfillment of her maternal function. Household duties are a concomitant responsibility which her husband seldom shares with her.

In addition to caring for her children and her home, the woman usually assists her husband in his work. The Chinese do not have a background of chivalry, and consequently no man, whatever his status, would normally consider his wife's economic activities as a threat. On the contrary, most Chinese in America expect their wives to contribute directly to the economy of the family. While American males may attribute the success of a woman to her feminine charms,[36] the Chinese male would hardly suspect his woman of resorting to such devices. The latter's charms are ordinarily displayed only to her husband.[37]

The Orientals in America have been so busy making a living under adverse or discriminatory circumstances that social activities have been relegated to a subordinate position. Traditionally, a wife

[34] "The Women," *Time* (April 26, 1954), 63:37.
[35] *Ibid.*, p. 38.
[36] Cf. Mills, *op. cit.*, p. 175.
[37] Cf. Hsu, *Americans and Chinese, op. cit.*, p. 155.

never assumes any share in her husband's social obligations.[38] In America she tends to have few opportunities to meet her husband's friends and business associates socially, and even though she has the opportunity, she usually prefers the company of women of her own group.[39]

If the mother spends much of her time working outside the home, a housekeeper may be employed. There is usually cheap labor available within the ethnic group, and the traditional family pattern makes provision for servants. Very often, however, the home adjoins the business establishment and the mother fulfills the domestic and the economic function simultaneously. Strangely enough, the kinds of business in which Orientals customarily engage—laundries, groceries, restaurants—would be considered "women's work" and beneath the dignity of the male in China.[40] In America, however, the Chinese father's decisions regarding business opportunities are governed by economic necessity and discrimination.

Mexican Maternal Role

The Mexican woman's place, like that of the Oriental, is traditionally within the home. She is expected to be submissive, faithful, devoted, and respectful toward her husband,[41] and to take the major responsibility for rearing the children. She is the chief reli-

[38] Confucius did not believe in the social intermingling of men and women and his example and teaching have had a marked influence on Chinese culture. Cf. Latourette, *op. cit.*, p. 678.

[39] Within the last century Chinese diplomats abroad had to inform the foreign offices of some of the Western countries to which they were attached that their wives could only associate with the women in the families of native officials. Hsu, "The Family in China," *op. cit.*, p. 88.

[40] Hsu, *Under the Ancestor's Shadow, op. cit.*, p. 262.

[41] Lewis, "Husbands and Wives in a Mexican Village," *American Anthropologist, op. cit.*, 51:602.

gious influence in the home and attempts to inculcate good morals in her children.[42] A good wife is not supposed to be critical, curious, or jealous of her husband's activities outside the home.[43] She is not expected to be a companion for her husband or to share in his activities in political, economic, or social life—unless they are home-centered. Women who overtly challenge the authority of their husbands, who "answer back," or offer resistance are criticized by women as well as by men.[44] Wives are even supposed to take their beatings without a struggle, and they seldom report such happenings outside the family system.[45]

The practice of chaperonage has certainly not fostered the development of the companionship role. A duenna accompanies the future wife in order to preserve the good name of the latter, and the kinds of association permitted between engaged couples is not conducive to companionship. It has been said that while the Mexican husband "makes an ideal lover because of his delicate attentions and consideration," he fails to make as satisfactory a husband inasmuch as he does not make his wife a companion or confidante.[46]

To a certain extent, the Mexican woman's traditional role is derived from Spanish and Aztec patterns. The inferior position of women in Spain was matched by their almost complete submission among the Aztecs.[47] It is believed that the Spanish were influenced by the Moors whose women went about with veils over their faces.[48]

Women in Mexico do very little reading, but they may belong to a club where other persons give them "book reviews." An Ameri-

[42] Burma, *Spanish-American Groups in the United States, op. cit.,* pp. 85-86.

[43] Lewis, *op. cit.,* p. 602.

[44] *Ibid.,* p. 603.

[45] Cf. *Ibid.,* p. 605; note also attitudes toward punishment, *supra,* Chapter 11, p. 235.

[46] Nevin O. Winter, *Mexico and Her People of To-Day,* Rev. ed., Boston, L. C. Page & Co., 1923, p. 173.

[47] Hayner, "Notes on the Changing Mexican Family," *American Sociological Review, op. cit.,* 7:489.

[48] Winter, *op. cit.,* p. 162.

can woman living in Mexico made the following observation: "Once during World War II when I said something about 'the war,' one of my sisters-in-law looked up from her mending to ask 'What war?'" Mexican women "are sorry if someone tells them that children are starving in Timbuktu, but they are so busy taking food to the families by the river bank who were flooded out of their homes . . . that they cannot be organized to do anything for Timbuktu."[49]

Many Mexican women in America assume roles according to the traditional pattern. They seldom assert themselves in public and rely on their husbands to take the initiative and represent the family in all matters outside the home. Inwardly, however, they may not be as submissive as they appear. The martyr complex is rather widespread among the women in Mexico. When they state that it is woman's unhappy lot to suffer at the hands of men, they give an indication of underlying conflicts between traditional and developmental roles.

The Mexican woman in the following case revealed hostile attitudes toward her husband when he was not present, but assumed a different role in his presence.

Mr. and Mrs. D. applied for financial assistance from a family agency because Mr. D. was ill and unable to work. There were seven children in the family and Mrs. D. was again pregnant. Mr. D. had a doctor's statement to the effect that he had an active duodenal ulcer and should not work for six weeks. It was evident that Mr. D. did not wish to put himself into the position of asking for help. He asked only that his family be helped, and said that he could stay with his mother.

At the time of the first home visit, Mrs. D. was at home alone; Mr. D. was at his mother's house. In talking with the wife I had the feeling that although she has a need for financial assistance, she still disliked having to ask for it or discuss it. She also showed some resentment toward her husband for being ill. In discussing his illness she said with a great deal of feeling, "He's been sick so long and he can only eat special food which

[49] De Treviño, *My Heart Lies South, op. cit.*, p. 165.

costs more than other food." I asked how long he has been ill and she said, "Oh, he has always had something wrong with his stomach."

Later, when Mr. and Mrs. D. came to the office Mr. D. was friendly and very talkative while his wife, who was also friendly, hardly spoke unless asked a question. She had talked a great deal when I visited the home and her husband was not there.

The woman who is too submissive, even in Mexico, may be regarded more as a fool than as an ideal. Women take pride in being able to assert themselves sometimes. Conflicting attitudes are evident in the fact that while women unanimously prefer submissive daughters-in-law, they do not always advise their own daughters to practice submission.[50]

The daughter-in-law is traditionally expected to live in the home of her husband's parents or adjoining it, and she is expected to perform her share of burdensome household tasks. Her mother-in-law acts as chaperon and is sometimes compared with a "policeman." When children are born, it is the mother-in-law rather than the young wife's mother who has the major responsibilities toward the mother and child.[51]

When the Mexican woman advances in age, her status is enhanced as her sons bring their wives home. Sometimes the mother's authority over her son is respected long after he is married, as the following case testifies.

The patient is a thirty-year-old Latin-American dental technician who is married to a Latin-American girl by whom he has five children. The patient was the first child of his family to have been born in this country, after his parents moved here. He feels that his sisters and brothers are jealous of him because he is a citizen and they are not.

His parents were strict disciplinarians and he learned early to respect them and to obey without question. After his marriage his father moved to Chicago to live, while his mother lived with him and his wife. Patient continued to obey her strict discipline in his own home and felt some-

---

[50] Lewis, op. cit., p. 603.

[51] Oscar Lewis, Life in a Mexican Village: Tepoztlán Restudied, Urbana, University of Illinois Press, 1951, p. 347.

what hesitant to make decisions without his mother's opinion. He described many instances when upon arrival home, his mother would be waiting up for him because he had stayed out too late. He said "an awfully lot" was expected of him because he was the first of their children to be born in this country and it was necessary for him to try to satisfy his parents' expectations.

A widowed Mexican woman may assume headship of her family, even though this is customarily the role of the eldest son. A third-generation Texas Mexican girl, whose family followed the traditional patterns in most other respects, indicates the role of her widowed mother in the following words:

My father died when his oldest child was twenty. He had planned to sell his grocery business in a small town and move to the nearby city, but he died suddenly about a month before we were to move. Although I had four grown brothers, my mother took over as the head of our family the day father died. Since that day, eighteen years ago, she has been father, mother, counselor, businesswoman, financier, etc., for our family. We moved as father had planned. My mother provided us with the opportunity to get a good education although it meant many sacrifices.

The Mexican woman may have the discomfort of knowing that her husband has a mistress. Most Latin-American women are brought up to expect infidelities, and they generally swallow their resentment and seek solace in their families or in church work. It is some consolation to know that their position as wives is unassailable, for divorce is not common[52] in the mother country. In America, however, women offer more resistance to their husbands' amorous expeditions.

Traditionally, the Mexican woman's role is one of subordination. Developmentally, however, she may be somewhat assertive beneath her passive exterior. An indication that her individuality is not completely merged in that of her husband is evident in the practice of retaining her own family name when she takes the name of her

[52] Maria Flores, *The Woman with the Whip: Eva Peron*, New York, Doubleday & Company, Inc., 1952, p. 38.

spouse.[53] The more assimilated the Mexican woman in America becomes, the more she tends to deviate from the traditional pattern.

EUROPEAN ROLES

Most European women are traditionally dependent upon and subordinate to their husbands. Again, woman's role is primarily that of homemaker. She is expected to be occupied, as is her German sister, with the three K's—*Kirche* (church), *Küche* (kitchen), and *Kinder* (children),[54] not with business and politics which are traditionally a man's sphere. In taking charge of the household, she generally holds the family purse. Italian women, it is said, have two outstanding functions: taking charge of their husbands' earnings and selecting wives for their sons.[55] The latter function has become less important in the American environment, but the Italian mother still manages the purse. She buys provisions and clothing, and plays an important role in dispensing funds for the children's needs. Traditionally, the unmarried child who is a wage-earner is expected to give his pay check to his mother,[56] but in the developmental Italian family this pattern has been altered.

The Greek women in Yankee City are not expected to be interested in anything outside of the home and children. There are no social organizations for women, and women themselves comment that "they aren't smart enough" for organized activities. They define their own role in these words: "Greek women . . . just stay at home, that's what they are for, to keep house and take care of the children."[57] Greek husbands, of course, do not encourage their wives

---

[53] Cf. Robert C. Jones, "Ethnic Family Patterns: The Mexican Family in the United States," *American Journal of Sociology* (May, 1948), 53:451.

[54] Anita Daniel, "It's Still the Three K's in Germany," *The New York Times Magazine*, March 28, 1954, p. 19.

[55] Williams, *South Italian Folkways in Europe and America, op. cit.*, p. 77.

[56] *Ibid.*

[57] Warner and Srole, *The Social Systems of American Ethnic Groups, op. cit.*, p. 109.

to participate in community social or political life. They believe that one trouble in America is that women have too much power. The women who vote, according to one spokesman in Yankee City, should be made to serve in the army. After work hours, the husband may seek social relaxation outside the home, but he expects his wife to remain at home with the children.[58]

The second-generation Italian woman receives a more formalized education than her mother, whose education was centered around homemaking.[59] She may also work for wages and belong to some clubs.[60] Among all the ethnic groups in Yankee City except the Irish and Jews, some first-generation wives are gainfully employed. As a rule, though, they are women whose children are in their teens or whose husbands are unemployed. In the first instance, the wife is not needed in the home as much as the woman with small children, and in the latter instance she is working to meet a critical situation.[61] Regardless of the circumstances, though, the ethnic wife seldom challenges her husband's dominant role.[62]

Second-generation Russian Molokans are less submissive, however. One employed wife remarked that as long as she worked outside the home her husband should "pitch in and help at home," and when she was tired he should "be willing to go to a restaurant."[63] The Molokan peasant woman, however, has a higher status by virtue of her religion than do other Russian women.[64]

Employment outside the home often serves as a wedge in giving the ethnic woman associations beyond the family and household. The Polish women of Yankee City, for instance, were ready to form an ethnic association for women after they began to work for wages.

Most Southern and Eastern European ethnic women feel little

---

[58] *Ibid.*

[59] Campisi, "Ethnic Family Patterns," *American Journal of Sociology, op. cit.,* 53:445.

[60] *Ibid.,* p. 444.

[61] Warner and Srole, *op. cit.,* pp. 109-110.

[62] *Ibid.,* p. 110.

[63] Young, *The Pilgrims of Russian Town, op. cit.,* p. 105.

[64] *Ibid.,* p. 107.

concern over the possibility of losing their husbands' affections. A Polish woman stated that within her group a wife "doesn't have to 'keep' her husband; it's all settled when they're married."[65] Most Italians feel the same way. Although they are generally demonstrative in speech and action, it is not customary among the first generation to show affection openly. They may tolerate some display of affection among their second-generation married children, but do not indulge in it themselves.[66]

First-generation European wives tend to be more subordinate to their husbands than the American wife and less subordinate than the Oriental or Latin-American woman. On the whole, European families seem to have a faster rate of assimilation than other ethnic types, and as the families become second- and third-generation Americans they tend to approximate more closely American family roles.

The Jewish Maternal Figure

Traditionally, the Jewish woman never approaches the status of her husband. Like the Chinese woman, her position depends to a large extent upon her motherhood, and the birth of a male child contributes considerably to status. Care of the household and of the children is primarily the mother's responsibility. She is the parent with whom the child has the most intimate contacts throughout childhood. Her "songs, lullabies, words of endearment, and admonition guide and direct the child toward the speedy acquisition of speech."[67] The mother not only clothes, feeds, and disciplines the child, but she also teaches him his prayers and trains him in Jewish ritual.

[65] Benedict, "The Family: Genus Americanum," op. cit., p. 164.
[66] Campisi, op. cit., p. 445.
[67] Bienenstok, "Authoritarian Attitudes in the Eastern European Shtetel Community," American Journal of Sociology, op. cit., 57:151.

The Jewish woman has an important religious function, according to one authority, since "the most impressive indications of Sabbath observance have always been of a domestic character."[68] Restoring the Sabbath to the Jewish home is believed to be "basic in any attempt to reinstate the Sabbath in modern Jewish living."[69]

An American Jewish mother tells of her own childhood religious training in the following words:

My oldest brother was coached very carefully from early childhood so that he could ably carry on the traditions of our religion. I recall how much pleasure my father derived at religious ceremonies, both at home and in the synagogue, when my brother was given the responsibility of reciting portions of special prayers.

As for the rest of us, we were all given instruction in Hebrew, read from the Scriptures assisted by a religious teacher, and were expected to participate at all ceremonies. At this point, I would like to say that it was expected that male children would assume a greater responsibility in connection with orthodox practices.

I know that I can never give to my children the spirit and devotion to our religion that we had from our parents. However, I am trying to teach my children, as Jews, to understand their background and history, and to follow the principal tenets of Judaism.

Traditionally, the Eastern European Jewish mother was both father and mother to her children inasmuch as the father was out of the home much of the time. Many Jewish fathers were peddlers, or they worked long hours in the factory, and therefore had little opportunity for establishing intimate relationships with the children.[70] An American Jew whose father came from Europe stated that the older men "didn't know the most elementary things about taking care of the house." He recalled the incident of a leaking faucet in his own home. "Mother asked father to fix the faucet, but

---

[68] Samuel H. Markowitz, *Leading a Jewish Life in the Modern World*, Cincinnati, Union of American Hebrew Congregation, 1942, p. 117; see also *supra*, Chapter 9, pp. 180-181.

[69] *Ibid.*

[70] Cf. Gordon, *Jews in Transition, op. cit.*, p. 193.

he didn't know how to replace the washer." According to this informant, the second-generation fathers seldom feel that they have any role in the household, either. This attitude is to be expected in view of the fact that some men tend to pattern their own roles after those of their fathers.

The Jewish mother is generally so occupied with domestic duties that she has no time for social life outside the home. In addition to household duties she may share the management of the family's business, but she seldom belongs to clubs or societies. Social life consists primarily in visiting relatives or neighbors and in attending the synagogue.[71]

Traditionally, then, the mother is the parent who shares the children's experiences and establishes close emotional ties with them. A Polish Jewess relates the role which her mother played.

With my adolescent life began a new task for mother. She became the buffer in our family life. I cannot think of mother except as of one who always stood between us and some unhappiness, or father. It was she who made it her task to explain us to father, to soften him to our desires.[72]

The mother assumed the role of buffer even though she herself could not speak English nor understand many of her daughter's ambitions. Insight into the intimate mother-daughter relationship is evident in the following passage:

Mother and I were always chums. Though she could not read one word of English there was not one book I read of which she did not know the narrative. She knew my "marks" at school. She knew my friends. She hated and loved my teachers as I did. It was as if she lived my life with me.[73]

The mother gloried in her daughter's success, and the relationship

[71] *Ibid.*, p. 194.
[72] Stern, *My Mother and I, op. cit.*, p. 76.
[73] *Ibid.*, p. 86.

between mother and daughter grew closer as new horizons became visible.

Mother and I grew closer than ever before. She was intensely proud of me. She would stand on the corner with her purchases of fish and chickens for the Sabbath and flaunt my wisdom and my knowledge before all her cronies. Every one knew when I won a prize, or read a "paper," or passed an examination. To mother there was but one student at high school, and that student was her daughter.[74]

Although first- or second-generation Jewish families are still tradition-oriented, there are many Jews who have long resided in America.[75] As the Jewish family has developed among the latter, it has become similar to that of the American family. The status of the Jewish woman in Minneapolis has changed perceptibly from the European pattern,[76] and the same holds true for the Jews of Yankee City.

It is generally easier for the Jewish family to adapt to the American economy and its concomitant network of relationships because the Jews, unlike other European immigrants, did not come from an agrarian economy. In contrast to other ethnic women, the Jewish woman did not become increasingly dependent upon her husband because she was insecure in a nonrural environment. The wife traditionally managed the household and the purse, and in America she continues to do so.[77] The Jewish wife has been likened to the purchasing agent and business manager of the family corporation

[74] *Ibid.*, p. 98.
[75] It is estimated that there were two thousand Jews in America at the time of the Revolution. David Emanuel, a Jew, became governor of Georgia in 1801. Early in the nineteenth century large numbers of Sephardic Jews came to America and about the middle of the century many Jews came from Germany and Western Europe. These Jews have become largely assimilated. The Eastern European Jews came in the latter part of the century and early in the twentieth century. Cf. Heywood Broun and George Britt, *Christians Only,* New York, Vanguard Press, 1931, p. 34.
[76] Gordon, *op. cit.,* p. 193.
[77] Warner and Srole, *op. cit.,* p. 112.

in which her husband is banker. In Yankee City leisure time is at her disposal and she is not employed in the economic system of the community since employment is antithetical to middle-class standards.[78]

Leisure-time activities correspond to those of the typical middle-class American woman. In Minneapolis there are said to be "few organizations and causes of either a civic or national character, general or Jewish, in which Jewish women do not participate."[79] Very few important decisions in regard to cultural, religious, or philanthropic work in the Jewish community of Minneapolis are made without her advice and assistance.[80] Only in the synagogue has the Jewish woman made no advance, for according to law there is a sacred area of the congregation which is a community of males only.[81] In nearly every other respect, though, the Jewish "husband-wife reciprocal appears in a form indistinguishable from that of the modern American family with its more equitable sharing of authority and control."[82]

ROLE OF NEGRO WOMEN

The Negro maternal family is a heritage from slavery. In the plantation domestic establishment, the woman's role was more important than that of her husband. The cabin was hers and rations of corn and salt pork were issued to her. She cooked the meals, tended the vegetable patch, and often raised chickens to supplement the rations. If there was a surplus to sell, the money was hers.

[78] Ibid., pp. 112-113.
[79] Gordon, op. cit., p. 196.
[80] Ibid., p. 197.
[81] Warner and Srole, op. cit., p. 116. See account of "first woman cantor in Jewish history" in Reformed congregation, Oceanside, Long Island. "Woman Cantor," Time (August 15, 1955), 65:36.
[82] Ibid., p. 113.

She made the clothes and reared the children.[83] If the family received any special favors it was generally through her efforts.[84]

Among lower-class Negroes today the family is still more often dominated by the woman than by the man. The proportion of Negro women heads of families is very high when compared with other family types. If the family lives on a farm or plantation in the rural South, the father has more status than the father in a rural village or larger community.[85] In rural nonfarm areas Negro families with female heads constitute from 20 to 30 percent of the families.[86] In the cities of the South, nearly a third of the Negro families have women as the head.[87] Compared with white families, 10.3 percent of Negro females as against 6.5 percent of white women were heads of households, and 9 percent fewer Negro females were wives of households.[88]

Children tend to be regarded as a value in themselves, whether born within wedlock or not. This attitude, as previously noted, may have its roots in Negro history, for the slave woman's value was largely dependent upon her fertility. Women are often congratulated on the birth of a child, even though a marriage has not taken place, since motherhood "signifies maturity and the fulfilment of one's function as a woman."[89] The childless woman inspires disparagement as well as commiseration.[90] Children are usually no barrier to remarriage; Negro men are said to accept readily children by former marriages or even illegitimate children.[91]

---

[83] Davie, *Negroes in American Society, op. cit.,* p. 207.

[84] King, "The Negro Maternal Family," *Social Forces, op. cit.,* 24:101.

[85] Davie estimates from 3 to 15 percent of Negro families in rural farm areas are without male heads. *Op. cit.,* p. 209.

[86] Johnson, *Growing Up in the Black Belt, op. cit.,* p. 80. Davie estimates 15 to 25 percent.

[87] Frazier, "Ethnic Family Patterns: The Negro Family in the United States," *American Journal of Sociology, op. cit.,* 53:437.

[88] *Ibid.,* p. 436.

[89] Frazier, *The Negro Family in the United States, op. cit.,* p. 95.

[90] *Ibid.*

[91] Johnson, *op. cit.,* p. 59.

As indicated earlier[92] the favored economic position of the Negro woman is an important factor. In the South the Negro woman maintains a virtual monopoly in domestic service positions.[93] Poorly paid as these jobs are, they nonetheless bring in more than the odd jobs upon which the father has to depend. In the South, more Negro women than men take out insurance, and very often the policy makes provision for the husband as well as for the children.[94] An indication of the significance of the mother is evident in the Negro expression of referring to a relative "on the sure [mother's] side."[95]

In many households where women are heads of families, the Negro head often classifies herself as widowed. Some of these women undoubtedly have been deserted or are unmarried mothers.[96] Others are separated from their husbands. The majority, however, are probably deserted.[97] The Negro woman often has to take love on male terms; she cannot compete with the attractive woman who gets a man to support her, nor with the prostitute. Hence, she may enter into unstable common-law marriages of relatively short duration.[98] Her husband's shortcomings are tolerated for the sake of affection and companionship. Even when legally married, she is hesitant to use legal force to compel her husband to assume responsibilities. The following case gives insight into these attitudes.

Mrs. W., a Negro woman with seven children became known to the agency when it was reported that she left her three small children at home alone while she worked. She had full responsibility for the children since she was separated from her husband.

Mrs. W. was born on a farm and married at the age of twenty. Mr. W. had never given her support. Shortly after marriage he left her,

[92] See Chapter 11, pp. 243-244.
[93] Davie, *op. cit.*, p. 208.
[94] *Ibid.*
[95] *Ibid.*
[96] Frazier, *The Negro Family in the United States, op. cit.*, p. 247.
[97] *Ibid.*
[98] Drake and Cayton, *Black Metropolis, op. cit.*, p. 584.

but he always returned. She became pregnant after each return. Because he was such a poor provider, she divorced him, but even after the divorce she permitted herself to become pregnant again. Her explanation was that she loved her husband, even though he "treated her bad." She always hoped that things would be better.

At one time Mr. W. contributed $40.00 monthly to the support of the family, but when the case was opened he was contributing only a few dry beans a week. The District Attorney's office was unable to bring an indictment against him because Mrs. W. was unable to follow through on requirements—she would accept the beans weekly and resisted filing charges against her husband.

The D.A.'s office is attempting to put pressure on Mr. W. for support. When Mrs. W. thought of what part she would have to play in the indictment she complained about not wanting to miss work as she could not afford to lose the money. Likewise, court upsets her. She gets upset and vomits every time she thinks of it. This feeling is partly due to her feeling for Mr. W. and her wish not to force him to the family support which she probably considers punishment for him.

The Negro woman, then, tends to be independent and may not wish to use coercion on a recalcitrant husband. Her relationships with her children are generally satisfying and of relatively more value than those with her husband.

13

Children's Roles and Parent-Child Relationships

AMERICAN PATTERNS

STATUSES of parents and children have little variation, inasmuch as the parent-child relationship is an "ideal type" in the "superiority-subordination" classification.[1] Yet, there are degrees of variation within a narrow range, depending upon cultural differences within specific family systems. Parent-child relations are important, for the individual's "modes of response to and effect upon others" are believed to be "determined to a very large degree by the nature of the relationships he has with his parents, or those who have taken the role of parents."[2] Attitudes toward authority,[3] religion, economics, and all other social institutions are hypothesized to originate and evolve in the course of the child's training in the family setting.

The American child is traditionally expected to be diligent, obedient, respectful toward his parents, and regardful of their wishes. He avoids doing anything that would displease or embarrass

[1] Cf. Warner and Srole, *The Social Systems of American Ethnic Groups, op. cit.*, p. 124.

[2] Shaw and Ort, *Personal Adjustment in the American Culture, op. cit.*, p. 6.

[3] Bienenstok, "Antiauthoritarian Attitudes in the Eastern European Shtetel Community," *American Journal of Sociology, op. cit.*, 57:150.

his parents, and shows the effect of parental training by being polite and mannerly. Traditional expectations also include studiousness, good morals, and participation in church activities. (See Table 3, p. 274.)

A century ago the American child probably conformed more closely to these traditional concepts than he does today. Families were larger and the country was predominantly rural. The child tended to make a direct contribution to the family economy; there were certain tasks that could be allotted to the preadolescent child

"I can't come out. I'm taking a nap." (Courtesy of Bil Keane and *The Saturday Evening Post.*)

TABLE 3.   Typical Responses of Respondents Revealing Traditional and Developmental Conceptions of a Good Child[a]

Respondent	Traditional Role Conceptions	Developmental Role Conceptions
Father	1. Learns to work and respect authority	1. Learns to consider and weigh the advice and experience of others and the family
	2. Takes schooling seriously and works for good ratings	2. Learns to develop personality and sense of humor along with formal education
	3. Is always truthful and honest	3. Considers mother and father as pals
	4. Attends and takes part in church activities	4. Shows signs of growing security and happiness
	5. Tries to do nothing that would embarrass parents	5. Learns to do own thinking
Mother	1. Obeys parents	1. Develops a good spirit of give and take
	2. Tries to do well in school	2. Shows signs of being well adjusted—happy and secure
	3. Respects the wishes of parents	3. Lets mom and dad know just how he feels about them
	4. Is reverent and learns God is to be worshiped	4. Shares joys and sorrows with parents
	5. Avoids doing that which displeases parents	5. Develops and uses social capabilities
Adolescent	1. Tries to obey his parents	1. Takes an active interest in family group activities
	2. Has respect for his mother and father	2. Feels close to his family but is becoming increasingly independent
	3. Does chores around the house	3. Is willing to coöperate with his family for the betterment of all
	4. Lives within the moral standards of the family	4. Is considerate of parents as he realizes they have their own lives to live, too
	5. Is polite and mannerly	5. Helps his siblings in their social adjustment rather than hindering them

[a] Table derived from study by Connor, *et al.,* "Parent-Adolescent Relationships," *Journal of Home Economics, op. cit.,* 46:189.

such as feeding the poultry or helping with household tasks. As the American family became more and more urbanized, however, children became an economic liability rather than an asset. Families decreased in size and, like all rare commodities, children became dearer.

Contemporary American culture tends to be looked upon as child-centered.[4] "From every point of view," remarks an Oriental, "this country is a paradise on earth for children."[5] Children's "needs, their wishes, and their performances are regarded as central and worthy of adult attention."[6] The child's influence is evident in the family's choice of food, magazines, and radio programs. Advertisers exploit the family's willingness to take into account the preferences of children in nearly every decision that is made.[7]

America is said to have a youth culture because of the recognition given youth and the value placed upon the qualities of youth. The young, unmarried girl is the center of attraction. Other societies regard men, often the old men, or mothers as ideal symbols.[8] Such qualities as energy, enthusiasm, resilience, inventiveness, and resourcefulness rank high in the scale of values. These are the qualities which characterize youth and which are believed to be typical of Americans in general, inasmuch as they played an important role in the development of the country.[9]

Perhaps one of the factors largely responsible for the glorification of childhood and youth is that the American family has few children. The contemporary American family has an average of about

[4] This is the attitude of Europeans according to Sirjamaki, *The American Family in the Twentieth Century*, *op. cit.*, p. 105.

[5] Hsu, *Americans and Chinese*, *op. cit.*, p. 71.

[6] Margaret Mead, "The Contemporary American Family as an Anthropologist Sees It," *American Journal of Sociology* (May, 1948), 53:457.

[7] *Ibid.*, p. 458.

[8] John Sirjamaki, "Culture Configurations in the American Family," *American Journal of Sociology* (May, 1948), 53:467.

[9] *Ibid.*

three children,[10] and parents tend to lavish affection on their children and to have regard for the individuality of each child. (See Table 3.) The small family also means that the family will have a higher standard of living. In fact, some parents acknowledge that they have limited family size in order to "give everything" they can to their children.

American children are reared in a child's world where they mature slowly, develop their abilities, indulge in play, and occasionally perform small tasks—often of an artificial nature. Generally they are protected from adult responsibilities, and laws and custom prevent their too early gainful employment. Concerning the kind of training the American child receives, one analyst notes:[11]

. . . my impression is that if you are what they used to call a severe disciplinarian with children, you get known to the neighbors as a crank. There is a sort of cheerful, unstated assumption that children will grow up and be polite soon enough and that there's no sense for the first fifteen years or so in pretending they are anything but inhabitants of the jungle. (There is a certain family pride in seeing your child become king or queen of the jungle.) The children themselves are of course not aware of being particularly bad or violent or ill-mannered. They have no other system to compare themselves with, and like all children don't even know that any other system exists.

A type of control commonly used by American parents is the bribe or fine. Once a child realizes that money has value, parents

[10] The recent rise in the birth rate is believed to be the result of temporary causes and, consequently, of a temporary nature. Marriages were postponed during the decade of the thirties, or married couples simply postponed raising a family. During the decade of the forties, the number of marriages was above normal, hence "borrowed" from the future. These new marriages always affect the number of births, especially first births. The net result was a temporary rise in the birth rate, made up chiefly of first, second, and third births. Cf. Kingsley Davis, "The American Family: What It Is—and Isn't," *The New York Times Magazine*, September 30, 1951, p. 41. See also "Small Families Are Still the Fashion," *The New York Times Magazine, op. cit.*, by the same author.

[11] Cooke, *One Man's America, op. cit.*, p. 258.

tend to use it as a convenient means of control. Money is given for good conduct such as making high grades in school, doing household chores, or being kind to siblings. Parents tend to "buy the conduct" of their children more often than by showing appreciation for achievement by a gift (even a monetary gift) at the end of the school year, or after a prolonged effort on the part of the children.[12] A small child made the following complaint about his parents:

I don't get enought money for the work I do. And my sister is always bothering me. And my fathers always teasting me about my girl friend. My mother never lets my cat in the house, she always calls my cat flea-bag or powderpuff. And she wont let me have a Dog.[13]

Child training, then, tends to give children an early appreciation for money. Private property is also valued. Wherever possible the child has his own room. Clothes, books, toys, and tools are regarded as personal property which other family members respect. If the child earns money for odd jobs, this money is also his personal property, and he is relatively free from constraint in spending it. The adolescent who has finished school and is working full time may agree to contribute a nominal sum to the family for room and board, but very often the young person takes parental support for granted, even after he is well into his twenties.[14] It is not uncommon for young couples to be supported by their parents in whole or in part, particularly if they are still in school.

The American father's role in child training appears to be two-fold: a fraternal relationship, especially with the son, and the part of a rather infrequent, unpredictable disciplinarian. Support may

[12] Baber, Marriage and the Family, op. cit., p. 266. See also Nora Smaridge, "Don't Let Children Become Money-grubbers," America (July 24, 1954), 91:415-417.
[13] Dorothy Barclay, "Children's Thoughts on Parental Behavior," The New York Times Magazine, May 9, 1954, p. 54.
[14] Cf. Commager, The American Mind, op. cit., p. 423.

be given the child when the mother's demands are excessive or when she is unwilling to let the child grow up.[15] The father's fraternal role may be evidenced in fishing or hunting excursions with his son, and sometimes in participation in ball games or neighborhood gang activities. In the latter instances, moreover, the father may be assuming an interest which he does not have, in order to be a pal to his son. Theodore Roosevelt has been held up as a model for the American father. In an introduction to a collection of the letters of Roosevelt, the editor says that no matter how great the pressure of public duties or how severe the strains of public office placed upon the President, this devoted father found time to send weekly a long letter to each of his absent children.

From the youngest to the eldest, he wrote to them always as his equals. As they advanced in life the mental level of intercourse was raised as they grew in intelligence and knowledge, but it was always as equals that he addressed them. He was always their playmate and boon companion, whether they were toddling infants . . . or growing schoolboys, or youths standing at the threshold of life. Their games were his games, their joys those of his own heart.[16]

It is the American mother, however, who plays the major role in child training. Many of the young American's conflicts result from the mother's "inevitable oscillation between demanding achievement as a proof of the child's love and threatening to withhold her love if the child does not achieve."[17] Ethical and emotional training tend to be primarily in the mother's sphere. A negative rather than a positive tone often prevails, and punishments may be given for disapproved behavior.

Areas of greatest conflict between the adolescent and his parents

[15] Mead, "The Contemporary American Family as an Anthropologist Sees It," *American Journal of Sociology, op. cit.,* 53:458.

[16] Joseph Bucklin Bishop (ed.), *Theodore Roosevelt's Letters to His Children,* New York, Charles Scribner's Sons, 1919, 4.

[17] Mead, "The Contemporary American Family as an Anthropologist Sees It," *op. cit.,* 53:457.

appear to be in relation to dating and to standards and values. Young people report that they have differences with their parents concerning whom to date and the hour to return home after a date. Daughters seemed to have different standards and values from their mothers in such areas as conduct, personal appearance, and health.[18] In general, adolescents complain of "nagging" by their parents. Compared with children of other cultures, however, American youngsters have an enviable position.

ORIENTAL PARENT-CHILD RELATIONSHIPS

While America is believed to be the country which accords the greatest privileges to childhood, China is the country in which children come last.[19] Chinese parents have traditionally had a free hand with their children. While the American parent can get involved in legal action for using harsh punishment, the Chinese parent is rarely penalized, even for infanticide.[20]

The two basic relationships in China are that between parents and children (with the emphasis on the sons) and that between the son and his wife. Ideally, the two should be complementary, but if they are not, the parent-son relationship takes precedence.[21] A son may even be expected to divorce his wife if there is a conflict in the two basic relationships, for filial piety is the most important virtue.[22]

The essence of the father-son relationship—filial piety—requires that a son serve his parents with devotion and respect, honor and support them, and carry on the family name through offspring.[23]

[18] Connor, et al., op. cit., p. 185.

[19] Hsu, Americans and Chinese, op. cit., p. 70-71.

[20] Ibid., p. 71.

[21] Yang, A Chinese Village, op. cit., p. 67.

[22] Hsu, Americans and Chinese, op. cit., p. 74.

[23] Ch'eng-K'un, "Families the Foundation of Chinese Social Organization," Social Forces, op. cit., 23:51.

After the parents' death it is the son's duty to provide a proper funeral and enter into ancestor worship.[24] The filial child, then, will not "talk back" to his parents, ignore their commands, or thwart their wishes. He will not, moreover, criticize their actions, even though these actions are wicked.[25] "Parents are always right" according to the Confucian dictum,[26] and it is the child's duty at all times and under all circumstances to show respect and regard for them.

Legends which have filial piety as their theme are numerous. Even though they are only legends, they are, nonetheless, dear to the majority of Chinese and are still narrated. Though the events are probably fictitious, the mere fact of their persistence attests to their importance in child training. According to one of these legends, a son lay naked on ice in the middle of winter in order to melt the ice because his ailing father wanted to taste some fish.[27] Other legends give accounts of filial sons who rushed into their burning homes to rescue their aged parents, leaving their children to die.[28] If a parent is sentenced to prison, the filial son will arrange to take the place of his parent.[29]

Piety also motivates the parent in caring for the child. The Japanese parents consider that they repay their forebears by passing on to their children the care which they themselves received.[30] In educating and training one's children, one repays *one's own* parents.

Very small children are generally indulged, especially the boys. About the age of six, however, the parents begin to exercise restraints. Japanese, as well as Chinese, culture places a premium on discipline, in contrast to American culture where individual

[24] Hsu, "The Family in China," *op. cit.*, p. 73.
[25] Ch'eng-K'un, *op. cit.*, p. 51.
[26] Hsu, *Americans and Chinese*, *op. cit.*, p. 73.
[27] Hsu, "The Family in China," *op. cit.*, pp. 73-74.
[28] *Ibid.*, p. 74.
[29] Hsu, *Americans and Chinese*, *op. cit.*, pp. 73-74.
[30] Queen and Adams, *The Family in Various Cultures*, *op. cit.*, p. 90.

initiative is encouraged.[31] An old Chinese proverb says that "filial sons are produced at the end of canes."[32] There is little "reasoning" with children, even after they are in their late teens.[33] Parental techniques consist of strict orders or prohibitions designed to make children conform to rigid norms. Sometimes parents resort to corporal punishment, but very often they use a more subtle type of compulsion consisting of group ridicule and laughter.[34]

The Oriental child is seldom praised. He is *expected* to follow the percepts of proper conduct and to give honor to the family. In fact, the Japanese parent often withholds praise and compares the child unfavorably with others in order to encourage the child to greater efforts.[35] The Chinese parent uses similar techniques, as is evident from the following statement by a second-generation Chinese:

I, for instance, was constantly reminded of my shortcomings, but seldom praised for my virtues. Not even as a child had Father ever commended me personally. True to the Chinese character, Father, despite his Americanism, never expressed his affection personally. Since infancy, I had never kissed him, in Occidental fashion, on the lips. Nor had he ever made similar overtures, since that would have been unthinkable, undignified, and thoroughly un-Chinese.[36]

Once when Pardee Lowe was giving public lectures, he learned that his father was coming into the hall to join the audience occasionally. The father never made any comments to his son, however, to indicate how the latter was performing. One day a stranger sat beside the father in the audience and remarked to him on the excellence of the speaker. Still the father made no comment. Only

---

[31] Smith, *Americans from Japan, op. cit.,* p. 51.
[32] Hsu, "The Family in China," *op. cit.,* p. 83.
[33] LaViolette, *Americans of Japanese Ancestry, op. cit.,* p. 22.
[34] *Ibid.,* p. 23.
[35] *Ibid.,* p. 25.
[36] Lowe, *Father and Glorious Descendant, op. cit.,* p. 287.

when the stranger asked outright for the identity of the speaker did the father acknowledge any relationship.

Describing his father's role and the relationship existing between parent and child, Pardee Lowe says:[37]

. . . He was unusually successful in his role of the severe and exacting parent, always commanding respect from us, even in our most rebellious moments, which were many. On the other hand, we children could never get it through our muddled Americanized heads that we were expected to act the part of filial sons and daughters. To us this meant becoming emotionless automatons, miniature editions of repressed and inhibited men and women. It meant forswearing laughter and play and the pleasures of the American "funny papers" for the seriousness of study, work, or meditation upon the Classics.

For all his strictness, everybody in Chinatown knew that he loved us. Everybody, that is, except ourselves. We were to make this discovery only after our marriages, when the added responsibilities and care of family life opened our eyes to the fact that Father was not the family villain of the piece, but a deeply affectionate parent ever ready to counsel and guide us.

The sooner the Oriental child acts like an adult, the better. Parents take pride in children who act older than they are. Chinese children unobtrusively enter into the world of adults, for they accompany their families to all kinds of gatherings—wedding feasts, funeral breakfasts, religious celebrations, and purely social or business events.[38] Children are not excluded from either the joys or the sorrows of the family. If there is a death in the family, economic difficulty, or domestic strife, the parents do not hide these troubles from the children. One analyst contrasts the American practice with that of the Chinese by remarking that American parents face a world of reality but create a near ideal realm for their children, whereas the Chinese children share the same world with their parents.[39]

[37] *Ibid.*, p. 288.
[38] Hsu, *Americans and Chinese, op. cit.*, pp. 80-81.
[39] *Ibid.*, pp. 81-82.

Since Oriental children are primarily an integral part of the family system, they do not have "children's parties" where they are the center of attention while the adults wait on them. A Chinese child's birthday party is a family affair, and the child is certainly not the center of attention.[40] When the Chinese child enters school he has no psychological urge to become part of a "gang." Secure in the shadow of his ancestors, he seeks no alliance outside the family group.[41]

Within the family a child's relations with his father are marked by reserve and submission, while the relations with his mother are warm and intimate. By way of comparison with American parents, Chinese parents are both undemonstrative, but the father is more so than the mother.[42] A father rarely has much to do with his daughter.[43] He may have genuine affection for her, especially if she lives up to his expectations, but affection between father and daughter is restrained. The father comes to know his daughter indirectly through the girl's mother.[44]

With his son the father is traditionally dignified and formal. Unquestioned obedience and submissiveness are expected of the child. When the son is small his father may take him out or may walk with him in the fields, but as the boy approaches adolescence the father becomes more formal and severe. Father and son seldom speak together except on business and rarely seek each other at recreation or at street gatherings.[45]

The mother, however, is much closer to the children. When the little girl is about six years old she starts accompanying her mother about the house, helping with minor duties. As the girl gets older she becomes more helpful and, generally, the intimacy between

[40] *Ibid.*, p. 81.
[41] *Ibid.*, p. 101.
[42] Cf. Blackey, "Some Cultural Aspects of Social Casework in Hawaii," *op. cit.*, p. 51.
[43] Hsu, "The Family in China," *op. cit.*, p. 83.
[44] Yang, *A Chinese Village, op. cit.*, p. 60.
[45] *Ibid.*, pp. 57-58.

mother and daughter increases. The mother is held responsible if her grown daughter does not work well or misbehaves, for villagers look upon the daughter's personality as a reflection of her mother's.[46]

Between the mother and son there is also a close relationship. Since the boy tends to have no female companions and few opportunities for recreation, he spends much of his free time talking with his mother. He may complain of the father's harshness or question his mother about marriage plans. If the boy's marriage threatens the intimacy of the mother-son relationship, the mother may become jealous and vent her feelings on her daughter-in-law.[47]

As the Oriental family has developed, especially in America, children tend to hold their own views and to disagree or argue with their parents.[48] Concerning such matters as a career, choice of marital partner, and religion, the child may be inflexible. Parents who have received a Western education or who have come into close contact with Western culture may be amenable to consultations with their children on matters which were traditionally legislated by the parents.[49]

Parents may allow children to keep their earnings or to use them for personal purposes instead of contributing everything to the common purse.[50] Many second- and third-generation children would like to have more intimate relationships with their parents, such as they observe among American parents and children. Sometimes an older brother or sister who has experienced the need for greater parental attention will attempt to substitute for a parent. A sixteen-year-old Chinese girl, for instance, said that her ten-year-old brother had withdrawn from the Cub Scouts because her parents never participated. She said that she was trying to remedy matters by acting as proxy for her mother at the P.T.A. meetings. "I wear

---

[46] *Ibid.*, pp. 59-60.
[47] *Ibid.*, p. 58.
[48] Cf. Hsu, "The Family in China," *op. cit.*, p. 83.
[49] *Ibid.*
[50] Lang, *Chinese Family and Society*, *op. cit.*, p. 338.

hose and heels and put on a hat," she said, "and I'm sure I look old enough to be Joe's mother." She further revealed her feelings in the following excerpt from a letter written to an older sister:

Mom went back to work last week, and so soon after the operation. She really didn't have to since we had enough help and since she really wasn't well enough to work—but she insisted. Of course, at this point, I sorta lost my temper. I had explained so many times before how important it is for the kids to come home and find Mom in the house once in a while. She always had the excuse that we didn't have enough help at the store. Well, now we do have the help, but she still insists on going down. That means that the cooking and cleaning falls to us, especially to me since you shoved the glorious position of being the oldest on me. This I don't mind so much, but I can't give Joe the security that he needs and can find in Mom. He's still so young! What upset me so much was Mom's argument for not staying home. She said, and I quote, "You all are old enough to take care of yourselves. Why, Joe can even fix his own breakfast." Yes, we are capable of taking care of ourselves, but at ten, Joe isn't old enough to realize that Mom's absence is not neglect, but concern for our material welfare. I realize that Mom's motives are good and it is her way of taking care of us, but it's hard for the kids to realize it. That's what I tried to tell Mom. It only provoked an argument, though, and hard feelings between us.

It is usually very difficult for a first-generation Chinese parent to conform to the roles of the contemporary American parent. Even the second- and third-generation parent finds such a transformation hard, for the Chinese conception of formalized parent-child relationships is directly opposed to the intimate, comradely American pattern.

MEXICAN PATTERNS

Traditional Mexican patterns of parent-child relationship are somewhat akin to those of the Oriental. Emphasis is on respect and authority.[51] At one time children were trained to kiss the hands of their elders in greeting, but this custom has gradually fallen into disuse.[52] Small children are expected to be "quiet, passive, and unobtrusive," while older children should be "obedient, self-controlled, and helpful."[53]

Respect for the father is engendered by the mother. Children are taught an attitude of respect and avoidance of intimacy.[54] A father seldom carries an infant—except in an emergency—and he rarely plays with the children. On the whole, he gives them little attention.[55] When he is home, the children are generally "obedient, subdued, controlled, and inhibited in his presence."[56] The father's anger is to be feared and he is to be revered simply because he is the father, rather than for any positive personal qualities.[57] Sometimes there are reasons for fearing to displease the father, as the following case history of a second-generation Mexican girl illustrates.

My father is a strong-willed man who clings tenaciously to his ideas and to the customs and traditions of his forefathers. Imbued with the beliefs of his Spanish father and Mexican mother, he has made himself the head, the only head of the family, to whom all respect and obedience are due. Although he has lived in the United States for more than thirty-five years he is still a Mexican citizen and has been unaffected by the American way of life. He is still a Mexican in spirit, manner, conduct, and beliefs.

From his sons and daughters my father expects total obedience and respect. My brothers have been trained to follow in his footsteps and have the same idea of the woman as he has. We, as girls, must never work outside the home and must always be ready to do what our father or brothers want. But just as the woman must be the slave of the man, the husband and sons must give her all love and respect.

[51] Lewis, *Life in a Mexican Village: Tepoztlán Restudied, op. cit.,* p. 329.
[52] *Ibid.*
[53] *Ibid.*
[54] *Ibid.,* p. 332.
[55] *Ibid.,* p. 333.
[56] *Ibid.,* p. 332.
[57] *Ibid.,* pp. 330-331.

My father has never tolerated the will of any other member of the family. He is the only one that can give orders and they must be obeyed.

Seeing that there was no future in staying at the ranch, that father would never let them work, and that it was impossible to make him change his mind, my two older sisters, after their graduation from high school, left home. My father did not stop them but forbade the rest of us to have anything to do with them. He never spoke to them and he never went to see them. My sisters could not come to the house to see us. However, they came when my father was not at home.

When my eldest sister was going to be married she wrote a letter to father asking him to come to the wedding and give her at the altar. My father refused to have anything to do with her. He said my sisters had to come home and beg his forgiveness. They had to say they had been wrong and that they were sorry.

Ten years have passed since my sisters left home. Yet my father has never visited my married sister's home. He claims they are in the wrong. He will never make a move toward reconciliation because he firmly believes he is right.

The child is usually closer to the mother, for mothers are regarded as "softer" by nature than the "harder" fathers.[58] A mother may be quite demonstrative in her affection for the small child, kissing and fondling the youngster. As the child gets older she shows her affection by not informing the father of his misdeeds or by intervening when the father is meting out punishment.[59]

Corporal punishment is frequently used both in the home and in school.[60] In the first-generation family there may be more toleration and less physical punishment. Many first-generation Mexican families, however, have not developed to the extent that they can accept the American patterns of parent-child relationship in regard to punishment. In one such family, a twelve-year-old boy who ran away from home was referred to the Juvenile Office. The parents told the social worker that he should be "kept in an institution." They declared further that they "found it impossible to be going

[58] *Ibid.*, p. 332.
[59] *Ibid.*, p. 333.
[60] See Chapter 4, pp. 81-82.

out looking for the boy" since they cannot afford the money for bus fare.

Mrs. S. wants Pedro held in the institution until he is sixteen and maybe he will do better. The boy wants to go on the streets and sell papers, but Mrs. S. is afraid he will get into trouble and then the police will blame the father.

When asked about the discipline in the home, Mr. S. said he could not have the children running and playing through the house as they might break something or might fall and get hurt. He would like to buy a TV set, but can't afford the down payment.

Not all parents are as harsh as Pedro's. Sometimes the parents cannot understand the American custom of labeling a teen-age boy delinquent for missing school or loafing on the street corners. In Mexico it is customary for men to idle on the street corner, for "the street corner is the illiterate's newspaper."[61] The boy who follows this practice in America, however, is liable to be accosted by a representative of the law. In such instances, the boy's family usually protests that the boy is not bad.

In the developmental Mexican family the adolescent girl is generally more cause for concern. She may refuse to accept chaperonage and insist on recreation in mixed groups of boys and girls. Pedro's sister, aged fourteen, had also rebelled against her overrestrictive parents. According to the case record:

Mr. S. said that Candelaria had come home around 11:00 P.M. the other night after being told again and again to come straight home from school. He had to get up to unlock the door to let her in. He told her the next time it happened he would have her locked out all night. A girl her age should stay home or she would get in trouble.

Although the Mexican parent tends to be a strict disciplinarian, especially the father, there are cases of "spoiled children." In the following instance, superstition rather than real affection accounts for parental indulgence.

[61] Burma, *Spanish-Speaking Groups in the United States, op. cit.,* pp. 116-117.

Mr. and Mrs. T. requested help with their twelve-year-old daughter, E., who runs away from home and who is frequently picked up by the police and has been often to the Juvenile Department. There is no problem of sex-delinquency here—E. just rejects her whole family and enjoys the turmoil she is creating with the wild fantasies she relates as having occurred. She has actually left home and gone straight to the police station. She dominates the whole family—there are eight other children—and is in complete control of the situation and says she will not, under any circumstances, remain at home. On one of her truancies she went voluntarily to the Juvenile Department and informed the worker there that she refused to stay at home.

The mother is a frail, sickly woman, passive and frightened. She wants her child back in the home—she says she has no idea why the child leaves. Her idea of affection is the bestowal of material gifts. When E. was returned home after being gone for three days, she bought her many gifts, thereby increasing the family indebtedness. There is no real love and warmth evident. Mrs. T. has been married before and she believes that E. has come under the influence of an aunt—a sister of Mrs. T.'s first husband—who is a "witch." Mrs. T. is very, very much afraid of this "witch" and insists she has put E. under a "spell." In all of her conversations, Mrs. T.'s fear of witchcraft and her deep-rooted superstitions are evident. She fails, absolutely, to realize that there is complete lack of discipline in her home and that she is letting a child rule the house. She says the witch has placed a curse upon her and her family and unless it can be raised there will be nothing but trouble. She burns "witches' candles" to overcome the "voodoo." Mrs. T. is very neurotic and immature but her concern for E. seems genuine, though she seems more frightened even of this "witch's" influence than she does of the loss of E.

The average Mexican parent is more flexible than the Oriental parent, but much more rigid than the American parent. Proximity to the mother country and frequent trips there tend to reinforce original cultural patterns. The Mexican ethnic group is, moreover, concentrated in ethnic colonies in the Southwest where there are fewer contacts with American cultural patterns than if the group were more scattered geographically.

EUROPEAN PATTERNS

Traditional roles of European family members vary from one group to another. On the whole, however, parents are expected to provide for the child's needs and the child, in return, is supposed to be docile and obedient. Among most European peasants, the child shares in the economic activities of the family at an early age. In Poland, according to a Yankee City informant, children "work all the time."[62] Family reputation is generally contingent upon the behavior of the children according to long-established norms. The father's position, though, more than that of any other single family member determines the family's status. Most European ethnic societies are societies of fathers, and the personalities of mother and children are identified with that of the family head. The average ethnic father, then, conceives his role in "patriarchal and authoritarian terms."[63]

When the European family comes to America, the father is obliged to surrender some of his traditional prerogatives. The first-generation father is generally reluctant, though, to compromise original cultural patterns, and the child tends to assume "the important function of absorbing change for the family."[64] Since the child learns to speak English in the schools and associates with American age-mates, he often becomes more familiar with the dominant culture than his parents. Fathers, in particular, resent the role of accepting information from the child.

They could remember how they themselves had feared and respected the father; and they were embittered by their own failure to evoke the same fear and respect from their children. Beyond the loose behavior

[62] Warner and Srole, *op. cit.*, p. 125.
[63] *Ibid.*, p. 143.
[64] *Ibid.*, p. 144.

at the table and in the streets, these parents sensed the tones of ridicule. In their eyes the young Americans were undisciplined and ungrateful, good only for throwing stones and snow at strangers. When the boys and girls were small, it was still possible to curb their rebelliousness; the swift punishment of the strap held them temporarily in line. But as age increased their power, they were not so amenable to authority. As they grew in knowledge and in craftiness, as their earnings rose above those of the head of the family, they ceased to bow to restraints and would no longer be ordered about.[65]

European ethnics usually find it difficult to allow their children to use initiative. Children are considered a part of the family system which is dominated by the father. When the children's "freedom" extends to choice of a marital partner without the consultation and approbation of elders, such an action is interpreted as a "madness of the reason."[66] "To many a saddened father and mother it seemed that their sons and daughters had moved gross passion to the center of marriage," remarks Oscar Handlin, "and had thereby obscured the true end of the family, perpetuation of the succession of generations."[67]

In Yankee City among the less assimilated ethnic groups, many of the traditional patterns still prevail. Greek fathers place great emphasis upon their dignity and authority. Neither joking nor argument is permitted to occur within the family, for joking involves informality and a certain "give and take" that should exist only among equals. Even if a visiting adult jokes with the father in the latter's home, it would be considered improper, since such behavior would lead the child "to question or doubt the father's dignity and authority."[68]

Second-generation Polish children still relinquish their pay checks to their parents and are then given the money that they need for

[65] Handlin, *The Uprooted, op. cit.,* p. 254.
[66] *Ibid.,* p. 256.
[67] *Ibid.*
[68] Warner and Srole, *op. cit.,* p. 130.

special purposes.[69] One father criticized the practice of having the children pay a certain amount for board and room and retain the remainder of their earnings. "Whatever my girls spend," he said, "I know about it."[70] Appropriation of children's earnings is general among the Poles, Russians, Greeks, and Armenians of Yankee City.[71] It has also persisted to a certain extent among the Italians.[72] Sometimes the children "hold out" on some of the money, but this practice is not considered right.[73]

Between second-generation parent and child, then, there is usually a cultural conflict. The child cannot depend solely upon his parents for cultural orientation. The converse is true; parents come to depend upon the child and to resent this dependence. American culture is, in the final analysis, given higher status since it is the "host" culture, and the child is more closely identified with it than are his parents. When parent and child are at cultural odds and attempt to exert pressure one upon the other, conflict is inevitable.[74]

Third-generation European ethnics tend to have resolved many of these cultural differences.[75] Americans of Western European descent experience few, if any, cultural conflicts. Eastern and Southern European ethnics, however, are less assimilated and will probably continue to cherish traditional cultural values and roles.

JEWISH PARENT-CHILD RELATIONSHIPS

Traditionally, the Jewish child owes his parents deference, respect, and obedience. Jewish law prescribes death for the child who

---

[69] *Ibid.*, p. 128.
[70] *Ibid.*
[71] *Ibid.*, p. 129.
[72] See Chapter 9, p. 179.
[73] Warner and Srole, *op. cit.*, p. 130.
[74] *Ibid.*, pp. 144-145.
[75] See Campisi, "Ethnic Family Patterns," *American Journal of Sociology, op. cit.*, 53:444-446.

fails to show the proper respect for his parents' wishes.[76] The child is under obligation to marry and have children, and to conduct himself in a way that will bring honor to the family. He is expected to observe and cherish Jewish religious practices and to see that they are transmitted to the next generation.

Parents have an obligation to train the child, especially in religious observances. To a son, the father owes a series of religious ceremonies, beginning in infancy with circumcision.[77] The mother, too, shares the responsibility for religious training inasmuch as many religious practices are centered in the home and she is with the child almost continuously during his formative years.

Toward a son the parents owe a good education, but an adequate marriage settlement or dowry is of more importance to a daughter.[78] Economic support, of course, is also the responsibility of the parents. A father can seldom impose his will by the threat of withholding economic support. Such an action would inevitably be censured by the Jewish community, for an integral relationship is supposed to exist between father and son.[79]

The father-daughter relationship is generally a distant one, involving such responsibilities on the part of the father as finding a suitable husband and providing a dowry for the daughter. If the daughter remains at home too long, the ethnic group tends to be critical.[80] A second-generation Polish Jewess, whose ambition was to receive a high school education, relates her father's reactions in these words: "Then in a voice of rare tenderness father told me that he wished me to grow up a pride to our people, quiet, modest, a good home maker, I was to marry; I too could be another Rachel, another Rebecca."[81]

[76] Tennenbaum, "Jewish Parents in a Child Guidance Clinic," *Smith College Studies in Social Work, op. cit.,* 10:56.
[77] Joffe, "The Dynamics of Benefice," *Social Forces, op. cit.,* 27:241.
[78] *Ibid.*
[79] Bienenstok, *op. cit.,* p. 154.
[80] *Ibid.,* p. 153.
[81] Stern, *My Mother and I, op. cit.,* p. 84.

The relationship between father and son is traditionally less intimate than that between mother and son. Since the European Jewish father is out of the home a great deal of the time, the son has infrequent associations with his father. Very often, when the father is at home, he wishes to spend his time in quiet study. Consequently, if the father is expected to act as disciplinarian, the child may have more fear than love for him. Chastisements are traditionally severe, but punishment seldom implies the threat of parental rejection.[82]

The mother or grandparents usually soften the father's punishments by some kind of sentimental indulgence. Very often the mother acts as a mediator between the child and his father. The only son, a second-generation Jew in a large family, recalls his own interfamilial relations in these words:

My mother took great pride and pleasure in waiting on me, almost to the point of slavery. The same relationship prevails between my wife and son. I can remember how the girls were expected to do all kinds of chores, whereas mother delighted in waiting on me, hand and foot. Father never spent much time with us. He was busy all the time, either with his business or with his gambling. About the only part father took in the lives of us children was to "strap" us. If mother left the strap hanging in the hall, it was an indication that one of us had been "bad," and that one was in for a strapping.

I have tried to play with my children and follow the American customs, but it hasn't been easy. When I was younger I found it easier to relate to women than to men, but I am now beginning to feel more comfortable in my dealings with men.

The mother-daughter relationship is also an intimate one. A second-generation Jewish girl relates some of her experiences as follows:

. . . After every school pleasure [mother] . . . would meet me with the query: "Did you enjoy it?" No day was too hot for her to spend

[82] Bienenstok, *op. cit.*, pp. 151-152.

at the ironing board; no price was too large for her to expend upon any garment. . . .

It was as if she had a vicarious thrill and joy in my pleasures and achievements. She did not in the least understand what basketball was, but how her eyes shone when I ran in to her with the unbelievable tidings that I had been put on the scrub team![83]

As the Jewish family has developed, even in Eastern Europe, the interfamilial relationships have become more like the American patterns. Children show respect for the father, and may refrain from handling his books or using his chair.[84] But they often argue, remonstrate, or try to use persuasion with all persons in authority. Parents tend to rely on reason rather than on arbitrary orders in dealing with their children.[85] Sometimes, if the mother is the dominant parent, there is relatively little discipline. The following case extract illustrates this situation.

Mr. S., who had been in the service for several years, complained that when he returned home his family was completely lacking in discipline. Every time he attempted to use discipline, his wife dissolved into tears and there was a "family scene."

He believes that his wife's reactions are due, in part, to her home training. She comes from a first-generation Russian Jewish family of three boys and two girls. Her father was a baker who worked evenings and slept all day. As a result, the family was a "strict matriarchy." The baker was regarded by everyone as "a swell fellow with little to say at any time." His wife was a "very generous, wonderful person who allowed everyone to do as he pleased."

In Yankee City the Jewish youth closely approximate American youth patterns, but they often lack parental approbation, especially from the father. A Jewish high school boy remarks, for example, that he said the Lord's Prayer in school "because when in Rome do as the Romans do."[86] Jewish parents, like American parents,

---

[83] Stern, *op. cit.*, pp. 102-103.
[84] Bienenstok, *op. cit.*, p. 155.
[85] *Ibid.*, p. 156.
[86] Warner and Srole, *op. cit.*, p. 141.

have ambitions for their children and are anxious to have the children receive a good education.[87] Children are less respectful than their fathers would like them to be, but the mothers often excuse the children's behavior.[88] A father complained that he could not even talk to his children. "And if I should tell them what to do," he added, "they would look at me as if I belonged in an insane asylum." Any remonstrations on the father's part were met by the rejoinder that "everybody does it and so can they."[89]

Second- and third-generation Jews seem to have become more acculturated than Oriental, Mexican, or Southern European ethnic groups. Among the recent first-generation Jewish immigrants, however, the traditional patterns tend to be more prevalent than American patterns.

NEGRO PARENT AND CHILD

Among lower-class Southern Negroes the child's relationships with the mother have traditionally been more important than those with the father. The Negro maternal family, it has been noted, has its roots in Negro history when, under slavery, the father had few responsibilites toward the mother or the children. Perhaps the African heritage of polygyny in which the attachments between mother and child were closer than those between father and child also played a part in the dominance of the Negro mother.[90] Under slavery, Negro children took their status from their mother,[91] with whom they were more closely identified than they were with their father.

[87] *Ibid.*, p. 150.
[88] *Ibid.*, p. 151.
[89] *Ibid.*, p. 152.
[90] Davie, *Negroes in America Today, op. cit.*, p. 206.
[91] *Ibid.*, p. 207.

Few restrictions tend to be placed on the actions of Negro adolescents, except in upper-class families or in families where religion is a value.[92] Children are frequently left at home alone or in the care of an older sibling while the mother is at work. They may have duties to perform around the house, but they are generally unsupervised, except when they work in the fields with their parents.[93] Children are economic assets, especially in the rural South. At the age of seven or eight they start to hoe and pick cotton, and at the age of twelve they begin to plough.[94]

Adolescents from lower-class Negro society have little opportunity for recognition through education or the acquisition of money, and they may seek "self-assurance in free sexual activity, in a reputation for physical prowess . . . and in other forms of antisocial behavior."[95] Since the acquisition of status appears to be a hopeless quest, the Negro adolescent may indulge in a kind of "free living that acknowledges little responsibility to accepted standards."[96] The Negro youth, however, does learn from his parents some useful techniques for getting along in a white man's world.

The Negro father-child relationship is not a close one, as a rule. Conditions during slavery were not conducive to the formation of intimate father-child relations. Some Negro fathers, of course, assumed an active role within the family after emancipation, and those who stayed in rural-farm areas often established close relationships with their children. Fathers of families who moved into rural nonfarm communities or into towns, however, were economically unable to assume or retain a position of dominance in the family.[97] Many of these fathers accepted their position philosoph-

---

[92] Johnson, *Growing Up in the Black Belt, op. cit.,* p. 65.
[93] Burgess and Locke, *The Family, op. cit.,* p. 173.
[94] *Ibid.*
[95] Johnson, *op. cit.,* p. 99.
[96] *Ibid.*
[97] See Chapter 11, pp. 243-244.

ically and with a sense of realism. One father remarked, "We can't feed all these children, but having children is the only freedom we got."[98]

The Negro father's inability to provide economic security undoubtedly affects his status in the eyes of his children. Some children try to understand the situation, though, as the child who said that her father was doing "the very best he can," which meant that he provided "a place to stay and something to eat."[99] One young man whose father had deserted his mother and whose mother was "too young" to raise him, nonetheless had strong affectional ties with both parents. According to the case record:

S. is the son of parents who were not legally married, and he was their only child. Since his mother was "too young" to care for him, an "auntie" took him. His parents separated and he never learned the whereabouts of his mother until three years ago. "I found her, we were reunited, and she told me she never wanted to give me up when I was a baby. I was just took from her." He appears to have close affectional ties with his mother, and she has visited him several times since his hospitalization.

The patient's father has been mentally ill and spent much of his time in "asylums." The last six months of the father's life, S. took care of him. With the father as well as with the mother, affectional family ties had significance to the patient.

Some children reject a father who deserts the family or is unable to offer them economic security. One teen-age Negro boy stated that a man "had no business getting married unless he could support a family." This young boy had a girl friend, but he severed the friendship because "no girl wants a boy that can't take her out." He believed that he should prepare for some kind of career "in order to make money and be prepared to assume the responsibilities of marriage." This boy's eldest sister rejected not only her father, but also all male figures with whom she had had any contact. She

[98] Johnson, op. cit., p. 99.
[99] Ibid., p. 100.

has had to share many of the responsibilities of the family, since she is the oldest child, and has suffered many privations. As a consequence, she is bitter. She had been engaged, but broke the engagement on the eve of the marriage. She quarreled constantly with her oldest brother, insisting that he did not contribute enough to the family purse. When the case was transferred to a male social worker, she refused to keep appointments and the mother admitted that the girl was "uncoöperative" with men.

Negro children's adjustment scores seem to be related to the economic and occupational status of their fathers. Children whose fathers are in professional occupations were found to have a low home maladjustment score. If their fathers are in the "servant" group, they are also well adjusted in the home. Where the father is a white-collar worker or unemployed, the children have a high maladjustment score.[100]

Of all family types, the Negro family seems to have the most tenuous parent-child relations. Between father and children the ties are generally very loose; between mother and children a closer relationship exists, but it seldom measures up to that of other family types. Children grow up relatively freer of constraint than do children of the dominant American group, a fact which undoubtedly contributes to the higher rate of delinquency among Negroes.

[100] *Ibid.*, p. 69.

14

Differential Sex Roles

AMERICAN SEX ROLES

WHEN a child is born one of the first queries pertains to the baby's sex. "Is it a boy or a girl?" ask relatives and friends. The sex of the child may be a cause of rejoicing or of disappointment to the family. The average American family seems to prefer at least one boy and one girl, and may register disappointment if all the children are of the same sex. Most parents tend to rejoice more over the birth of a son, unless they already have several sons. The observant little girl may note that enthusiastic congratulations are heaped on the fathers of new sons, but when a daughter is born, the event may be passed off with a comment such as "Isn't that lovely!"[1]

For the first two years there is a considerable parallelism in the treatment of boys and girls, but by the time the child reaches his second year sex typing becomes more marked. By the time the child is five years of age, it is very apparent.[2] Sex typing is evident in the way the child is dressed. The small boy wears trousers and the girl a dress, although it must be admitted that the advent of blue jeans and slacks have altered the traditional pattern. Choice of toys is also indicative of sex typing. The girl is given dolls, toy

[1] Dorothy Barclay, "For the Girls of the Family," *The New York Times Magazine*, April 9, 1950, p. 38.

[2] Shaw and Ort, *Personal Adjustment in the American Culture, op. cit.*, p. 254.

dishes, and the equipment for playing house. A boy is discouraged from engaging in these feminine activities. Stuffed animals are substituted for dolls, and mechanical toys or tools are considered masculine playthings.

Sex typing is seen in the behavior expected of the boy and the girl. The parents urge the boy "not to be a sissy," and yet he is told "not to fight." As soon as an argument arises among his playmates, both parents watch anxiously to see if he shows signs of "being a quitter," or of "not being able to take it."[3] Even little girls are expected to settle their childish problems in much the same fashion as their brothers.[4] Parents hope that the boy will "make good at school, in sports, and, later on, in his job."[5] The boy is encouraged to "be nice to his sister" and look after her.

The little boy learns about masculine patterns from his father and his older brothers. Some "rough-housing" and hearty banter are to be expected from the sterner sex. From his father the boy learns that "relationships with men require putting forth all your strength, taking buffets good-humouredly, getting in and pitching, small as you are—and that this is fun."[6] He also learns that it is "unmanly" to cry, and that he is supposed to hide his fright.[7]

Maternal approval is very important to the small child. He receives rewards in the form of praise—or cookies—when he is "healthy, achieves, learns independence . . . [and] skill in the management of things."[8] Masculine style becomes culturally defined by women as well as by men. This style is characterized by independence, forthrightness, assertiveness, and strength.[9]

The little girl tends to be flattered and spoiled by an indulgent

---

[3] Mead, *Male and Female, op. cit.,* p. 278.
[4] *Ibid.*
[5] *Ibid.,* p. 276.
[6] *Ibid.*
[7] Shaw and Ort, *op. cit.,* p. 43.
[8] Mead, *Male and Female, op. cit.,* p. 276.
[9] Shaw and Ort, *op. cit.,* p. 252.

father who seldom enforces discipline.[10] She learns that crying is not necessarily "unwomanly" and that it is a very useful device for achieving her own will.[11] Her mother generally gives her few domestic responsibilities except to keep her personal belongings orderly and perhaps help with minor tasks such as the dishes.

The small girl is also busy at not "being a sissy." She learns to roller-skate, coast, and swim. Dressed in blue jeans, she no longer has to keep her legs demurely crossed,[12] but is encouraged to engage in rather strenuous activity. As she approaches her teens, however, she is told not to be a "tomboy"—get involved in fights, climb trees, play boys' games, and "run wild."[13] She learns that men and women behave differently. Men go to work and women stay at home and take care of the house. Comments are seldom made about a man's appearance, but people notice a woman's beauty and exclaim over her new clothes. Men tend to form their own circles at social gatherings and they talk about business or politics or community affairs. Women talk about children and shopping and cooking, and other homey topics.[14]

By the time the boys and girls reach junior high school they begin to date. The two-sex dating pattern is occurring earlier and earlier. "Last year," says the harassed teacher, "it was the seventh grade, this year it's started in the sixth."[15] During adolescence when young people are dating they tend to engage in some sexual experimentation,[16] and loss of virginity is not necessarily a hindrance to marriage.[17]

[10] Mead, *Male and Female, op. cit.*, p. 278
[11] Shaw and Ort, *op. cit.*, p. 43.
[12] Mead, *Male and Female, op. cit.*, p. 279.
[13] *Ibid.*, p. 277.
[14] Komarovsky, *Women in the Modern World, op. cit.*, p. 53.
[15] Mead, *Male and Female, op. cit.*, p. 280.
[16] Austin L. Porterfield and H. Ellison Salley, "Current Folkways of Sexual Behavior," *American Journal of Sociology* (November, 1946), 52:215. The findings of this study are based on an analysis of young people following careers which society respects and honors, such as students for the ministry, nurses, teachers, and social workers.
[17] See Chapter 10, p. 195.

When the adolescent girl begins dating she discovers that American culture is full of contradictions and inconsistencies where women's roles are concerned.[18] At the beginning of adolescence, the girl is supposed to assume a "quiet, demure, rather lady-like demeanor." By the time she is fifteen she discovers that such behavior will relegate her to the status of a "wall flower." The most popular girls of her age are active, talkative, and somewhat aggressive—an adaptation to the hesitant social approaches of boys.[19] In later adolescence the girl must again make an adaptation to the more mature, aggressive social approaches of the male.[20]

During middle and late adolescence the young girl becomes aware of the general disposition of American society to give her adulation and chivalrous attention. She is wined and dined, adored and entertained, all of which give her a sense of personal worth and charm.[21] Chivalrous attitudes toward American women and the high status which they have traditionally enjoyed are rooted in early American history. The colonizers from Spain and France brought few of their women with them, and the imbalance of the sexes caused a premium to be placed upon the fairer sex.[22] Parents tend to be more indulgent of their daughters than they are of their sons. The girl receives money for little luxuries, has her expenses at college paid, while her brothers are expected to earn their spending money and work their way through college.[23]

The American girl may envy the social emancipation of her brother, though, who is freer to play away from home, to choose his own activities, and to take a job away from home.[24] Boys have

---

[18] Baber, *Marriage and the Family, op. cit.*, p. 384.

[19] Harold E. Jones, "Adolescence in Our Society," *The Family in a Democratic Society*, New York, Columbia University Press, 1949, p. 81.

[20] *Ibid.*

[21] Sirjamaki, *The American Family in the Twentieth Century, op. cit.*, p. 64.

[22] Herbert Ingram Priestley, *The Coming of the White Man, 1492-1848, A History of American Life*, I, eds. Arthur M. Schlesinger and Dixon Ryan Fox, New York, The Macmillan Co., 1929, pp. 112, 238-239.

[23] Mirra Komarovsky, "Functional Analysis of Sex Roles," *American Sociological Review* (August, 1950), 15:512.

[24] *Ibid.*, p. 511.

more privacy in their personal affairs; they are not expected to relate the details of a telephone conversation and their mail is not censored.[25] The girl also has more family obligations—running errands for relatives and observing family birthdays or other social occasions.[26]

The adolescent boy prepares for his role outside the home by being given more independence than his sister. He is allowed to "take a paper route" and can find himself a summer job.[27] Such economic activities are a foreshadowing of his adult role as breadwinner. A man is expected to work gainfully, and the job becomes an important factor in his life. Unemployment, seasonal labor, or a low-paid job can cause anxiety when a man has family responsibilities.[28]

As a consequence of training for sex roles, the American boy develops such traits as competitiveness, independence, dominance, and aggressiveness.[29] The role of the American girl is not as clearly defined and adolescent girls have "considerable confusion about the feminine role."[30] As one analyst remarks, the well-adjusted American girl

is intelligent enough to do well in school but not so brilliant as "to get all 'A' 's"; informed and alert but not consumed by an intellectual passion; capable but not talented in areas relatively new to women; able to stand on her own feet and to earn a living but not so good a living as to compete with men; capable of doing some job well (in case she does not marry or, otherwise, has to work) but not so identified with a profession as to need it for her happiness.[31]

[25] *Ibid.*

[26] *Ibid.*

[27] Komarovsky, *Women in the Modern World, op. cit.,* p. 61.

[28] Sirjamaki, *The American Family in the Twentieth Century, op. cit.,* p. 88.

[29] Komarovsky, "Functional Analysis of Sex Roles," *op. cit.,* p. 511.

[30] Dorothy Barclay, "How Girls Judge Mother's Role," *The New York Times Magazine,* June 21, 1953, p. 32.

[31] Mirra Komarovsky, "Cultural Contradictions and Sex Roles," *American Journal of Sociology* (November, 1946), 52:189.

Girls appear to be emotionally more attached to their parents and more dependent upon both parents as patterns to be imitated and to direct and channel behavior than are boys.[32]

ORIENTAL PATTERNS

Among both the Chinese and the Japanese the male child is definitely regarded as superior to the female. A Chinese proverb states that the most beautiful and gifted girl is not so desirable as a deformed boy. Sometimes Chinese boys are given girls' names to protect them from evil spirits, for it is believed that the spirit will be deceived by the name into thinking that the child is a girl, and will pass him by.[33]

The eldest son is especially important for he is the one who is heir to family tradition and responsibility.[34] He carries on the family line and preserves family honor and possessions. If a father could not transfer the trusteeship of the family to a son, his own role would have been played in vain.[35] While the father is still alive, he acts as the ancestor's agent, but upon his death he merely becomes one of the ancestors "whose influence remains the most potent factor to control the younger man's life."[36] Father and son, then, are both under ancestral authority. A son is needed to carry on ancestor worship—the cornerstone of the Chinese family.[37]

A family which has no son will endeavor to adopt one from a poor family with several boys. Among the Japanese, a single daughter can continue the family name through *yoshi*-marriage, that is,

[32] Komarovsky, "Functional Analysis of Sex Roles," *op. cit.*, p. 512.
[33] Latourette, *The Chinese: Their History and Culture, op. cit.*, p. 679.
[34] Queen and Adams, *The Family in Various Cultures, op. cit.*, p. 90.
[35] Benedict, *The Chrysanthemum and the Sword, op. cit.*, p. 255.
[36] Hsu, *Under the Ancestor's Shadow, op. cit.*, p. 258.
[37] Latourette, *op. cit.*, p. 678.

binding a son-in-law through adoption, with assumption of the family name.[38]

Boys are also preferable from an economic standpoint. They remain within the family and are producers throughout their lives,[39] while girls become a part of the family system into which they marry. Confucianism is largely responsible for the traditional position of women in China.[40] Chinese metaphysics recognizes two forces at work in life: the *Yang* or dominant male element which is associated with good fortune and the *Yin* or subordinate female element which is associated with darkness and evil.[41]

Many traditional ceremonies indicate the relative importance of the sexes. A Japanese wife bows to her husband, a child bows to his father, younger brothers bow to older brothers, and the sister bows to all her brothers—whatever their ages.[42] Even the infant strapped to his mother's back has his head inclined by his mother's hand when his father makes his entrance.[43] The Book of Rites and Ceremonies says: "Men and women do not sit in the same room, do not hang their clothes on the same hook; they do not pass an object from hand to hand."[44]

The eldest son shares many of his father's prerogatives, inasmuch as he is destined to become family head. When the Japanese wish to express utter confusion, they say it is neither "elder brother nor younger brother," which is tantamount to the American expression that something is "neither fish nor fowl."[45] The elder brother de-

[38] Marvin K. Opler, "Cultural Values and Attitudes on Child Care," *Children* (March-April, 1955), 2:47.

[39] Latourette, *op. cit.,* p. 678.

[40] See list of seven deadly sins against women in Jack Belden, *China Shakes the World,* New York, Harper & Brothers, 1949, p. 311.

[41] *Ibid.;* Latourette, *op. cit.,* p. 678.

[42] Queen and Adams, *op. cit.,* p. 90.

[43] Benedict, *The Chrysanthemum and the Sword, op. cit.,* p. 48.

[44] As quoted in Han Suyin, *A Many-Splendored Thing,* Boston, Little, Brown & Co., 1952, p. 184.

[45] Benedict, *The Chrysanthemum and the Sword, op. cit.,* p. 52.

cides what is best for his younger siblings and may not show too much consideration in enforcing it.[46]

The inferior status of Chinese girls is attested to by the practice of infanticide.[47] Even in the absence of female infanticide, the mortality rate among little girls is much higher than it is among boys, which would indicate that girls are not as well fed or cared for as boys.[48] "The saddest thing in life," runs an old Japanese proverb, "is to be born a woman."[49] When the first-born child is a daughter, people say politely, "That is fortunate—now, when the son is born, there will be a nursemaid to carry him about."[50] Binding the feet of the Chinese girl—a practice now in disuse—has been interpreted as a gesture symbolic of her "unconditional surrender."[51] The Japanese woman walks behind her husband, and though husband and wife may observe Western customs when in Western garb, when the woman puts on her kimono she lets her husband precede her through the doors.[52]

Girls, even among the upper classes, usually take for granted parental preference for boys.[53] The small Chinese girl learns early in life that she is not as important as her brothers. A Chinese girl relates her experience in these words:[54]

One day at new year's, First Uncle took an iron box from its drawer in the cabinet in the reception hall where our ancestral tablets were kept and unlocked it with a key he carried. We children crowded around to see.

"These," he said, producing a book, "are our ancestral records."

[46] Queen and Adams, *op. cit.*, p. 90.
[47] Latourette, *op. cit.*, p. 679.
[48] Lang, *Chinese Family and Society, op. cit.*, p. 253.
[49] "The Women," *Time, op. cit.*, 63:37.
[50] Handley, "Social Casework," *Journal of Social Casework, op. cit.*, 28:45.
[51] Yang, *A Chinese Village, op. cit.*, p. 63.
[52] Benedict, *The Chrysanthemum and the Sword, op. cit.*, p. 53.
[53] Lang, *op. cit.*, p. 253.
[54] Su-Ling Wong and Earl H. Cressy, *Daughter of Confucius*, New York, Farrar, Straus and Young, 1952, pp. 86-87.

"I am now going to record the birth of my first grandson," he told us proudly. "He is the number one of his generation, and is the first son of the first son of the first son."

We all watched as he made the entry.

"Am I in the book?" I inquired when he had finished.

He nodded.

"Where? I want to see," I said, edging past the others.

He turned the pages. "Here you are," he said, and held the book where I could see.

I put my finger on a character. "I know that word," I said, "it is 'San.'"

"That is your second brother, Wong San-lo," said First Uncle.

"Show me my name," I said impatiently.

"Here," he said, pointing.

"I can read it," I said triumphantly. "*Chih nu*—seven, female."

"Right," he said approvingly.

"But I am Ling Ling and that is only a number," I told him. "Where is my name?"

"You are a girl," he said, unconsciously dashing my enthusiasm and merely stating a fact. "Boys have a name and a serial number. Girls have a number only. When you grow up and marry, the words will be added, 'married to so-and-so,' and your name will also be entered on the record book of your husband's clan."

Chinese girls are traditionally given a type of education very different from that of their brothers.[55] As a rule the girl's training revolves around managing a household, the duties she owes her husband, her mother-in-law, and her husband's family.[56] After a girl reaches the age of twelve, she is not allowed to associate with any boys other than her brothers or the cousins who live in the household.[57] Because contacts with other boys are so limited, brother and sister may become close companions. The boy feels that it is his duty to protect his sister, and she accepts his protection and companionship.[58]

[55] Latourette, *op. cit.*, p. 679.
[56] *Ibid.*
[57] Yang, *op. cit.*, p. 63.
[58] *Ibid.*

In families of the poor the Chinese girls may play a more dominant role. They act as little mothers for the younger siblings and
are expected to protect their brothers at play, at home, and at
school. Early in life little girls develop tendencies toward independence and learn to play a strong, protective role.[59]

Among America's Orientals the girls often assume such a maternal, protective role for the younger children. A Chinese girl
whose older brothers were in service during World War II became
dominant in the family. She could speak English and her parents
had to rely upon her in the absence of her brothers. When the boys
returned home, this daughter continued to play the dominant role.

Oriental girls in America are better educated than those in the
mother country. They go to schools where they mix freely with the
opposite sex, a fact which disturbs many of their parents.[60] Parents
are still strict about their daughters' dating with boys, but older siblings are "blazing the way" for the younger children.[61]

According to tradition, girls do not inherit any immovable property. One Chinese girl commented on the fact that her family had
given her costly jewels and furs as birthday gifts, since she was
ineligible for any other property gifts. Even America's Chinese girls
do not expect to have an equitable share in the family inheritance.
Many girls feel that under these circumstances they are entitled to
educational advantages and to relatively free access to family sav-
ings while they are still under the parental roof. When a Chinese
girl protested at the elaborate wedding which her family was planning, her girl friend reminded her, "Let them do it up big, the way
they plan. After all, the boys will inherit everything. This is about
all you'll get."

According to Oriental custom, then, girls are clearly at a dis
advantage. The male is preferred for he carries on the family line,

[59] Lee, "Research on the Chinese Family," op. cit., p. 502.
[60] Cf. LaViolette, Americans of Japanese Ancestry, op. cit., p. 50.
[61] Ibid.

he is an economic asset, and is destined ultimately to be a mediator for the family in the realm of the ancestors.

MEXICAN DIFFERENTIAL SEX ROLES

Like the Orientals, the Mexicans traditionally have regarded boys as preferable to girls. Boys learn the pattern of male dominance from their fathers and put it into practice in their relations with their sisters.[62] When a girl becomes old enough to do chores, her brothers begin to give her orders. She is expected to serve her brothers "by washing, ironing, and mending their clothes, by preparing and serving their food, and in other little ways."[63]

The first-born son and the last born seem to be favored over the other children.[64] Favoritism is shown by the unequal distribution of food and clothing, greater leniency in punishing, and more attention when a child is ill or injured. Children who are not favored usually show resentment, even of the eldest son, and react by quarreling, fighting, and avoidance of one another.[65]

When boys and girls reach the age of seven or eight years, they are not allowed to associate freely outside the family group.[66] The girl is expected to help her mother with tasks around the home. The burden of household duties tends to fall on the eldest daughter, but all girls over ten years of age are pressed into continual service in the home.[67] When a girl is twelve or thirteen she may be kept home from school, for fear of involvements with boys.[68]

[62] Lewis, *Life in a Mexican Village: Tepoztlán Restudied, op. cit.,* p. 344.
[63] *Ibid.*
[64] *Ibid.*
[65] *Ibid.*
[66] Nathan L. Whetten, *Rural Mexico,* Chicago, University of Chicago Press, 1948, p. 393.
[67] Lewis, *Life in a Mexican Village: Tepoztlán Restudied, op. cit.,* p. 389.
[68] *Ibid.*

Although boys and girls in Mexico formerly attended the same school, a revision of the federal school laws in 1942 requires that education be unisexual beyond the second grade.[69] Girls tend to associate going to school with freedom and pleasurable activity. They are away from the surveillance of their mothers and have an opportunity to form friendships.[70]

Boys often regard school as confining, and play truant to go swimming, play games, or loiter. Most boys look forward to the time when they will not have to go to school.[71] Boys generally have more freedom to play than do their sisters, and in the absence of their fathers, the mothers may have difficulty in controlling them.[72] When a boy is about sixteen his parents tend to relax controls over him so that he may become a man. After he has his "fling" at sex, liquor, and some violence, he will be expected to settle down.[73]

Girls are much more sheltered than boys, and as they grow older they are supervised more closely.[74] If a girl has premarital sexual relations, willingly or otherwise, it is considered a major family tragedy.[75] This attitude toward the preservation of the virginity of unmarried girls prevails throughout most of Latin America.[76] A father may be very stern with a wayward daughter, because she has dishonored the family. As a punishment she may be forced to leave home,[77] or her father may refuse to speak to her.[78] In rural areas, there is little that could be called courtship, but in villages

[69] Whetten, op. cit., p. 393. See also De Treviño, My Heart Lies South, op. cit., p. 49.

[70] Lewis, Life in a Mexican Village: Tepoztlán Restudied, op. cit., p. 387.

[71] Ibid., p. 388.

[72] Ibid., p. 389.

[73] Burma, Spanish-Speaking Groups in the United States, op. cit., p. 117.

[74] Whetten, op. cit., p. 395.

[75] Ibid., p. 397.

[76] Cf. Emilio Willems, "The Structure of the Brazilian Family," Social Forces (May, 1953), 31:340.

[77] See case, Chapter 10, pp. 203-204.

[78] Lewis, Life in a Mexican Village: Tepoztlán Restudied, op. cit., p. 339.

the walk around the plaza on Sundays constitutes a kind of court-ship.[79]

Brothers assume the role of protectors of their sisters' reputation and morality, and a brother may beat his sister if he discovers her with a boy.[80] The eldest brother, especially, regards the preservation of family honor as his role. If the father is dead or absent, a girl's suitor must ask her elder brother's consent to the marriage. This occurs even among second- and third-generation ethnics in America.[81]

The following case excerpt reveals the pride with which a Mexican boy fulfilled his traditional role:

Serapio, aged 12, is the eldest son. When his father was sent to the State Hospital, the family moved with the grandparents and things ran smoothly. The boy described in detail his shoe shine business, from which he made from $4.00 to $6.00 a week, and on Saturday he turned the money over to his mother. He also worked at a flower shop and the lady was very nice to him. He was very proud of the fact that his mother would give him a full day off work on Sunday—just like a grown person. She generally gave him fifty cents. He would first go to Church and in the afternoon he would take his little brother to a movie. These were the good days when he made money, looked after his brothers and sisters, and gave his mother financial help.

Then his father came back and things changed. His father sits around the house all day doing nothing. He becomes very angry when the children make noise playing, and whips them. Serapio would not mind his father's whipping him with a belt, paddle, or switch, but his father uses his fist. The father forbids the children to go out anywhere after school; they are supposed to come right home and stay quiet all the rest of the evening. For a short time they had a TV and things weren't so bad, but they couldn't buy the TV and the people took it back. Serapio says he will continue to run away as long as his father forbids him to do things and hits him.

The eldest Mexican son tends to lose his prerogatives in America.

[79] Whetten, op. cit., p. 395.
[80] Lewis, Life in a Mexican Village: Tepoztlán Restudied, op. cit., p. 344.
[81] See Chapter 10, p. 202.

To a certain extent, the same thing is occurring even in the mother country.[82] Girls in America assume a more important role. They attend school with their brothers and obtain jobs outside the home. Even the young teen-age girl easily procures domestic work where she is paid wages. She may demand and receive less chaperonage and greater freedom from patriarchal controls.

On the whole, though, the male still tends to dominate in the Mexican ethnic group. A group worker's record makes the following comment on the leader of a particular group:

> The leader is lucky to be a male and to have recognition as a leader in other athletic programs. Being a male has been an advantage in exercising authority over other club members, since the Mexican culture tends to vest authority in the male rather than in the female. These authoritarian patterns have been detrimental to self-government within the group, but in time this habit should be modified.

EUROPEAN ROLES

Material on the sex roles of children within the various European families is meager. As infants both sexes play together, but at the age of seven or eight the little girl begins to be excluded from mixed groups and has little to do with boys.[83] Girls are expected to help their mothers and become adept at womanly duties. They are generally educated to perform domestic functions rather than to participate in civic and social life.[84]

Very often the fathers complain that their American-born daughters are not helpful around the house. A French-Canadian father in Yankee City said that his daughter would probably wait until she married to learn how to cook, sew, and clean house, and a

[82] See the novel by Josephina Niggli, *Step Down, Elder Brother,* New York, Rinehart & Company, Inc., 1947.

[83] Handlin, *The Uprooted, op. cit.,* p. 254.

[84] See Chapter 12, pp. 262-263.

Polish mother commented that her daughter never worked hard.[85]

Boys are generally valued more than girls, since a boy carries on the family name. The eldest son has traditionally had the preferred position, for primogeniture—the right of the first-born son to inherit the family estate and title of nobility—has prevailed in Western Europe for centuries. Among Italians, many privileges and responsibilities given are given the eldest son.[86] He is the one who brings his bride home to live and he is the one who assumes the role of family head when the father dies.[87]

While girls are protected and supervised rather closely, their brothers are allowed freedom to gather in groups outside the home and enjoy themselves. Boys may drink, play games, and engage in arguments and discussions,[88] but girls and women have their recreation primarily in the home. In America, however, ethnic women observe freedom of association between men and women, and they eventually revolt against restrictions.[89]

Adolescent girls are traditionally under surveillance lest they lose their virginity before marriage. Italian families place a high value on virginity in their unmarried daughters,[90] and the men of the family are expected to protect their women and avenge the honor of the family in the event that it is stained. A young man never makes sexual advances toward a well-brought-up girl who might be a possible wife;[91] it is only with bad women that he can seek sexual satisfaction before marriage.

European parents tend to be concerned over American courtship patterns.[92] They cannot guide their children by the "safe rules of

[85] Warner and Srole, *Social Systems of American Ethnic Groups, op. cit.,* p. 126.
[86] Williams, *South Italian Folkways in Europe and America, op. cit.,* p. 76.
[87] *Ibid.,* p. 78.
[88] Cf. Child, *Italian or American? op. cit.,* p. 25.
[89] Handlin, *op. cit.,* p. 254.
[90] Child, *op. cit.,* p. 30.
[91] *Ibid.*
[92] See case analysis, Chapter 10, pp. 199-200.

the Old World," and the children know too much—boys as well as girls.[93] Information about sexual matters is seldom given by the parents; it is contrary to the cultural pattern.[94] Even among second-generation parents there is constraint in discussing sex.[95]

As the second-generation children mature and become parents themselves, they make adaptations to American culture. Girls are allowed more freedom and may even select their mates without parental consent. Boys are still regarded as superior to girls, but girls also have high status. Children need not contribute toward the family income by handing over their pay checks. Personality development, after the American pattern, receives increasing stress, and girls are educated to be more than competent housewives.[96]

JEWISH PATTERNS

Among the Jews, boys have traditionally been preferred to girls. Throughout the boy's life there are religious ceremonies to mark every important event. Eight days after birth the "covenant of circumcision" takes place. On the thirty-first day after birth the first son is redeemed. Redemption, the occasion of a happy gathering, consists in making a gift which will probably be used for charitable purposes.[97] When the male child is thirteen years of age he publicly assumes religious responsibility at the ceremony of *Bar Mitzvah*. He reads the law in the synagogue and chants a portion of the hymns.[98] The male child also studies the Torah or Jewish

[93] Handlin, *op. cit.*, p. 255.
[94] Cf. Child, *op. cit.*, p. 29.
[95] Campisi, "Ethnic Family Patterns," *American Journal of Sociology, op. cit.*, 53:446.
[96] *Ibid.*, p. 445.
[97] Tennenbaum, "Jewish Parents in a Child Guidance Clinic," *Smith College Studies in Social Work, op. cit.*, 10:55.
[98] *Ibid.*, p. 56.

law.[99] He is the one who recites *kaddish* for his parents after their death and carries on the family name.[100]

As soon as the little boy can talk, he is taught the blessings and most important prayers. He is usually sent to school before he is five years of age. Even earlier he is taken to the synagogue where he is taught to participate in the religious rites.[101] A Jewish father needs a son, for the boy is his spiritual heir. "Without a son," says one analyst, "life is empty, all labor is in vain, all energy is poured into the void; for there is then no one to whom family traditions and one's own unfinished work can be handed down, to be continued in posterity."[102]

The Jews never practiced female infanticide, nor did they abandon their baby daughters as did the Greeks and Romans.[103] But girls have not been traditionally regarded as important as boys. According to the Talmud:

A daughter is a vain treasure to her father. From anxiety about her he does not sleep at night; during her early years lest she be seduced, in her adolescence lest she go astray, in her marriageable years lest she does not find a husband, when she is married lest she be childless, and when she is old lest she practice witchcraft.[104]

Compared with her brother, a little girl's reception into the Jewish community is very simple. Her birth is merely announced in Hebrew in the synagogue on the Sabbath following her birth.[105] The duty of parents to teach their sons the Torah is of primary importance, but the girl is exempted from any such intensive study.

[99] Weiss-Rosmarin, *Jewish Survival, op. cit.,* p. 348.
[100] *Ibid.*
[101] Mark Zborowski, "The Children of the Covenant," *Social Forces* (May, 1951), 29:359-360.
[102] Bienenstok, "Antiauthoritarian Attitudes in the Eastern European Shtetel Community," *American Journal of Sociology, op. cit.,* 57:153.
[103] Weiss-Rosmarin, *op. cit.,* p. 348.
[104] Tennenbaum, *op. cit.,* 10:55.
[105] *Ibid.,* p. 56.

Her educational training aims to mold her character according to Jewish ethical ideals rather than to develop her reasoning faculties.[106]

Jewish girls are meant to be mothers. A Russian Jew describes a girl's traditional training and purpose as follows:[107]

A girl's real schoolroom was her mother's kitchen. There she learned to bake and cook and manage, to knit, sew, and embroider; also to spin and weave, in country places. And while her hands were busy, her mother instructed her in the laws regulating a pious Jewish household and in the conduct proper for a Jewish wife; for, of course, every girl hoped to be a wife. A girl was born for no other purpose.

Traditionally, Jewish women were not part of the cult "either as functionary or administrator or as member of the cult fellowship." In the Temple was a woman's court, a public place for those who had no share in the ritual, but the synagogue had no women's compartment "simply because no woman was there as one of the religious fellowship but as a visitor, as a guest, who came irregularly."[108]

Jews who have long resided in America tend to place less emphasis on the importance of the male child. In the synagogue, he will probably continue to retain his superiority,[109] but a Jewish informant said that women have even taken their places in the pulpit. In one instance the woman, a resident of a Southern state, was the wife of a rabbi and she took her husband's place when he died. Another indication of the vanishing sex differential among America's Jews is the ceremony of *Bas Mitzvah* which parallels that of *Bar Mitzvah* for the boys. "Sex distinctions have outlived their usefulness among the Jews in America," remarked one commentator.

[106] Weiss-Rosmarin, *op. cit.*, p. 347; Louis M. Epstein, *Sex Laws and Customs in Judaism*, New York, Bloch Publishing Co., Inc., 1948, p. 84.
[107] Antin, *The Promised Land, op. cit.*, p. 34.
[108] Epstein, *op. cit.*, pp. 80-81.
[109] Cf. Warner, p. 116.

NEGRO SEX ROLES

Few objective studies of Negro sex roles have been made, and analyses of Negro family life place little emphasis on this aspect of family living. Therefore the following generalizations are based on limited studies.

Children are generally welcomed by the Negroes—whether in or out of wedlock—whatever their sex. Since the Negro family tends to be predominantly matriarchal, the small Negro girl should not have feelings of inferiority because of her sex. As the girl grows up, she is often left unsupervised and is relatively free in selecting her companions and in determining what she wants to do. Should she have an illegitimate child, this occurrence tends to be looked upon as a part of the normal process of maturation.[110] She finds domestic work readily enough, and tends to exercise considerable freedom in the matter of marriage. Sometimes girls feel that their mothers are too vigilant, and they may complain that the boys are given more freedom.[111] Except in highly disorganized families, attempts are made to keep girls "out of trouble," but when trouble comes, it is generally accepted with equanimity.

Negro boys probably feel less restraint from their mothers than do their sisters. Just how advantageous they consider maleness is problematical—coupled as it is with the liabilities associated with their race. Observation of the lower-class Negro father would hardly give the boy grandiose ideas about male superiority. Economic restrictions, even though the boy has skills and education, should also act as a depreciating factor.

Sex differentials, when viewed within the ethnic group, vary from one group to another. It is probable that the Negro girl has

[110] See Chapter 10, pp. 205-206.
[111] Johnson, *Growing Up in the Black Belt, op. cit.,* p. 66.

higher status within her group than the girl within any other
ethnic group, including the dominant American group. The Oriental boy probably ranks highest in status because of his sex. More
empirical studies of sex roles among ethnic types need to be made
in order to verify these generalizations.

15

Roles of Other Family Members

THE AMERICAN FAMILY

THE American family and kin group "have become among the smallest to be found anywhere in the world today."[1] At most, the effective kin group embraces the immediate members of nuclear families linked by blood and marriage through three generations—grandparents, parents, and children.[2] The segregation of the immediate family from other relatives is characteristic of all industrial societies, but in America it has progressed further than anywhere else, and it "affects every aspect of our family life."[3]

The newly married couple is expected to set up a household apart from the parents of either spouse. As a rule, the newly established household is not adjoining that of the parental families, and very often it is in another community. Americans are known as a mobile people. The Census Bureau reports that one fifth of the native population lives in a state different from that of its birth and that one out of every five adults changes his residence each year.[4]

[1] Sirjamaki, *The American Family in the Twentieth Century, op. cit.,* p. 100.
[2] *Ibid.,* p. 85.
[3] Davis, "The American Family: What It Is—and Isn't," *The New York Times Magazine, op. cit.,* September 30, 1951, p. 18.
[4] *Ibid.*

320

This perpetual mobility serves to drive a wedge between the young couple and their respective parental families. When great distance separates family members, there are fewer opportunities for association. The time and expense involved in travel may become pro-

"When is she coming and how long is she staying?" (Courtesy of Bob Barnes and *The Saturday Evening Post*.)

hibitive, and the older people who have leisure time may not have the health to travel even if they have the financial means.

Factors other than mobility and industrialization have left their impact on the size of the American family system. According to Western cultural norms, husband and wife owe primary fealty to each other. An American wife does not become a part of her husband's extended family, nor does her husband have prior responsibility to his parents.[5] Sometimes one spouse or the other has a dislike for a parent-in-law, or a young person who formerly felt constrained under the parental roof feels freer after marriage to release aggressive feelings.[6] If these conditions prevail the young couple will probably have fewer associations with the older generation.

Associations with in-laws tend to be infrequent. If a young couple must make their home with either parental family, this situation is usually regarded as an emergency which must be borne for a short time. Should a widowed or aged parent take up residence with the couple, it is likewise considered unfortunate. Complaints about mothers-in-law form so clear a pattern that there is said to be a "mother-in-law syndrome." In the order of frequency some of the symptoms constituting the syndrome include: interfering, possessive, critical, indifferent, immature, uncongenial, and thoughtless.[7]

The gap between generations is also a force in restricting interfamilial relations. In American society where mobility is very high, the younger generation may have ideas and attitude dissimilar from those of their elders. Rather than argue with the older generation or listen to their remonstrances, the young people merely keep their distance and visit infrequently.

Social mobility is also a factor in widening the wedge between generations. Younger people are generally better educated than their parents and as a consequence they often occupy a higher class position. In one community, for instance, less than 10 percent of the professional men had fathers who were in professional pursuits, and only 39 percent of the skilled workers had fathers in skilled trades.[8] Differing class position as well as age differentials account for varying attitudes and standards of living between generations.

---

[5] No more than 7 percent of married couples in 1950 doubled up with parental families. Sirjamaki, *The American Family in the Twentieth Century, op. cit.,* p. 84.

[6] *Ibid.,* p. 83.

[7] Evelyn M. Duvall, "How to Get Along with Any In-law," *Collier's* (October 1, 1954), 134:34-35.

[8] Davis, "The American Family: What It Is—and Isn't," *op. cit.,* p. 18.

Earlier in American history when the country was predominantly rural, the family system was more extensive in that grandparents generally resided under the same roof with some of their children, and uncles, aunts, and cousins very often lived nearby. One index of the continuing isolation of the conjugal family is the comparatively recent advent of the baby sitter. When children were left in the care of grandparents, uncles and aunts, cousins or younger sisters, there was no need to coin a term to denote their function. Older persons within the home accepted child care as a matter of fact. Today, however, "people 'sit' in order to get into homes . . . lounge in an upholstered chair and look at the fire; and . . . all the people in homes are trying to get out of them, for at least one evening a week, and get a sitter in."[9]

The small, conjugal family system as it prevails in America has its disadvantages. When crises arise, aid from relatives is never invariably certain. Each marital unit is independent and is expected to handle its own finances; a well-to-do brother is not expected to help a less able brother buy a home. If one sibling assists another financially in a crisis, the assistance is often considered as a loan. There are no reciprocal familial responsibilities and controls beyond the conjugal unit.[10] Some families have only the pay envelope to rely upon when sickness, unemployment, or inflation falls to their lot.[11] Emotionally, too, the channels for response are united to a narrow family circle, and when death or desertion strikes, it may remove the sole emotional props. A small family circle is a disadvantage not only in times of trial and tribulation, but also in times of rejoicing. Joys are not as keen if they cannot be shared with loved ones.

The elderly person in American culture today has lost many functions which his parents enjoyed. Urban living with its com-

[9] Margaret Mead, "What Is Happening to the American Family," *Journal of Social Casework* (November, 1947), 28:326.
[10] Cf. Cavan, *The American Family, op. cit.,* p. 149.
[11] Cf. Benedict, "The Family: Genus Americanum," *op. cit.,* p. 166.

plexity, congested living quarters, high rate of mobility, and emphasis upon youth and productivity, is not conducive to the status of the aged; older people tend to feel "left out of it."[12] Orientals who observe American practices in regard to the old are shocked at the lack of reverence shown them. The reactions of a young Chinese student are reported as follows:

When Linda Tsao Wen-Mei arrived in San Francisco, she saw *old* people walking *alone* on the streets! Where were their children? Had young people in America no shame? White-haired grandmothers lunching in restaurants—alone![13]

Americans retire from a job rather abruptly, and have few opportunities to improve status by virtue of their own accomplishments once the age for retirement has been reached.[14] Failure to reach goals which they had set for themselves is a blow to their self-esteem, for Americans tend to evaluate personal worth in terms of promotion, prestige, recognition, and social position.[15] As a consequence of such attitudes, Americans do not like to get old. Among women, the refusal to grow old is most evident even at the age of thirty. Women, it has been noted, pretend to be twenty-nine for several years.[16]

Geographical isolation from children and grandchildren accentuates the plight of the older person in American society. Although elderly people may prefer to maintain a separate home of their own,[17] many are unable to bear the financial strain. If they have lived apart from their children over a period of years, they may not feel welcome in the latters' homes, or may feel that they are a

[12] Parsons, "Kinship Systems," *American Anthropologist, op. cit.,* 45:37.
[13] W. L. White, "The Way We Look to Them," *Reader's Digest* (January, 1952), 60:17.
[14] Cf. Winch, *The Modern Family, op. cit.,* p. 107.
[15] Shaw and Ort, *Personal Adjustment in the American Culture, op. cit.,* p. 237.
[16] Cf. *ibid.,* p. 235.
[17] Davis, "The American Family: What It Is—and Isn't," *op. cit.,* p. 41.

burden to their children.[18] Studies of the attitudes of college students gave support to the hypothesis that the obligation of children to support aged and needy parents is no longer well established in the mores. Children take into consideration the nature of their personal reaction before they arrive at a decision as to whether or not they will help their parents.[19]

Despite these weaknesses, there are ties which exist between the generations as well as between relatives. The strongest bond (and one which is rather vulnerable) is that of mutual affection.[20] There is, moreover, a marked degree of identification with kinfolk as such, regardless of what they are like. Friends are of our own choosing, but we are born to our kin.[21] According to the findings of one study, relatives felt they had a right to drop in unexpectedly, to help themselves to food in the kitchen, use personal belongings, and make comments on the household management and behavior of family members. Relatives furthermore tend to regard one another as custodians of the family reputation. They voluntarily assume responsibility for one another in matters of social etiquette and in occupational and professional guidance.[22]

In the American family, then, it seems as though both emotional and financial security are vested in the small conjugal unit. Parents have responsibilities toward their children, but when the parents grow old the responsibilities which children have toward them is contingent largely upon the strength of emotional ties. Since the number of elderly persons in the population is steadily increasing,

[18] See case illustrations in Ollie A. Randall, "The Older Person in the World of Today—In the Family," *New Goals for Old Age*, ed. George Lawton, New York, Columbia University Press, 1943, pp. 50-70.

[19] Robert M. Dinkel, "Attitudes of Children Toward Supporting Aged Parents," *American Sociological Review* (August, 1944), 9:378-379.

[20] Sirjamaki, *The American Family in the Twentieth Century, op. cit.*, p. 84.

[21] James H. S. Bossard and Eleanor S. Boll, "The Immediate Family and the Kinship Group: A Research Report," *Social Forces* (May, 1946), 24:380.

[22] *Ibid.*

the problem of caring for the aged is one that needs careful consideration by social scientists and social workers.[23]

ORIENTAL FAMILIES

In China the circle of kin embraces the paternal kin within five degrees of kinship, and a few of the closest relatives on the mother's and wife's side.[24] Within this larger circle there is a smaller one which includes: parents, brothers and their families; paternal uncles and their children; married sisters and paternal aunts; and the maternal grandmother.[25] Within one household are ordinarily found parents, brothers, and their families, and probably the third-generation males with their children.

Members of this extended family system have mutual responsibilities and privileges.[26] Even in America the Chinese tend to preserve traditional attitudes toward relatives whom Americans would regard as distant. Pardee Lowe says that his home "took in at times, particularly on feast days, every available member of our clan . . . to be found in the city." The men came to consult Father "as Senior Elder," and many who came for a talk "stayed not only overnight but for weeks—even in some cases years." The family's dry-goods store was "a perpetual Chinese work-relief project."[27] If a family is economically secure the probabilities are that members will have better health and live longer. What is more, the family will be

---

[23] Cf. Elizabeth Ogg, *When Parents Grow Old,* New York, Public Affairs Committee, 1954, and Ernest W. Burgess, "The Growing Problem of Aging," *Living Through the Older Years,* ed. Clark Tibbitts, Ann Arbor, University of Michigan Press, 1949, pp. 7-25.

[24] Lang, *Chinese Family and Society, op. cit.,* p. 166.

[25] *Ibid.*

[26] See Chapter 9, p. 168.

[27] Lowe, *Father and Glorious Descendant, op. cit.,* pp. 66-67.

recognized by kinsmen, for a poor Chinese remarked that the "poor have few relatives, the rich have many."[28]

Support of aged parents is not a matter of magnanimity, but a moral duty.[29] The fact that sons tend to live under the paternal roof is, of course, an important consideration. Apart from moral duties, a son could hardly disregard his parents if he is still financially dependent upon them.

Within this large household children establish strong effective ties with many adults. They are not dependent solely upon their parents for any of their needs.[30] The relationship between grandparents and grandchildren is especially close. "The happiness of having a grandchild is the goal of all middle-aged parents," says one analyst.[31] Sometimes the Oriental grandmother uses her influence over a child to dominate her daughter-in-law.[32] The grandmother has more leisure to devote to the child and she can give the child presents which the mother cannot manage to get.[33] Even in cases where the grandparents do not share the same roof, during brief visits the older couple can do almost anything they wish in regard to the children. The liberty taken by Chinese grandparents, uncles, and in-laws would probably break up the average American family. They can do "almost anything they see fit in regard to the children, even if it means going over the parents' head."[34]

Constant association with many relatives with whom one has close relationships gives the child a feeling of security. Should a parent be ill or deceased, there will be other adults upon whom the child can rely. These relationships provide a richness and security which children who are brought up in cribs and play pens cannot

[28] Lang, *op. cit.*, p. 167.
[29] Hsu, "The Family in China," *op. cit.*, p. 83.
[30] Hsu, *Americans and Chinese, op. cit.*, p. 78.
[31] Yang, *A Chinese Village, op. cit.*, p. 66.
[32] Benedict, *The Chrysanthemum and the Sword, op. cit.*, p. 265.
[33] *Ibid.*
[34] Hsu, *Americans and Chinese, op. cit.*, p. 78.

possibly have.[35] Outsiders or baby sitters are never called in. A Japanese commentator makes the following observation about the practice of using baby sitters:

One of the strangest institutions of American life seems to us to be the baby sitter. Among Japanese, children and the home are the most precious part of living. We would not give them up merely to dash off to a movie or a dance or a cocktail party. Much less would we think of paying someone to take over for us the most wonderful part of our lives.[36]

Another striking contrast between American and Oriental cultures is the attitude toward age. While an American may refuse to acknowledge his age, the average Chinese feels that old age marks the beginning of a loftier and more respected status.[37] When a wife reaches fifty or sixty years of age she has several daughters-in-law under her domination, is the grandmother of a long line of children, and is also overseer of a large household.[38] Although the old father may not have an increase in responsibilities, he still performs many useful functions and is regarded as important to his country's as well as his family's welfare long after he has passed his prime.[39]

In China and Japan, then, old people are the repositories of wisdom. They are respected for their age and remain useful members of the family. To a lesser extent, these attitudes still prevail among the Orientals in America. All people belong in the home, and suggestions to place the ill or mentally disturbed in an institution would probably be rejected.[40]

[35] Cf. Murphy, In the Minds of Men, op. cit., p. 50.
[36] Sumiko Kawachi, "A Japanese Speaks Up," The Catholic Digest (April, 1950), 14:91.
[37] Hsu, Americans and Chinese, op. cit., p. 327.
[38] Yang, op. cit., p. 57.
[39] Lang, op. cit., p. 10.
[40] Cf. Pearse, Social Information Report, op. cit., p. 10.

Mexican Family

In many respects the Mexican family system resembles that of the Oriental. The Mexican family is not as extended as the Chinese, but it does embrace a wide circle of aunts and uncles, cousins, in-laws, and even godparents. Social roles are derived from kinship status, as is the case in Oriental societies, rather than from the occupational system as is the case in American society.[41]

The household customarily includes parents and unmarried children, as well as married sons and their families. In America, the sons may not live under the same roof with their parents, but wherever possible they construct a domicile adjoining it. Very often there is inadequate space in cities, and this practice has contributed to the congested conditions in slum areas.

The following excerpts from a case record on a Mexican family residing in a large Southwestern community gives insight into the nature of the extended Mexican family:

Juan's case came to the attention of the Juvenile Office when school authorities reported that the boy had been absent from school for several weeks. The boy's parents are separated, and he is in the custody of his mother. The mother is unacquainted with the child's whereabouts, but she thinks he is with his father who has no suitable home for a child.

When Juan was located he said that he had been living with his father. He didn't know the exact address. He says he works with his father cleaning yards, and that the father gives him money. Apparently the child does not wish to return to his mother's house; the only reason he gives is that his mother beats him.

Juan's mother explained that she had let the boy go to his cousin's house to play the accordion the day that he disappeared. His father

[41] Cf. Florence Kluckhohn, "Cultural Factors in Social Work Practice and Education," *Social Service Review, op. cit.,* 25:45.

denied that the boy was with him, and the mother believes the boy stayed with his paternal aunts and uncles.

When Juan's mother came to get the boy, she was accompanied by her maternal aunt who lives next door to her. The aunt took the initiative and said Mr. M. was not worthy to be a father. He was a drunkard who made life miserable for her niece. He didn't come around to bother his wife any more, because he knew the family would send the police after him if he did.

Mrs. M. thinks the only reason why Juan prefers to stay with his father is the fact that the latter gives the boy spending money, and the paternal relatives have influenced the child by telling him that his mother is no good. I asked Mrs. M. if her aunt was very nice to the children. The mother said that sometimes her aunt scolded the children and Juan resented his aunt's authority over him. I told her that this might be a factor in keeping the boy away from home, and it might be well to let her aunt know that the boy was to be treated differently.

In a visit to the home after Juan's return there, the boy complained about his aunt's interference. He said that he didn't want his aunt always telling him what to do. At this time I noticed an elderly lady who was bedridden. Mrs. M. explained that this was her grandmother who was very sick and needed a great deal of care. She has assumed the responsibility for her grandmother.

Mexico is predominantly rural and mobility is not high. Roads and transportation systems are poorly developed in many parts of Mexico, a fact which contributes to isolation.[42] In such a society elderly people retain their status and are useful members of society. The older male who is unable to work in the fields always manages to find tasks to perform around the house. Grandmothers occupy a respected position in the household because of their long experience and skills. Traditionally "reverence for parents increases with the passing of the years."[43] Both men and women "have a definite feeling of usefulness" as they get older, and an "assurance that they are respected and wanted by their children."[44]

[42] Fraga and Kennedy, "Recreational Needs of the Senior Latin-American in San Antonio," op. cit., p. 56.
[43] Winter, Mexico and Her People of To-Day, op. cit., p. 164.
[44] Fraga and Kennedy, op. cit., p. 97.

A young person, however, need not be entirely truthful about age, especially a woman. "Never tell your age," an American woman was warned by her prospective Mexican mother-in-law. "Always tell at least five years less, for everybody will automatically add on five anyhow, because everybody automatically subtracts five. You understand?" cautioned the older woman.[45]

Mexican attitudes toward the aged, though, were admired by this young American who lived in Mexico after her marriage. She comments that "one of the sweetest qualities of the Mexican family is devotion to the old," and adds:

Countless are the Mexican homes to which I have made visits . . . in which I have found, pridefully displayed like . . . a jewel in a case, an old lady or gentleman upward in the eighties. . . . They are given the best chair, the best view of everything, the first refreshments, the affection and deference of everyone present. . . . It is unheard of that any old person who has any connection whatsoever with the family should be left alone, sad and bewildered, when the shadows of life are descending.

Even more shocking, to Mexicans, than sending one's "old ones" off to homes for the aged, would be to send them away to sanitariums, rest homes, or hospitals, when they become ill, a burdensome care, or even senile. No, this is when the *viejitos* need love and understanding, now, if ever. . . .

Nobody supposes that young children are injured by the presence in the home of the old, senile, or even slightly demented. On the contrary, they learn that we all grow old and feeble and foolish. This is reality. And they are taught compassion and patience, both very beautiful qualities.[46]

The traditional system of *compadrazgo* establishes two sets of relationships: one between the spiritual godparents and the child, the other between the parents and godparents. Social, political,

---

[45] De Treviño, *My Heart Lies South, op. cit.,* p. 81.
[46] *Ibid.,* pp. 167-169.

and economic factors enter into the selection of godparents. A well-to-do, influential person is desired inasmuch as he will be of greater assistance in time of need. The more godchildren a man has, the wider his influence. Godparents are chosen for baptism, confirmation, and marriage.[47] In Tepoztlán every possibility for extending the godparent relationship has been utilized.[48] Among less isolated groups in Mexico, however, these relationships are rapidly breaking down.[49] Mexicans residing in an urban Southwestern community indicated that these relationships had little if any importance to them. In many instances their compadres were not geographically close to them, and isolation had impaired the relationship.[50] Undoubtedly the political value of the relationships would be practically meaningless in an urban American environment, even if the economic values remained.

Other changes are occurring within the ethnic group in America. The older person feels that he does not receive from his grandchildren the same degree of respect that he accorded his elders. He is concerned, moreover, about his grandchildren's freedom from parental control, though he might not be aware of the repercussions this tendency will have on his children when they grow older.[51] The older Mexican is also aware of the fact that he no longer has the close association which he formerly enjoyed with his children and grandchildren.

A Mexican grandmother in a Texas community exemplifies the reaction of some aged people in her ethnic group toward their changing status.

Mrs. S., a widow, continues to live in the family home with her youngest child, a nineteen-year-old son. She refused to speak English, although she is well able to converse in English and understands it

[47] Lewis, *Life in a Mexican Village: Tepoztlán Restudied, op. cit.,* p. 350.
[48] *Ibid.,* p. 351.
[49] Whetten, *Rural Mexico, op. cit.,* p. 399.
[50] Fraga and Kennedy, *op. cit.,* pp. 80-81.
[51] *Ibid.,* pp. 97-98.

perfectly. Four of her children are married to Anglos. She complains of being lonesome and seems to resent the fact that she is not a highly revered and respected grandmother who rules the family. She says she is "tied down" with the responsibility of caring for her youngest son, but he seems to be well able to care for himself, financially and otherwise. Because this son does not accept all her attentions and because her other children are married outside the ethnic group, Mrs. S. has withdrawn more or less into a shell and complains endlessly about having no one with whom to talk. She appears to be in poor mental as well as physical health, probably because she cannot reconcile herself to her loss of status as matriarch of her family.

European Families

Data on the degree of extension which prevails within the various European families is meager. Primogeniture—the prerogative of the eldest son to inherit the family estate and title—has prevailed throughout much of Europe. Under this system, the eldest son only is favored and the extension of the family to other members is more nebulous. In rural areas, however, isolation and close association with relatives generally strengthen and extend family ties. Among the Italians the extended family includes blood relatives of both parents, provided the relatives live in the same community or visit it, as well as godparents.[52]

Among most Catholic peoples of Southern Europe spiritual relationships with godparents have significance.[53] As a rule, godparents are chosen only for baptism and confirmation.[54] Influential persons who are able to be of assistance to the family are generally selected. So strong is this tie that some older Italians expect to meet their spiritual rather than their fleshy parents in heaven.[55]

[52] Child, *Italian or American?*, op. cit., p. 45.
[53] Cf. Campisi, "Ethnic Family Patterns," *American Journal of Sociology*, op. cit., 53:444.
[54] Williams, *South Italian Folkways in Europe and America*, op. cit., p. 79.
[55] *Ibid.*

The names *compare* and *comare* are used to designate the spiritual relationship.[56] Very often these godparents are blood relatives, a fact which reinforces the strength of the relationship.[57] Sometimes the children are named after one of their godparents, a practice which has fallen into disuse in America because of the un-American names of the older generation godparents.

In America these beliefs and attitudes have not been appreciably modified. To refuse to become a godparent is regarded as a deep insult.[58] As a rule, though, parents make inquiries about the availability of potential candidates for the honor beforehand. If godparenthood should impose additional responsibilities—financial or otherwise—upon a person who felt reluctant, the parents would never make the proposal.[59]

The rule of primogeniture is optional and variable among the Italians in America. Success is generally more important than being the first-born male.[60] Parents may live with the eldest son, but sometimes they choose to reside with the youngest son.[61]

Older people tend to be highly respected according to tradition, and parents who are no longer able to work expect their children to care for them. Traditionally, this responsibility has rested primarily on the eldest son and his wife.[62] The only persons who went to institutions in Italy were those who had no relatives, and the whole community felt bound in charity to aid them.[63]

In America, too, elderly Italians are seldom found outside their children's homes. Caring for the aged, ill, or mentally disturbed relatives may be a burden; mothers may grumble about the extra work and fathers complain about the strain on family income, but

---

[56] *Ibid.*
[57] *Ibid.*, p. 80.
[58] *Ibid.*, pp. 94-95.
[59] *Ibid.*, p. 95.
[60] Campisi, *op. cit.*, p. 444.
[61] Williams, *South Italian Folkways in Europe and America, op. cit.*, p. 190.
[62] *Ibid.*, pp. 184-185.
[63] *Ibid.*, p. 184.

if a professional worker suggests that these dependents be institutionalized, the family would probably be horrified.[64] If parents die, leaving an ailing unmarried child, the responsibility tends to be assumed by brothers and sisters.

European families in America are probably not as closely knit as Oriental or Mexican families, but they tend to have greater strength than the American family.

JEWISH FAMILY

The Jewish family is still less extended than the average European family. In many respects, it approximates the American family. Hospitality is valued, and relatives tend to be more welcome than friends. An American Jew describes the situation prevailing in her family in the following words:

There has always been a close and warm feeling of affection among the members of our family which I feel is an outgrowth of the strong feeling of unity inculcated by my parents. This closeness also extended to our relatives. I recall many a Sabbath meal at my home shared with an unexpected relative or friend. This was not an uncommon occurrence and our guests were always welcome. The Sabbath and its ceremonies bring back many nostalgic memories.

American Jewish parents do not customarily live in the homes of their children. One informant who has an unmarried brother commented that his mother "wouldn't think of living with her children." Although the mother bemoans the fact that one son is unmarried and "has no one to care for him," she nonetheless refuses to live with him herself, lest it appear that she is dependent upon him.

Spiritual relationships such as that which exists between godparents and a child are a part of Christian rather than of Jewish

[64] *Ibid.*, p. 193.

culture. The practice of naming a child after a sponsor, particularly if the latter is a relative, is common among Mexicans and some Europeans. Jews, too, often name a child after relatives. A Jewish informant remarked:

It is traditional that Jewish children be named after relatives who are deceased, usually grandparents, and of course all of the children in my family received names of grandparents and other close relatives. My children, and the children of my sisters and brothers, are named after our parents.

American Jews who have become largely assimilated may not continue this custom, for dead relatives often have Biblical names that are "too revealingly Jewish."[65] Some parents compromise by selecting an "American" name that is vaguely suggestive of the Hebrew original, so that Isaac becomes Irving or Aaron becomes Arthur. In this way, respect is paid to the family ancestors, and at the same time the child is spared a too Jewish name.[66]

Traditionally, parents are respected by their children and old age is regarded as a blessing. In Minneapolis the Jews make every effort to satisfy the needs of their parents who are no longer able to care for themselves. One Jew made the following comment:

When my father was taken ill, I saw that he was given every medical attention and I know that both my parents feel that all of us children would do all we can for them. I have been maintaining the home for them. They live alone because it's better for them. That's what they want.[67]

There is an old saying among the Jews to the effect that "one father supports ten children, but ten children can't support one father." That Jewish children have an obligation to support their parents is by no means taken for granted;[68] in this respect the Jews

[65] Steinberg, *The Making of the Modern Jew, op. cit.,* p. 241.
[66] *Ibid.*
[67] Gordon, *Jews in Transition, op. cit.,* p. 138.
[68] Joffe, "The Dynamics of Benefice," *Social Forces, op. cit.,* 27:241-242.

resemble Americans. Another factor is involved in the Jewish practice, however. To be the recipient is humiliating to the Jew. Hence, a dependent old person might prefer to accept assistance impersonally from a social agency rather than be dependent upon the charity of his children. These attitudes explain the willingness of the Jewish aged to live in institutions, despite the pleas of their children that they reside with them. Even gifts may not be accepted by aged or needy parents. One Jewess commented that every time she gave her mother a gift, the latter felt bound to reciprocate—usually with something more expensive.[69]

The Jews, then, are closely akin to the American pattern in the matter of the extended family. In fact, the American Jews not only limit the family to the nuclear, conjugal unit where responsibility to other family members is negligible, but old parents also prefer to ignore any overtures of assistance which their children might make.

Negro Family

The Negro family is said to have an "amorphous" character since it may extend not only to "uncles, cousins, and other persons related by 'blood,' such as illegitimate children, but even adopted children."[70] Regardless of how small or how crowded a Negro home is, there is "always room for a stray child, an elderly grandmother, an indigent aunt, a homeless friend."[71]

The following case excerpt illustrates the numerous placement possibilities of an orphaned Negro girl:

When Mary's mother died she was placed in an orphanage, but she failed to make a satisfactory adjustment, and relatives asked to remove her. Immediately after leaving the orphanage, Mary lived a few weeks

[69] *Ibid.*, p. 242.
[70] Frazier, "Ethnic Family Patterns: The Negro Family in the United States," *op. cit.*, 53:437.
[71] Davie, *Negroes in American Society, op. cit.*, p. 209.

with her uncle, Mr. W. The home was crowded and Mary had differences with her aunt. After a few weeks she decided to stay with a cousin. This arrangement lasted for less than a month, and she went to live with another uncle, Mr. S. The latter was separated from his wife and living with a cousin. Here the child made a better adjustment and stayed for three years.

The conjugal unit is not as important in delineating the limits of the Negro family as it is among Americans and Jews. Since many marriages are of the common-law variety, the father is not necessarily as integral a part of the family as might be expected. The head of the household is usually the mother, grandmother, or even the great-grandmother. A Nashville study revealed that grandmothers were present in 61 of the 342 families studied, but the grandfather was also present in only 25 of the families.[72] Among the simple people in a folk society, the old grandmother is regarded as a repository of wisdom. She is familiar with means of warding off the "dangers of ill luck" and can be relied upon to ease the pains of childbirth.[73] The Negro grandmother "stands today, as of old," says Frazier, "as the 'oldest head' in the House of Mother."[74]

In contrast to other families, the Negro family is an elastic, extended one with ill-defined boundaries. The aged are not only respected, but they also tend to dominate the household. Old men, of course, may not have as much security as grandmothers, but the family ties of lower-class Negro men have never been strong. If economic security is somewhat tenuous within the Negro family, because of low income, whatever the family does have tends to be shared by all members.

[72] Frazier, *The Negro Family in the United States, op. cit.*, p. 123.
[73] *Ibid.*, p. 119.
[74] *Ibid.*, p. 124.

Part IV

CONCLUSION

16

Review and Assessment

THE PURPOSE: IN RETROSPECT

A KNOWLEDGE of cultural values and an appreciation of their significance to those who hold them is hypothesized to be helpful and, at times, essential for effective practice with ethnic clients. Within the framework of the social institutions—the organized system of practices developed around values—the teacher or practitioner in the helping profession can conceptualize the relative importance of specific ethnic values. When ethnic group values are viewed against American cultural values, the professional person will, it is believed, be better able to appreciate the quandary in which members of cultural groups often find themselves when faced with a choice between two systems of values.

In generalizing about the cultural values of specific ethnic groups, American values may be envisioned at one extreme of a conceptual pole or continuum, while Oriental values are at the opposite pole. Other ethnic groups approximate one or the other pole in varying degrees.

CULTURAL VALUES OF SPECIFIC ETHNIC GROUPS

American Values

The American family is a small one in which children are individualized and consulted. To peoples of other cultures it appears

341

that American children are "spoiled" and reared in a dream world where they are shielded from the harsh realities of life. In late adolescence they are expected to establish a home of their own apart from that of the parents, and to become relatively independent. Parents may have no voice in the choice of their children's marital partners and parental approbation is not necessarily mandatory.

American family life is characterized by companionship and affectional ties. Husband and wife are supposed to be emotionally interdependent, and when emotional satisfaction begins to wane or to disappear, divorce may be obtained on the grounds of "incompatibility." Of all family types, with the exception of the Negro, the American family is the most unstable.

Parents are often "pals" to their children and expect to share the confidences of their offspring. Reserve or aloofness from the children is not valued by either parent. To observers from other cultures it appears as though American parents demand little respect or obedience from their children. Parents and children seem to be on more of a peer level than is found among other cultural groups. Even the father plays with his child, assists in caring for his physical needs, and enjoys sharing his experiences. Children do not customarily relinquish their earnings to the family purse, nor do they necessarily engage in the economic activities of the family.

The fairer sex has a predominant position in American society, and boys are not favored more than girls within the family. An attractive young woman is an effective gimmick used by advertisers to sell everything from mouthwash to lawn mowers. The mother tends to be dominant within the home and she also participates in political, economic, and social life. She may engage in a profession if she so desires, and at the same time be a mother and housewife. Since her husband may cast sidelong glances at comely young ladies with whom he associates during work hours, it behooves the American wife to retain her own physical charms.

Youth rather than old age is glorified in America. In a highly industrialized, ever mobile society the elderly members—like outmoded machinery—tend to feel obsolete and useless. Arbitrary retirement abruptly terminates an active life in the business world. By the time a person reaches the age of retirement, the home to which he retires is generally an empty shell, for his children are married and living in homes of their own. If he needs financial or medical aid, his children are not obligated to assist him and he may be forced to rely upon welfare agencies.

Elderly people, as well as the very young, appear to find more satisfaction in religion than those in the prime of life. But to most Americans religion does not rate high in the scale of values. Americans tend to be relatively unfamiliar with dogma, to attend services in church irregularly, and rarely to engage in religious devotions within the home. The Sunday School appears to have displaced the home in imparting religious knowledge, and perfect Sunday School attendance records are rare. For the most part, religious affiliations are most significant for rites of passage. When the American is looking for a place to be married and a place to be buried, the church affords a proper setting for an elaborate ceremony.

American attitudes toward authority are nurtured in the home. To other ethnic peoples it appears that children are much too vocal in the affairs of the home and that they have very little respect for the wishes of their parents. These same attitudes prevail among adult Americans toward all persons in authority—teachers, employers, policemen, and professional workers. The person in authority is often suspected of using his position for individual gain. Politicians, especially, have this reputation. If a politician is entirely honest, however, and fails to take personal advantage of his position, he is apt to be labeled a "sucker." "Putting one over" on the policeman or any other person is considered good sport. Fun is poked at the person who fails to maintain the authority with which he is vested. To some extent, democracy is responsible for these attitudes, since democracy implies equality. While Americans look out for their own rights and pay lip service to democracy, however, they simultaneously restrict the rights of ethnic group members.

Economic values tend to rate high in American society, and this country is renowned for the achievements and inventions which have made it the most prosperous nation in the world. Money, success, and power are the epitome of American ambition. Almost everything is calculated in monetary terms, time expended (for time is worth money), recognizable material achievements, and the accruing prestige and power. Despite the prevailing high standards of living, many Americans still are not satisfied and persist in the race to "keep up with the Joneses." The more money they have acquired—with all that money can buy—the greater their success and the higher their prestige. Economic considerations influence nearly every action, from the number of children one will have to the number of cars in the garage.

Recreation has become an increasingly important value in American urban life where working people are often confined to dull, monotonous jobs in factories and offices. Much of this recreation is commercial—in keeping with the stress placed upon money—and much of it is enjoyed with age or sex groups. Americans like to be with groups of other people and they crowd into movies, stadia, and swimming places in order to recreate. The tendency to join organizations is another index of gregariousness. Recreation need not be productive of anything but sheer relaxation, and at the tempo Americans live and work, the relaxation obtained in recreation is undoubtedly a value.

Education, too, is becoming more and more of a value in American life. Americans receive many years of schooling, though the purpose for which they are being educated is often hazy. True, education is essential for high-powered jobs and the professions, but some Americans go to school primarily for the social life which it offers and to be able to say that they have a degree. Intellectuals are not as highly esteemed as are competent businessmen, and the absent-minded professor tends to be the butt of many a joke.

Americans may be envisioned as a polar type characterized by a monogamous, small, somewhat unstable conjugal family whose members place a high value on economic institutions and recreation. The importance of education is not too clearly defined, and persons in authority often are only tolerated. Religion tends to be even more of a nebulous value than authority; it is useful primarily during crises or for rites of passage.

Values of Orientals

At the opposite conceptual pole one might place the Orientals. Chinese and Japanese families are large, extended systems which have retained such traditional family functions as religion, education, recreation, and economics. Children are highly valued, and status is determined, in part, by the number of offspring one has to carry on ancestor worship. Sons, however, are preferable to daughters, for the latter eventually become a part of the family into which they marry.

Solidarity is high, and divorce or desertion is a rare occurrence. The family is a functioning unit which is designed to meet every crisis and provide for every emergency—unemployment, sickness, and old age. Marriage is a family contract and the marital partners traditionally have little or nothing to say about the choice of a mate. If the marriage is emotionally unsatisfactory, the husband may take a concubine—provided the family is able to support her.

Old people are highly respected and generally exercise authority over their children and grandchildren as long as they live. They retain economic control of the household and direct all family activities. Eventually the aged parents will become ancestors and will be in an influential position in the hereafter; hence, it would be foolhardy to ignore or displease them.

Religion is a value inasmuch as it is so closely related to the family practice of ancestor worship. Even in America the Chinese continue this practice. The Chinese have made many contributions to social thought in the realms of religion and philosophy. Confucianism, for instance, continues to make an impact upon Chinese life.

Authority is not something to joke about among the Orientals. The Japanese have an elaborate ceremonial code which is designed to show the proper amount of respect toward the proper persons. Authority, too, is associated with the family. In many parts of rural China the actual political authority stems from family heads, toward whom respect is always shown. Even sons do not presume to establish a joking relationship with their fathers.

Education is highly valued by the Chinese, for it has usually been a prerequisite for political office. For the young child, especially the girl, education is often family-centered. Recreation, too, revolves around the family. Birthdays, weddings, and funerals are occasions for recreation. On holidays and festivals the whole family recreates as a unit, with small children joining in the merriment.

The economic system has some importance to all peoples because it is through this system that the necessities of life are provided. Among the Orientals the economic system is interwoven with the family structure. Most Chinese and Japanese value land in preference to hard cash. They like to have sufficient financial means to meet the requirements of status, but once this goal has been achieved, they do not continue to direct their efforts toward piling up money. Prestige is more intricately involved with family honor than with material things.

In many respects, then, Oriental societies appear to be at opposite poles from the American family. The large, extended family system permeates every aspect of life and determines, in large part, cultural values.

Mexican Values

The Mexican is closely akin to the Oriental in many respects. Many Mexicans are in whole or part Mongoloid like the Oriental, for they are descendants of the Mongoloid Indian aborigines. Culturally as well as biologically, then, the Mexicans bear some resemblance to the Orientals.

Mexican families are extended, but not to the same degree as the Chinese. Five generations are seldom calculated in the Mexican family. Grandparents, parents, and children, however, are often within the same household, and the sons traditionally bring their wives into the parental homes. In one respect the Mexican family extends beyond that of the Oriental, for Mexicans include the spiritual godparents of their children as a part of the family.

Sons are valued more than daughters, and the aged are generally loved and esteemed. Family size is seldom limited, for children are regarded as important in all extended family systems.

Like the Orientals, the Mexicans have a great respect for authority. The family head traditionally symbolizes authority, and he demands respect from all family members. Mexicans dislike getting involved with the law, especially in America. Law generally appears a bit arbitrary, and it is not something to be disregarded.

Religion may be more of a value in Mexico than it is in America because in the mother country religion, like the family, is associated with all events of life. Recreation, for instance, is often provided by religious festivals. The godparent relationship is formed through religion, and all the rites of passage tend to be of a religious nature.

Among the rural Mexicans economic values as Americans know them become important only after they have been cultivated on American soil. When the simple material needs of the family have been met, there is little stimulus for the acquisition of tomorrow's needs; the *mañana* attitude prevails. Time is not worth money; it is to be spent leisurely.

Formal education, too, has little significance for the average Mexican. Like economic values, however, the need for a formal education may be appreciated when a family begins to become acculturated to the American way of life. Most education is informal in nature and is received within the home.

Values of European Ethnic Groups

Since the majority of ethnics from Northern and Western Europe have been in America for three or more generations, they have become largely assimilated. Southern and Eastern Europeans, however, immigrated in large numbers around the turn of the twentieth century; hence, cultural differences are more pronounced, and generalizations refer primarily to these groups.

European families are not as extended as the Orientals or Mexicans, but they often include the spiritual relationship between godparents and children. Family solidarity is strong, at least until the families are second- or third-generation American ethnics. For the most part, old people and children are cherished family members and are not regarded as liabilities or nuisances. The eldest son has a privileged position traditionally, but in America his status is also dependent upon his personal qualities.

Families are traditionally patriarchal, and the father is obeyed and respected. Attitudes toward the father are usually carried over to other persons vested with authority. Religion was more of a value to the first-generation immigrants than it is to the third generation, for the latter often acquires American attitudes. Rites of passage, however, usually remain associated with religion. Even if the ethnic is not a practical church-goer, he wants to get married and be buried properly.

Economic values rank higher among this group than among the Mexicans. Many European ethnics came to America to make money and then expected to return home. Education and recreation, too, assume relatively important places because most Europeans settle in cities where they feel the full impact of American culture.

Jewish Values

Of all ethnic groups, the Jews most closely approximate the Americans—recent Jewish immigrants and some of the early twentieth century immigrants excepted. The Jewish family is a small, conjugal unit with the same tenuous bonds of the American family. Boys usually have more status than they do in the American family, however, for the religious function is traditionally reserved for the male.

Religion is a value at least to the extent that it is a factor in identifying the ethnic group. Orthodox Jews place more importance upon traditional religious observances than do the Reformed or Conservative Jews. Like Americans, the Jews place emphasis upon the economic institution. Education is highly valued, and has been throughout Jewish history. The security of the ethnic group often hinges upon education and adequate finances.

There is little evidence that Jewish attitudes toward authority and recreation are dissimilar from those of the dominant American group. Even in Eastern Europe the Jews tended to be antiauthoritarian. Parents reasoned with their children, and although punishments were often severe, this fact was seldom interpreted as rejection. Recreation is valued by all urban peoples who have any leisure time, and the Jews have traditionally been an urban people.

In most respects, then, the Jews seem to have values much like those of the dominant American group. Perhaps there is more emphasis on religion and on education, but in economics, government, and recreation the variations are slight.

Values of American Negroes

The Negro group probably has fewer cultural differences than any of the other major ethnic groups, because the Negroes have resided in America for centuries. Of all groups, however, the Negro family is the most unstable and the family boundaries are most elastic. Other traditional family systems emphasize solidarity and censure divorce and desertion. The Negro family in America, however, lacks these traditional strengths because under slavery the Negroes had few rights as family members. Husbands were separated from wives and Negro women became the mistresses of their white masters.

Since family limits are not too rigidly defined, the Negro family extends beyond the conjugal unit to aunts, uncles, cousins, and grandparents. In-laws are generally not as important as they are in the average extended family, because many marriages are of the common-law variety.

The Negro family gives even more status to the mother than does the American family. Fathers were never considered as dependable as mothers, and economic conditions in the South have not been conducive to high status or security for the Negro male. At birth, girls are just as welcome as boys, and it may make little appreciable difference whether or not they are born in wedlock.

Religion served a very important function in the lives of earlier Negroes, since they could release their feelings quite openly in their own churches. Today, however, it seems that this social institution is less important.

As for values associated with the other institutions, the Negro appears to resemble the lower classes of the dominant group. Rural, lower-class people generally place little emphasis on formal education and on commercialized recreation.

On the whole, then, the Negro ethnic group veers toward the dominant American group—on a lower class level—in the institutional areas of authority, recreation, education, and economics. Religion may be more important, however. The greatest deviation from the dominant cultural pattern is in the family system.

Importance for the Professional Person

Significance of Culture in Establishing Relationships

The professional person who hopes to be of assistance to a client must first of all establish a satisfactory working relationship with him. Knowledge and appreciation of cultural values are believed to facilitate the formation of such a relationship, inasmuch as they eliminate much of the searching and probing into the reasons for an action or a social situation, and, furthermore, tend to give the client the impression of being understood. A relationship, as the term is used here, refers to "the dynamic interaction of feelings and attitudes" between the professional person and the client "with the purpose of helping the client achieve a better adjustment between himself and his environment."[1]

Prejudice and insincerity often permeate the social climate when two different cultures come into contact with each other. It is difficult, for example, to establish rapport between a professional person representing the dominant American culture and a Negro client. The same difficulty prevails when the client belongs to an ethnic group that is numerically strong in a given locality. Since relationship is a dynamic, reciprocal process, the nature of the relationship established between the professional worker and the client will be contingent upon the attitudes and responses of one toward the other. Attitudes are revealed not so much by reassuring speeches on the part of the professional worker as by an inflection of the voice, a facial expression, or the selection of language. A worker who makes use of epithets or who chooses to speak English to a Spanish-speaking client when he is able to converse in Spanish,

---

[1] Felix P. Biestek, S.J., "An Analysis of the Casework Relationship," *Social Casework* (February, 1954), 35:58. In italics.

for instance, will not readily establish rapport. Teachers and those who deal with youth might bear in mind the assumption that attitudes are caught more frequently than they are taught,[2] and that a teacher's views tend to influence those of his pupils.

Teachers, social workers, counselors, and others in the helping professions who desire to establish sound working relationships need to have an acceptance of the client and to create an atmosphere in which the latter can express his feelings. The client ought to receive the impression, moreover, that he has dignity and worth as an individual, and will be dealt with accordingly; that he will not be judged as a failure or a weakling; that his confidence will be respected; and withal that the professional worker has sympathetic understanding. If such are the professional worker's attitudes, the client undoubtedly will feel more freedom to express his fears and apprehensions.

An individual "can be rightly known," it has been said, "only in his own cultural milieu."[3] In establishing a working relationship with an ethnic client, the professional worker might profitably bear in mind the importance of the family and of the roles of family members in some other cultures. A nurse or social worker, for example, who attempts to plan a diet or a budget with a Mexican or Italian mother before the man of the house has been consulted may find little response on the part of the wife; in patriarchal families the wife traditionally does not exercise initiative. Similarly, a teacher might be prepared to expect an Oriental or Greek child to have difficulty in entering into play groups, inasmuch as the child's contacts are traditionally family-centered. The presenting

[2] Laurence DeFee Haskew, "The Role of Education in Improving Human Relations," *Cultural Groups and Human Relations,* New York, Columbia University Press, 1951, p. 185.

[3] Marrow, *Living Without Hate, op. cit.,* p. 34. Italics. There may be said to be a specific "cultural milieu" even for the profession. Cf. Kurt Freudenthal, "Our Culture: How to Integrate It into That of Our Community," *Social Work Journal* (January, 1955), 36:11-12.

problem is, at times, cultural in nature, and a knowledge of values is often basic to an understanding of the situation.

Although the sympathetic professional person may establish rapport at the initial social contact, the effectiveness of the subsequent relationship may also depend upon a knowledge of values. Feelings and attitudes, which are products of culture, can be evaluated only in the light of cultural knowledge. Such, for example, would be true in the following instances: the Indian or Mexican child who appears to be indifferent when the teacher administers timed tests; the Negro whose superstitious beliefs are responsible for acute anxiety; or the Mexican laborer who cannot hold a job because his value of time differs from that of the American. Even though the client may have a favorable first impression of the professional worker, the relationship will tend to lose tonicity if the latter cannot subsequently seem to understand cultural conflicts.

Aid in Treatment

The kind of adaptation which an ethnic makes will be dependent to a great extent upon the manner in which he resolves cultural conflicts and meets new situations. A professional worker who is unfamiliar with other cultures may not realize the number of adaptations which a client must make in a new environment. Such adaptations as using another system of transportation and communication, finding a place to live, and finding work may have been expected by the newcomer, but nonetheless they may be occasions for worry. Other adaptations, such as those involved in utilizing the equipment of the American home, factory, or school, may not have been anticipated as clearly.[4] The adaptations pertaining to such cultural values as the family and religious beliefs, however, will tend to generate the greatest anxiety. For example,

---

[4] For an analysis of problems facing the newcomer see Hertha Kraus, "The Newcomer's Orientation to the American Community," *New Emphasis on Cultural Factors*, New York, Family Service Association of America, 1948, pp. 9-13.

an Oriental or Mexican might reject with horror the suggestion that a mentally disturbed or aged member of the family be placed in an institution. Birth control as a solution to an ever increasing, malnourished family might also be wholly unacceptable because of religious or family values. That many ethnic peoples even seek professional services is surprising, since most ethnics tend to rely upon their own group organizations for mutual aid and support. The professional services which Americans seem to "take for granted" are often an integral part of American culture, and a pattern for which the past experience of other ethnics has not prepared them.

Under these circumstances, the professional worker needs to be cautious in suggesting measures or initiating procedures that are culturally unacceptable to the client. A knowledge of cultural values will afford insight into acceptable and unacceptable procedures. "Adjustment," it has been said, "has to start with people where they are, with their institutions, their outlook, the values they place on the events of life."[5] In setting the treatment goal, the professional worker may expect the client to go further in the process of change than his cultural limitations permit him to go.[6] Where values are concerned, change nearly always creates a crisis. A professional worker, for example, might be surprised at the reaction of a Mexican to the suggestion that a family member with active tuberculosis living in a crowded slum area be placed in a sanatorium. To the Mexican, the care of the ill is traditionally a family function and the unacculturated ethnic will not accept passively the suggestion by an outsider that the family be disrupted, especially if a loved one in need will be confined to a sanatorium.

Even in minor matters, a culture may make little provision for change. Until a century ago, China went so far as to restrict contacts with the outside world in order to preserve her culture as it

[5] McNickle, "A U. S. Indian Speaks," *Americas, op. cit.,* 6:27.
[6] Pollak, "Cultural Dynamics in Casework," *op. cit.,* 34:281.

was.[7] Even other Western peoples such as certain Europeans tend to adapt slowly when compared with Americans. As one indication of the rate of social change in many parts of Europe, consider the practice of passing the family home and estate from one generation to the next with little, if any, alteration. Another index of the rate of change is the tendency of a son to follow in his father's occupational footsteps. If such be the case with many Europeans—the forebears of most old Americans—how much more difficult must rapid social change be for members of other groups.

Some personality types will, of course, adapt with greater facility than others. Among cultural groups there is believed to be what is called a basic personality type comprising those elements which we share more or less in common with other members of our society.[8] The basic personality type sanctioned by one culture may not have the same approbation or status in another. For instance, the person whose past experience has led him to believe in the effectiveness of graciousness, mildness, and timidity may be sadly disillusioned or even panicky in the American aggressive, competitive cultural environment. Adaptation in this regard may shake the very foundations of emotional security or may result in apathy and a sense of futility.

Culture, A Basis of Security

Culture by its very nature plays a vital role in giving its adherents a feeling of security inasmuch as it prescribes what to do in a given

[7] For generations every schoolboy in China studied the following observation of Confucius: "To gather in the same places where our fathers before us have gathered; to perform the same ceremonies which they before us have performed; to play the same music which they before us have played; to pay respect to those whom they honored; to love those who were dear to them—in fact, to serve those now dead as if they were living, and now departed as if they were still with us: this is the highest achievement of true filial piety." As quoted in Herrymon Maurer, "The Trouble with China Is Confucius," Fortune (April, 1947), 35:128.

[8] Cf. Abram Kardiner, "The Concept of Basic Personality Structure as an Operational Tool in the Social Sciences," in The Science of Man in the World Crisis, ed. Ralph Linton, New York, Columbia University Press, 1945, pp. 107-122.

circumstance. Although culture is neither static nor simple, all cultures are organized to produce some degree of psychic security.[9] Like an insurance company, a cultural system "figures the threats and provides certain assurance that said threats may be avoided or neutralized if certain prescribed patterns are followed."[10] Of course, some cultural systems will balance threats and defenses more adequately than others. Among some cultural groups, for instance, too much attention is devoted to unreal "threats," and a great deal of energy is spent in "hunting witches" or "chasing ghosts." The normal individual in a properly functioning cultural system, however, will have the hazards of life and the defenses against them provided by cultural patterns.

Cultural security is contingent upon one's identification with or feeling of belonging to a cultural group. Belongingness is the assurance of being inwardly at home as well as outwardly accepted by a group. There is no fear of isolation or ostracism as long as one identifies with a group and conforms to its norms. The feeling of belonging gives a sense of linkage with the past and a hope of continuity through the transmission of one's culture to future generations. Not belonging, on the contrary, produces an individual shaky in his relationships, prone to anxiety and indecision—like a child reared without the security of parental love.

When culture change is too rapid or when divergent cultures conflict, a subsequent loss of predictability and hence of dependability in personal relationships results. It is impossible to play a game according to rules if there are disagreements as to what the rules of the game are. Culture prescribes rules, and when the stakes are high, that is, when the conflict involves values, the very foundations of security may be rocked. In areas of lesser import an uncom-

[9] Cf. Winch, *The Modern Family, op. cit.,* p. 164.
[10] John Gillin and George Nicholson, "The Security Functions of Cultural Systems," *Social Forces* (December, 1951), 30:179.

fortable or uneasy feeling may arise, yet not be sufficient to endanger basic security.

In the light of this analysis of cultural values, there are several questions which the person in the helping profession may ponder with profit, namely: does the professional worker always realize the significance of a cultural value to the client, or does the worker tend to regard certain values as mere idiosyncrasies? Are American cultural values, simply because they are "American," always to be preferred to the values of the client? Are pressures put upon the client to adopt the "American way"? Is the professional worker conscious of the incongruities which outsiders see in American culture? Does the professional worker envision Americans as products of culture and as representatives of that culture to the client? Is the professional worker aware of the imbalance that results from modifying certain cultural values and leaving other related values undisturbed?

These are some of the questions to which professional workers could profitably give serious consideration. In working with clients of differing cultural backgrounds, it would seem that effective treatment presupposes an awareness of the importance of cultural elements and a readiness to examine critically some of the cultural values of the dominant American society. The professional worker needs to bear in mind the fact that some values are deeply rooted and that many other cultures make less provision than does American culture for rapid change. Knowledge and skill in handling cultural values should, moreover, aid the professional person in establishing rapport with the client, and should prevent the worker from expecting the ethnic client to accept forms of treatment that are culturally unacceptable.

BIBLIOGRAPHY

Bibliography

Adamic, Louis. *From Many Lands.* New York: Harper & Brothers, 1940.
Adams, Elizabeth Laura. *Dark Symphony.* New York: Sheed & Ward, 1942.
"The American Way of Life." *Fortune* (February, 1951), 43:63-67.
"America's Chinese." *Life* (January 8, 1951), 30:71-77.
Anderson, Elin L. *We Americans.* Cambridge: Harvard University Press, 1938.
Anderson, Jackson M. *Industrial Recreation.* New York: McGraw-Hill Book Co., 1955.
Anon. "An Analysis of Jewish Culture." *Jews in a Gentile World.* Edited by Isacque Graeber and Steuart H. Britt. New York: The Macmillan Co., 1942, pp. 243-263.
Antin, Mary. *The Promised Land.* Boston: Houghton Mifflin Co., 1912.
Baber, Ray. E. *Marriage and the Family.* 2d ed. New York: McGraw-Hill Book Co., 1953.
"Backsliding." *Time* (July 24, 1950), 56:54.
Barclay, Dorothy. "Children's Thoughts on Parental Behavior." *The New York Times Magazine* (May 9, 1954), p. 54.
Barclay, Dorothy. "For the Girls of the Family." *The New York Times Magazine* (April 9, 1950), p. 38.
Barclay, Dorothy. "How Girls Judge Mother's Role." *The New York Times Magazine* (June 21, 1953), p. 32.
Barron, Milton L. *The Juvenile in Delinquent Society.* New York: Alfred A. Knopf, Inc., 1954.
Barry, Colman J. *The Catholic Church and German Americans.* Milwaukee: Bruce Publishing Co., 1953.

Barzun, Jacques. *God's Country and Mine*. Boston: Little, Brown & Co., 1954.

Beals, Ralph. "The Mexican Student Views the United States." *Annals of the American Academy of Political and Social Science* (September, 1954), 295:108-115.

"Beastly Rulings." *The New York Times Magazine* (August 8, 1954), p. 41.

Behrman, S. N. *The Worcester Account*. New York: Random House, 1954.

Belden, Jack. *China Shakes the World*. New York: Harper & Brothers, 1950.

Benedict, Ruth. *The Chrysanthemum and the Sword*. Boston: Houghton Mifflin Co., 1946.

Benedict, Ruth. "The Family: Genus Americanum." *The Family: Its Function and Destiny*. Edited by Ruth N. Anshen. New York: Harper & Brothers, 1949, pp. 159-169.

Benedict, Ruth. *Patterns of Culture*. New York: Penguin Books, Inc., 1934.

Benedict, Ruth. *Race: Science and Politics*. Rev. ed. New York: Modern Age Books, 1943.

Berry, Brewton. *Race Relations*. New York: Houghton Mifflin Co., 1951.

Bienenstok, Theodore. "Antiauthoritarian Attitudes in the Eastern European *Shtetel* Community." *American Journal of Sociology* (September, 1951), 57:150-158.

Biestek, Felix P., S.J. "An Analysis of the Casework Relationship." *Social Casework* (February, 1954), 35:57-61.

Black, Algernon D. *If I Marry Outside My Religion*. New York: Public Affairs Committee, 1954.

Blackey, Eileen. "Some Cultural Aspects of Social Casework in Hawaii," *Cultural Problems in Social Case Work*. New York: Family Welfare Association of America, 1940, pp. 38-58.

Bossard, James H. S., and Boll, Eleanor S. "The Immediate Family and the Kinship Group: A Research Report." *Social Forces* (May, 1946), 24:379-384.

Bosworth, Francis. "Settlements and Neighborhood Centers." *Social Work Year Book 1954*, pp. 470-474.

Bradford, Ben. "Rebirth of the Sunday School." *The New York Times Magazine* (September 19, 1954), pp. 30, 60.

Brasch, R. "Why Jews Cover the Head." *Commentary* (January, 1954), 17:37-40.

Brightbill, Charles K. "Recreation." *Social Work Year Book 1954*, pp. 439-448.

Brodersen, Arvid. "Themes in the Interpretation of America by Prominent Visitors from Abroad." *Annals of the American Academy of Political and Social Science* (September, 1954), 295:21-32.

Broun, Heywood, and Britt, George. *Christians Only.* New York: Vanguard Press, 1931.

Buck, Pearl S. *Pavilion of Women.* New York: The John Day Co., 1946.

Buitron, Anibal and Barbara. "What About Our Indians?" *Americas* (March, 1954), 6:3, 41.

Burgess, Ernest W. "The Growing Problems of Aging." *Living Through the Older Years.* Ed. by Clark Tibbitts. Ann Arbor: University of Michigan Press, 1949.

Burgess, Ernest W., and Locke, Harvey J. *The Family.* New York: American Book Company, 1950.

Burma, John H. *Spanish-Speaking Groups in the United States.* Durham, N. C.: Duke University Press, 1954.

Bush, Vannevar. "Today's Research and Tomorrow's World." *Congressional Record* (March 24, 1954), 100:A2246.

Campisi, Paul J. "Ethnic Family Patterns: The Italian Family in the United States." *American Journal of Sociology* (May, 1948), 53: 443-449.

"Can This Marriage Be Saved?" *Ladies' Home Journal* (December, 1953), 70:54, 88-91.

"Can This Marriage Be Saved?" *Ladies' Home Journal* (June, 1954), 71:55, 77-80.

Carter, William Eugene. "The Religious Drama of Mexico: Its Use in Program Planning in a Group Work Agency." Unpublished Master's dissertation. San Antonio: Our Lady of the Lake College, 1951.

Cavan, Ruth Shonle. *The American Family.* New York: Thomas Y. Crowell Co., 1953.

Chapin, F. Stuart. *Contemporary American Institutions.* New York: Harper & Brothers, 1935.

Chase, Stuart. *Mexico: A Study of Two Americas.* New York: The Macmillan Co., 1931.

Chen, Theodore H. E. "Racial Characteristics of the Chinese." *Sociology and Social Research* (January-February, 1940), 24:216-230.

Ch'eng-K'un, Cheng. "Familism the Foundation of Chinese Social Organization." *Social Forces* (October, 1944), 23:50-59.

Child, Irvin L. *Italian or American?* New Haven: Yale University Press, 1943.

Chin, Al-Li S. "Some Problems of Chinese Youth in Transition." *American Journal of Sociology* (July, 1948), 54:1-9.

Clark, Elizabeth W. "The Challenge of Transplanted People for Casework." *New Emphasis on Cultural Factors.* New York: Family Service Association, 1948, pp. 14-17.

Cohen, Eva, and Witmer, Helen. "The Diagnostic Significance of Russian Jewish Clients' Attitudes Toward Relief." *Smith College Studies in Social Work* (June, 1940), 10:285-315.

Commager, Henry Steele. *The American Mind.* New Haven: Yale University Press, 1952.

"Community Recreation in 1948." *Recreation* (June, 1949), 43:101-113.

Connor, Ruth, Johannis, Theodore B., Jr., and Walters, James. "Parent-Adolescent Relationships." *Journal of Home Economics* (March, 1954), 46:183-191.

Cooke, Alistair. *One Man's America.* New York: Alfred A. Knopf, Inc., 1952.

Coyle, Grace L. *Group Work With American Youth.* New York: Harper & Brothers, 1948.

Coyle, Grace L. "Social Group Work." *Social Work Year Book 1954*, pp. 480-486.

Cuber, John F. "Changing Courtship and Marriage Customs." *Annals of the American Academy of Political and Social Science* (September, 1943), 229:30-38.

Dale, Edward Everett. *The Indians of the Southwest.* Norman: University of Oklahoma Press, 1949.

Daniel, Anita. "It's Still the Three K's in Germany." *The New York Times Magazine* (March 28, 1954), pp. 19, 22-25.

David, Lester. "Should Husbands Do Housework?" *This Week Magazine* (July 4, 1954), pp. 5, 13.

Davidson, Gabriel. *Our Jewish Farmers.* New York: L. B. Fischer Co., 1943.

Davie, Maurice R. *Negroes in American Society.* New York: McGraw-Hill Book Co., 1949.

Davis, Allison. "Light from Anthropology on Intercultural Relations." *Cultural Groups and Human Relations.* New York: Columbia University Press, 1951, pp. 76-91.

Davis, Kingsley. "The American Family: What It Is—and Isn't." *The New York Times Magazine* (September 30, 1951), pp. 18, 41-42.

Davis, Kingsley. "Small Families Are Still the Fashion." *The New York Times Magazine* (July 11, 1954), pp. 17, 35.

De Treviño, Elizabeth Borton. *My Heart Lies South.* New York: Thomas Y. Crowell Co., 1954.

Dinkel, Robert M. "Attitudes of Children Toward Supporting Aged Parents." *American Sociological Review* (August, 1944), 9:370-379.

"Do Americans Want Their Children to Receive Religious Instructions?" *Catholic Digest* (September, 1953), 17:9-14.

Doyle, Bertram Wilbur. *The Etiquette of Race Relations in the South.* Chicago: University of Chicago Press, 1937.

Drake, St. Clair, and Cayton, Horace R. *Black Metropolis.* New York: Harcourt, Brace & Co., 1945.

Duffy, Joseph M., Jr. "Europe's Image of America." *The Commonweal* (July 9, 1954), 60:335-338.

Duteil, H. J. *The Great American Parade.* Translated by Fletcher Pratt. New York: Twayne Publishers, Inc., 1953.

Duvall, Evelyn M. "How to Get Along with Any In-Law." *Collier's* (October 1, 1954), 134:34-40.

Elder, Rachel Ann. "Traditional and Developmental Conceptions of Fatherhood." *Marriage and Family Living* (Summer, 1949), 11:98-100, 106.

Elliott, Mabel A., and Merrill, Francis E. *Social Disorganization.* 3d ed. New York: Harper & Brothers, 1950.

Epstein, Louis M. *Sex Laws and Customs in Judaism.* New York: Bloch Publishing Co., Inc., 1948.

Evans, Bergen. *The Natural History of Nonsense.* New York: Alfred A. Knopf, Inc., 1946.

Evans, Bergen. *The Spoor of Spooks and Other Nonsense.* New York: Alfred A. Knopf, Inc., 1954.

Fairchild, Henry Pratt. *Race and Nationality as Factors in American Life.* New York: The Ronald Press Company, 1947.

"Family and Family Life." *The Jewish Encyclopedia.* New York: Funk & Wagnalls Co., 1910, 5:336-338.

"Family and Family Life." *The Universal Jewish Encyclopedia.* Edited by Isaac Landman. Patrons Edition. New York: Universal Jewish Encyclopedia, Inc., 1941, pp. 242-244.

"Fast-Traveling Cardinal, His Fast-Growing Church." *Newsweek* (May 24, 1954), 43:54-57.

Fauset, Arthur H. *Black Gods of the Metropolis*. Philadelphia: University of Pennsylvania Press, 1944.

"Feature 'X'." *America* (March 13, 1954), 90:626-627.

Fei, Hsiao-T'ung. "Land as a Social Value." *Societies Around the World*. Edited by Irwin T. Sanders. New York: The Dryden Press, Inc., 1953, II, pp. 52-53.

"Feud Leads to Slaying of Mother, Son." *San Antonio Express* (September 20, 1953), pp. 1-2.

Flores, Maria. *The Woman With the Whip: Eva Peron*. New York: Doubleday & Co., Inc., 1952.

Folsom, Joseph K. *The Family and Democratic Society*. New York: John Wiley & Sons, Inc., 1943.

Folsom, Joseph K. "Changing Values in Sex and Family Relations." *American Sociological Review* (October, 1937), 2:717-726.

"Fourth in Importance." *Time* (May 24, 1954), 63:87.

Fraga, Felix, and Kennedy, John J. "A Study of the Recreational Needs of the Senior Latin-American in San Antonio, Texas." Unpublished Master's dissertation. San Antonio: Our Lady of the Lake College, 1954.

Frazer, James George. *The Golden Bough*. 1 vol., abr. ed. New York: The Macmillan Co., 1922.

Frazier, E. Franklin. "Ethnic Family Patterns: The Negro Family in the United States." *American Journal of Sociology* (May, 1948), 53:435-438.

Frazier, E. Franklin. *The Negro Family in the United States*. Rev. and abr. ed. New York: The Dryden Press, Inc., 1948.

Frazier, E. Franklin. "The Negro Family." *The Family: Its Function and Destiny*. Edited by Ruth N. Anshen. New York: Harper & Brothers, 1949, pp. 142-158.

Freudenthal, Kurt. "Our Culture: How to Integrate It into That of Our Community." *Social Work Journal* (January, 1955), 36:11-12.

Freymond, Jacques. "America in European Eyes." *Annals of the American Academy of Political and Social Science* (September, 1954), 295:33-41.

Galarza, Ernesto. "Program for Action." *Common Ground* (Summer, 1949), 9:27-38.

Gillin, John, and Nicholson, George. "The Security Functions of Cultural Systems." *Social Forces* (December, 1951), 30:179-184.

Ginsburg, Sol. W. "The Impact of the Social Worker's Cultural Structure on Social Therapy." *Social Casework* (October, 1951), 32:319-325.

Ginsburg, Sol W. *On Cultural Factors in Casework.* New York: National Travelers Aid Association, 1954.

Gioseffi, William. "The Relationship of Culture to the Principles of Casework." *Social Casework* (May, 1951), 32:190-196.

Gist, Noel P., and Halbert, L. A. *Urban Society.* 3d ed. New York: Thomas Y. Crowell Co., 1948.

"Global Food for Thought." *Newsweek* (November 29, 1954), 44:103-104.

Goldstein, Sidney E. *The Meaning of Marriage and Foundations of the Family: A Jewish Interpretation.* New York: Bloch Publishing Co., Inc., 1942.

Goodman, Mary Ellen. "The Anthropological Dimension." *Adult Leadership* (April, 1954), 2:13-16.

Gordon, Albert I. *Jews in Transition.* Minneapolis: University of Minnesota Press, 1949.

Gorer, Geoffrey. *The American People.* New York: W. W. Norton & Company, Inc., 1948.

Gosset, Pierre and Renée. "The U.S.A. Through a French Looking Glass." *Reader's Digest* (December, 1953), 63:33-44.

Greenleigh, Lawrence F. "Psychological Problems of Our Aging Population." Washington: Department of Health, Education and Welfare, 1952.

Hallenbeck, Wilbur C. *American Urban Communities.* New York: Harper & Brothers, 1951.

Hamilton, Gordon. *Theory and Practice of Social Case Work.* New York: Columbia University Press, 1940.

Handley, Katherine Newkirk. "Social Casework and Intercultural Problems." *Journal of Social Casework* (February, 1947), 28:43-50.

Handlin, Oscar. *The Uprooted.* Boston: Little, Brown & Co., 1951.

"Hard Work at Hip Wo." *Life* (April 25, 1955), 38:71.

Haskew, Laurence DeFee. "The Role of Education in Improving

Human Relations." *Cultural Groups and Human Relations*. New York: Columbia University Press, 1951, pp. 179-190.

"Have We Any Friends?" *Fortune* (February, 1951), 43:117-178.

Havemann, Ernest, and West, Patricia Salter. *They Went to College*. New York: Harcourt, Brace & Co., 1952.

Hayakawa, S. I. *Language in Thought and Action*. New York: Harcourt, Brace & Co., 1949.

Hayner, Norman S. "Notes on the Changing Mexican Family." *American Sociological Review* (August, 1942), 7:489-497.

Hayner, Norman S., and Reynolds, Charles N. "Chinese Family Life in America." *American Sociological Review* (October, 1937), 2:630-637.

Hendry, Charles E. *The Role of Groups in World Reconstruction*. New York: Whiteside, Inc. (Woman's Press), 1952.

Herskovits, Melville J. *The Myth of the Negro Past*. New York: Harper & Brothers, 1941.

Hertzler, J. O. "The Sociology of Anti-Semitism Through History." *Jews in a Gentile World*. Edited by Isacque Graeber and Steuart H. Britt. New York: The Macmillan Co., 1942, pp. 62-100.

Hertzler, J. O. "Toward a Sociology of Language." *Social Forces* (December, 1953), 32:109-119.

Hightower, Ann. "French Myths About America." *The New York Times Magazine* (February 27, 1949), pp. 15, 61.

A History of the Third Plenary Council of Baltimore. Baltimore: Baltimore Publishing Co., 1885.

"Hollywood Discovers the U.S. Business Drama." *Newsweek* (May 3, 1954), 43:90-91.

Horton, Paul B. and Leslie, Gerald R. *The Sociology of Social Problems*. New York: Appleton-Century-Crofts, Inc., 1955.

"How Real Can It Get?" *Time* (April 26, 1954), 63:104-105.

Howell, Clifford. *Of Sacraments and Sacrifice*. Collegeville, Minn.: Liturgical Press, 1952.

Hsu, Francis L. K. *Under the Ancestor's Shadow*. New York: Columbia University Press, 1948.

Hsu, Francis L. K. "The Family in China." *The Family: Its Function and Destiny*. Edited by Ruth N. Anshen. New York: Harper & Brothers, 1949, pp. 73-92.

Hsu, Francis L. K. *Americans and Chinese*. New York: Henry Schuman, Inc., 1953.

Hughes, Everett Cherrington, and Helen MacGill. *Where Peoples Meet.* Glencoe, Illinois: Free Press, 1952.

Humphrey, Hubert H., Jr. *The Stranger at Our Gate.* New York: Public Affairs Committee, 1954.

Hurok, Sol, and Goode, Ruth. *Impresario.* New York: Random House, 1946.

Hurwitz, Henry. "Chaos or Creation?" *Menorah Journal* (Spring, 1932), 20:1-11.

Hutchins, Robert M. "Do Americans Want a High Culture?" *St. Louis Post-Dispatch.* Seventy-Fifth Anniversary Supplement (December 13, 1953), p. 28.

Hutchins, Robert M. *Education for Freedom.* Baton Rouge: Louisiana State University Press, 1943.

Hutchinson, Paul. "The President's Religious Faith." *Life* (March 22, 1954), 36:151-170.

Inkeles, Alex, and Levinson, Daniel J. "National Character: The Study of Modal Personality and Sociocultural Systems." *Handbook of Social Psychology.* Cambridge, Mass.: Addison-Wesley Publishing Company, Inc., 1954, II, pp. 977-1020.

Irvine, May. "Communication and Relationship in Social Casework," *Social Casework* (January, 1955), 36:13-21.

"An Italian Family in America." *Life* (October 5, 1953), 35:134-148.

Jackson, Reid E. "Education in Black." *The Crisis* (October, 1945), 52:288-290.

Jacobson, Eugene, Charters, W. W., Jr., and Lieberman, Seymour. "The Use of the Role Concept in the Study of Complex Organizations." *Journal of Social Issues* (1951), 7:18-27.

Jacobson, Paul H. "Differentials in Divorce by Duration of Marriage and Size of Family." *American Sociological Review* (April, 1950), 15:235-244.

"Japanese Return to Shinto Faith." *The New York Times* (January 3, 1954), p. 20.

Joffe, Natalie F. "The Dynamics of Benefice Among East European Jews." *Social Forces* (March, 1949), 27:238-247.

Johnson, Charles S. *Growing Up in the Black Belt.* Washington: American Council on Education, 1941.

Jones, Harold E. "Adolescence in Our Society." *The Family in a Democratic Society.* New York: Columbia University Press, 1949, pp. 70-84.

Jones, Robert C. "Ethnic Family Patterns: The Mexican Family in the United States." *American Journal of Sociology* (May, 1948), 53: 450-452.

"Judaism." *Life* (June 13, 1955), 38:89-110.

Justman, Joseph. "Educational Services for Veterans at Brooklyn College." *School and Society* (September 20, 1947), 66:209-213.

Kane, John J. *Catholic-Protestant Conflicts in America.* Chicago: Henry Regnery Co., 1955.

Kane, John J. *Marriage and the Family.* New York: The Dryden Press, Inc., 1952.

Kane, John J. "Momma, What's Happened to Daddy?" *Jubilee* (July, 1954), 2:22-25.

Kang-Hu, Kiang. "The Chinese Family System." *Annals of the American Academy of Political and Social Science* (November, 1930), 152:39-46.

Kaplan, Mordecai M. *Judaism as a Civilization.* New York: The Macmillan Co., 1934.

Kardiner, Abram. "The Concept of Basic Personality Structure as an Operational Tool in the Social Sciences." *The Science of Man in the World Crisis.* Edited by Ralph Linton. New York: Columbia University Press, 1945, pp. 107-122.

Kardiner, Abram, and Ovesey, Lionel. *The Mark of Oppression.* New York: W. W. Norton & Company, Inc., 1951.

Kawachi, Sumiko. "A Japanese Speaks Up." *The Catholic Digest* (April, 1950), 14:90-93.

King, Charles E. "The Negro Maternal Family: A Product of an Economic and a Culture System." *Social Forces* (October, 1945), 24:100-104.

"Kingpin Costello, Gamblers' Gambler." *Newsweek* (November 21, 1949), 34:27-31.

Kluckhohn, Clyde. *Mirror for Man.* New York: McGraw-Hill Book Co., 1949.

Kluckhohn, Clyde, and Leighton, Dorothea. *The Navaho.* Cambridge: Harvard University Press, 1946.

Kluckhohn, Florence R. "Cultural Factors in Social Work Practice and Education." *Social Service Review* (March, 1951), 25:38-47.

Knapp, Patricia, and Cambria, Sophie T. "The Attitudes of Negro Unmarried Mothers Toward Illegitimacy." *Smith College Studies in Social Work* (March, 1947), 17:185-203.

Koenig, Samuel. "Second- and Third-Generation Americans." *One America*. Edited by Francis J. Brown and Joseph S. Roucek. New York: Prentice-Hall, Inc., 1945, pp. 471-485.

Komarovsky, Mirra. "Cultural Contradictions and Sex Roles." *American Journal of Sociology* (November, 1946), 52:184-189.

Komarovsky, Mirra. "Functional Analysis of Sex Roles." *American Sociological Review* (August, 1950), 15:508-516.

Komarovsky, Mirra. *Women in the Modern World*. Boston: Little, Brown & Co., 1953.

Kraus, Hertha. "The Newcomer's Orientation to the American Community." *New Emphasis on Cultural Factors*. New York: Family Service Association, 1948, pp. 9-13.

Kraus, Hertha. "Identifying Professional Requirements for Social Service Abroad." *Social Casework* (April, 1954), 35:147-154.

Kronenberger, Louis. *Company Manners*. Indianapolis: Bobbs-Merrill Co., Inc., 1951.

Kulp, Daniel H., II. "Chinese Continuity." *Annals of the American Academy of Political and Social Science* (November, 1930), 152: 18-29.

La Barre, Maurine Bois. "Cultural and Racial Problems in Social Case Work with Special Reference to Work with Negroes." *Cultural Problems in Social Case Work*. New York: Family Welfare Association, 1940.

"The Land Beggar." *Jubilee* (June, 1954), 2:10-19.

Landis, Judson T., and Mary G. *Building a Successful Marriage*. New York: Prentice-Hall, Inc., 1948.

Lang, Olga. *Chinese Family and Society*. New Haven: Yale University Press, 1946.

Lasker, Bruno. *Democracy Through Discussion*. New York: H. W. Wilson Co., 1949.

Latourette, Kenneth S. *The Chinese: Their History and Culture*. 3d ed., rev. New York: The Macmillan Co., 1946.

LaViolette, Forrest E. *Americans of Japanese Ancestry*. Toronto: Canadian Institute of International Affairs, 1945.

Lee, Dorothy. "Some Implications of Culture for Interpersonal Relations." *Social Casework* (November, 1950), 31:355-360.

Lee, Rose Hum. "The Decline of Chinatowns in the United States." *American Journal of Sociology* (March, 1949), 54:422-432.

Lee, Rose Hum. "Research on the Chinese Family." *American Journal of Sociology* (May, 1949), 54:497-504.

Leighton, Dorothea, and Kluckhohn, Clyde. *Children of the People.* Cambridge: Harvard University Press, 1947.

Lengyel, Emil. *Americans from Hungary.* Philadelphia: J. B. Lippincott Co., 1948.

Lewis, Oscar. "Husband and Wives in a Mexican Village: A Study of Role Conflict." *American Anthropologist* (October-December, 1949), 51:602-610.

Lewis, Oscar. *Life in a Mexican Village: Tepoztlán Restudied.* Urbana: University of Illinois Press, 1951.

Lindsay, Isabel Burns. "Race as a Factor in the Caseworker's Role." *Journal of Social Casework* (March, 1947), 28:101-107.

Little, Wilson. *Spanish-Speaking Children in Texas.* Austin: University of Texas Press, 1944.

"A Lively World's Last Days." *Life* (April 25, 1955), 38:137-145.

Loram, Charles T. "The Fundamentals of Indian-White Contact in the United States and Canada." *The North American Indian Today.* Edited by C. T. Loram and T. F. McIwraith. Toronto: University of Toronto Press, 1943, pp. 3-18.

Lowe, Pardee. *Father and Glorious Descendant.* Boston: Little, Brown & Co., 1943.

McEntire, Davis. *Leisure Activities of Youth in Berkeley, California.* Berkeley: Council of Social Welfare and University of California, 1952.

McEvoy, J. P. "America Through the Eyes of a Japanese War-Bride." *Reader's Digest* (April, 1955), 66:95-99.

McNickle, D'Arcy. "A U.S. Indian Speaks." *Americas* (March, 1954), 6:8-11, 27.

Mannes, Marya. "The Friendliest People in the World, Fundamentally." *The Reporter* (May 25, 1954), 10:35-36.

Mao, Natalie Siao-sieu. "Ceremonies and Rites of Chinese Marriage Before the Republic." Unpublished Master's dissertation. Washington: Catholic University of America, 1948.

Marden, Charles F. *Minorities in American Societies.* New York: American Book Company, 1952.

Markowitz, Samuel H. *Leading a Jewish Life in the Modern World.* Cincinnati: Union of American Hebrew Congregation, 1942.

Marrow, Alfred J. *Living Without Hate*. New York: Harper & Brothers, 1951.

Martinez, Sylvia. "How It Feels to Be a Puerto Rican." *Integrity* (July, 1955), 9:3-11.

Matsumiya, Kazuya. "Family Organization in Present-Day Japan." *American Journal of Sociology* (September, 1947), 53:105-110.

Matsuoka, Yoko. *Daughter of the Pacific*. New York: Harper & Brothers, 1952.

Maurer, Herrymon. "The Trouble with China Is Confucius." *Fortune* (April, 1947), 35:125-131.

Maynard, Theodore. *The Catholic Church and the American Idea*. New York: Appleton-Century-Crofts, Inc., 1953.

Mead, Margaret. *And Keep Your Powder Dry*. New York: William Morrow & Co., Inc., 1942.

Mead, Margaret. "What is Happening to the American Family?" *Journal of Social Casework* (November, 1947), 28:323-330.

Mead, Margaret. "The Contemporary American Family as an Anthropologist Sees It." *American Journal of Sociology* (May, 1948), 53:435-459.

Mead, Margaret. *Male and Female*. New York: William Morrow & Co., Inc., 1949.

Meerloo, Joost A. M. *Conversation and Communication*. New York: International Universities Press, Inc., 1952.

Michener, James A. "The Facts About the GI Babies." *Reader's Digest* (March, 1954), 64:5-10.

Michener, James A. "One Must Respect Korean Culture." *Reader's Digest* (April, 1954), 64:15-19.

Mihanovich, Clement S., Schnepp, Gerald J., and Thomas, John L. *Marriage and the Family*. Milwaukee: Bruce Publishing Co., 1952.

Mills, C. Wright. *White Collar*. New York: Oxford University Press, Inc., 1951.

Murphy, Gardner. *In the Minds of Men*. New York: Basic Books, Inc., 1953.

Myrdal, Gunnar. *An American Dilemma*. New York: Harper & Brothers, 1944.

Nelson, Lowry. "Speaking of Tongues." *American Journal of Sociology* (November, 1948), 54:202-210.

"The New American Domesticated Male." *Life* (January 4, 1954), 36:42-45.

"New School Rules in Switzerland Smack of Oriental Strictness." *The Asian Student* (December 25, 1953), 2:1.

"Newsmakers." *Newsweek* (May 31, 1954), 43:44.

Niggli, Josephina. *Step Down, Elder Brother*. New York: Rinehart & Company, Inc., 1947.

Nolan, Joseph. "Play as You Work." *The New York Times Magazine* (January 30, 1955), pp. 50-51.

Ogg, Elizabeth. *When Parents Grow Old*. New York: Public Affairs Committee, 1954.

"160,000,000 and Bigger by the Minute." *The New York Times Magazine* (August 23, 1953), p. 21.

Opler, Marvin K. "Cultural Values and Attitudes on Child Care." *Children* (March-April, 1955), 2:45-50.

Osborne, Ernest G. "Problems of the Chinese Family." *Marriage and Family Living* (Winter, 1948), 10:8.

Overstreet, Harry and Bonaro. "Democracy in Daily Experience." *Adult Leadership* (September, 1953), 2:24-26.

Papashvily, George and Helen. *Anything Can Happen*. New York: Harper & Brothers, 1945.

Park, No-Yong. *Chinaman's Chance*. Boston: Meador Publishing Co., 1940.

Park, Robert E. *The Immigrant Press and Its Control*. New York: Harper & Brothers, 1922.

Parsons, Talcott. "The Kinship System of the Contemporary United States." *American Anthropologist* (January-March, 1943), 45:22-38.

Passin, Herbert, and Bennett, John W. "The America-educated Japanese, I." *Annals of the American Academy of Political and Social Science* (September, 1954), 295:83-96.

Payne, Robert. "Flirtation Is a Serious Business." *The New York Times Magazine* (March 21, 1954), pp. 14, 62-64.

Pearse, Dorothy T. *Social Information Report in the Administration of Aid to the Permanently and Totally Disabled*. Washington: Department of Health, Education and Welfare, 1953.

"People." *Time* (May 24, 1954), 53:48.

"The People of the U.S.A.—A Self-Portrait." *Fortune* (February, 1940), 21:14, 28.

Pilch, Judah. *Jewish Life in Our Times*. New York: Behrman House, Inc., 1943.

Pollak, Otto. "Cultural Dynamics in Casework." *Social Casework* (July, 1953), 34:279-284.

Pollak, Otto. "Cultural Factors in Medical Social Work Practice—Part II." *Medical Social Work* (October, 1954), 3:139-152.

Porterfield, Austin L., and Selley, H. Ellison. "Current Folkways of Sexual Behavior." *American Journal of Sociology* (November, 1946), 52:209-216.

Powdermaker, Hortense. "An Anthropologist Looks at the Movies." *Annals of the American Academy of Political and Social Science* (November, 1947), 254:80-87.

"Pretty Jewish Girl Wins Legacy Fight." *San Antonio Express* (February 17, 1954), p. 1.

Priestley, Herbert Ingram. *The Coming of the White Man, 1492-1848.* Vol. I of *A History of American Life.* Edited by Arthur M. Schlesinger and Dixon Ryan Fox. New York: The Macmillan Co., 1929.

The Purposes of Education in American Democracy. Washington: National Education Association, 1938.

Queen, Stuart A., and Adams, John B. *The Family in Various Cultures.* Philadelphia: J. B. Lippincott Co., 1952.

Queen, Stuart A., and Carpenter, David B. *The American City.* New York: McGraw-Hill Book Co., 1953.

Randall, Ollie A. "The Older Person in the World of Today—In the Family." *New Goals for Old Age.* Edited by George Lawton. New York: Columbia University Press, 1943, pp. 50-70.

"Report Card." *Time* (May 31, 1954), 63:43.

"Report Card." *Time* (June 28, 1954), 63:73.

Reuter, Edward Byron. *Handbook of Sociology.* New York: The Dryden Press, Inc., 1941.

Riker, William H. *Democracy in the United States.* New York: The Macmillan Co., 1953.

Roosevelt, Theodore. *Theodore Roosevelt's Letters to His Children.* Edited by Joseph Bucklin Bishop. New York: Charles Scribner's Sons, 1919.

Rowan, Carl T. *South of Freedom.* New York: Alfred A. Knopf, Inc., 1952.

Ruesch, Jurgen, and Bateson, Gregory. *Communication.* New York: W. W. Norton & Company, Inc., 1951.

Sanders, Irwin T. "Characteristics of Peasant Societies." *Societies*

Around the World. Edited by Irwin T. Sanders. New York: The Dryden Press, Inc., 1953, II, pp. 19-24.

Saunders, Lyle. *Cultural Differences and Medical Care.* New York: Russell Sage Foundation, 1954.

Schwartz, Shepard. "Mate-Selection Among New York City's Chinese Males, 1931-38." *American Journal of Sociology* (May, 1951), 56: 562-568.

Scott, Franklin D. "The Swedish Students' Image of the United States." *Annals of the American Academy of Political and Social Science* (September, 1954), 295:136-145.

Sewell, William H., Morris, Richard T., and Davidsen, Oluf M. "Scandinavian Students' Images of the United States: A Study in Cross-Cultural Education." *Annals of the American Academy of Political and Social Science* (September, 1954), 295:126-135.

Shaw, Franklin J., and Ort, Robert S. *Personal Adjustment in the American Culture.* New York: Harper & Brothers, 1953.

Siepmann, Charles A. *The Radio Listener's Bill of Rights.* New York: Anti-Defamation League of B'nai B'rith, 1948.

Sirjamaki, John. "A Footnote to the Anthropological Approach to the Study of American Culture." *Social Forces* (March, 1947), 25:253-263.

Sirjamaki, John. "Culture Configurations in the American Family." *American Journal of Sociology* (May, 1948), 53:464-470.

Sirjamaki, John. *The American Family in the Twentieth Century.* Cambridge: Harvard University Press, 1953.

Slavson, S. R. *Recreation and the Total Personality.* New York: Association Press, 1946.

Smaridge, Norah. "Don't Let Children Become Money-grubbers." *America* (July 24, 1954), 91:415-417.

Smith, Bradford. *Americans from Japan.* Philadelphia: J. B. Lippincott Co., 1948.

Smith, John Caswell, Jr. "Understanding the Negro Client." *The Family* (May, 1946), 27:87-95.

Solender, Sanford. "Comments on Helen Green's Paper" on "Cultural Factors in Social Group Work." *Toward Professional Standards.* New York: American Association of Group Workers, 1947, pp. 78-85.

"Split Decision." *Time* (July 24, 1950), 56:62.

Steinberg, Milton. *The Making of the Modern Jew.* Indianapolis: The Bobbs-Merrill Co., 1934.

Steinberg, Milton. *Basic Judaism.* New York: Harcourt, Brace & Co., 1947.

Steiner, Jesse F. "Recreation in an Urban Society." *The Sociology of Urban Life.* T. Lynn Smith and C. A. McMahan. New York: The Dryden Press, Inc., 1951, pp. 557-572.

Stern, E. G. *My Mother and I.* New York: The Macmillan Co., 1917.

Stewart, George R. *American Ways of Life.* New York: Doubleday & Company, Inc., 1954.

Streeter, Edward. "Have Fathers Changed?" *The New York Times Magazine* (May 9, 1954), pp. 14, 41.

Stringer, William H. "The President and the Still Small Voice." *The Congressional Record* (April 26, 1954), 100:A2991-A2993.

Studt, Elliot. "An Outline for Study of Social Authority Factors in Casework." *Social Casework* (June, 1954), 35:231-238.

Suyin, Han. *A Many-Splendored Thing.* Boston: Little, Brown & Co., 1952.

Swift, Arthur L. "Religious Values." *The Family: Its Function and Destiny.* Edited by Ruth N. Anshen. New York: Harper & Brothers, 1949, pp. 393-405.

Tennenbaum, Ruth. "Jewish Parents in a Child Guidance Clinic: A Study of Culture and Personality." *Smith College Studies in Social Work* (September, 1939), 10:50-76.

"Texans Greet Ruling With Mixed Reaction." *San Antonio Express* (May 18, 1954), p. 10A.

Titiev, Mischa. *The Science of Man.* New York: Henry Holt & Co., Inc., 1954.

"To All on Equal Terms." *Time* (May 24, 1954), 63:22.

Treudley, Mary Bosworth. "American Cultural Themes and Social Work." *Social Forces* (March, 1950), 28:290-297.

Truxal, Andrew G., and Merrill, Francis E. *The Family in American Culture.* New York: Prentice-Hall, Inc., 1947.

Tyler, Elizabeth B. "Casework with Negro People." *The Family* (November, 1946), 27:265-273.

Tyre, Nedra. *Red Wine First.* New York: Simon and Schuster, Inc., 1947.

Useen, John, and Ruth Hill. "Minority-Group Pattern in Prairie Society." *American Journal of Sociology* (March, 1945), 50:377-385.

Valle, H. "Civilization in the United States from the Mexican Point of View." Translated by Henriette R. Van de Velde. *America Now.*

Edited by Harold E. Stearns. New York: Literary Guild of America, Inc., 1938, pp. 557-572.

Vendryes, J. *Language: A Linguistic Introduction to History*. Translated by Paul Radin. New York: Alfred A. Knopf, Inc., 1925.

Verin, Olga. "Racial Attitudes of Negro Clients." *Smith College Studies in Social Work* (September, 1945), 16:1-25.

Vickery, William E., and Cole, Stewart G. *Intercultural Education in American Schools*. New York: Harper & Brothers, 1943.

Ware, Caroline. *Greenwich Village*. Boston: Houghton Mifflin Co., 1935.

Warner, W. Lloyd, and Srole, Leo. *The Social Systems of American Ethnic Groups*. "Yankee City Series," Vol. 3. New Haven: Yale University Press, 1945.

Webster, H. T. *The Best of H. T. Webster*. New York: Simon and Schuster, Inc., 1953.

Weinstein, Marybeth. "Marriage by Go-Between." *The New York Times Magazine* (April 3, 1955), p. 47.

Weiss-Rosmarin, Trude. *Jewish Survival*. New York: Philosophical Library, Inc., 1949.

"What the U.S. Thinks of Life: Here and Hereafter." *Catholic Digest* (May, 1953), 17:74-81.

"What They Think . . ." *Newsweek* (May 24, 1954), 43:76.

Whetten, Nathan L. *Rural Mexico*. Chicago: University of Chicago Press, 1948.

White, W. L. "The Way We Look to Them." *Reader's Digest* (January, 1952), 60:16-19.

Willems, Emilio. "The Structure of the Brazilian Family." *Social Forces* (May, 1953), 31:339-345.

Williams, Phyllis H. *South Italian Folkways in Europe and America*. New Haven: Yale University Press, 1938.

Williams, Robin M., Jr. *American Society*. New York: Alfred A. Knopf, Inc., 1951.

Winch, Robert F. *The Modern Family*. New York: Henry Holt & Co., Inc., 1952.

Winter, Nevin O. *Mexico and Her People of To-Day*. Rev. ed. Boston: L. C. Page & Co., 1923.

Wolfenstein, Martha. "The Emergence of Fun Morality." *Journal of Social Issues* (1951), 7:16-25.

"Woman Cantor." *Time* (August 15, 1955), 65:36.

"The Women." *Time* (April 26, 1954), 63:37-38.

"Women Executives." *Time* (January 11, 1954), 63:72.

Wong, Su-Ling, and Cressy, Earl Herbert. *Daughter of Confucius: A Personal History*. New York: Farrar, Strauss & Young, Inc., 1952.

Wright, John J. "The Church and American Society." *Catholicism in American Culture*. New York: College of New Rochelle, 1954, pp. 39-44.

Wright, Richard. *Black Boy*. New York: Harper & Brothers, 1945.

Wu, John C. H. *Beyond East and West*. New York: Sheed & Ward, 1951.

Yang, Martin C. *A Chinese Village*. New York: Columbia University Press, 1945.

Young, Pauline V. *The Pilgrims of Russian-Town*. Chicago: University of Chicago Press, 1932.

Yutang, Lin. "Oriental: A Chinese-American Evening." *America Now*. Edited by Harold E. Stearns. New York: Literary Guild of America, Inc., 1938, pp. 545-556.

Zborowski, Mark. "The Children of the Covenant." *Social Forces* (May, 1951), 29:351-364.

INDEXES

INDEXES

Index of Names

Index of Subjects